John Milton's *Paradise Lost*

John Milton's epic poem *Paradise Lost* (1667), a reworking of the Biblical story of the loss of Eden, is a literary landmark for writers, critics and students around the world.

Taking the form of a sourcebook, this guide to Milton's complex work offers:

- extensive introductory comment on the contexts and many interpretations of the text, from publication to the present
- annotated extracts from key contextual documents, reviews, critical works and the text itself
- cross-references between documents and sections of the guide, in order to suggest links between texts, contexts and criticism
- suggestions for further reading.

Part of the *Routledge Guides to Literature* series, this volume is essential reading for all those beginning detailed study of *Paradise Lost* and seeking not only a guide to the poem, but a way through the wealth of contextual and critical material that surrounds Milton's text.

Margaret Kean is the Dame Helen Gardner Fellow in English at St Hilda's College, Oxford. She has published a number of articles on Milton's poetry.

Routledge Guides to Literature*

Routledge Guides to Literature offer clear introductions to the most widely studied authors and literary texts.

Each book engages with texts, contexts and criticism, highlighting the range of critical views and contextual factors that need to be taken into consideration in advanced studies of literary works. The series encourages informed but independent readings of texts by ranging as widely as possible across the contextual and critical issues relevant to the works examined and highlighting areas of debate as well as those of critical consensus. Alongside general guides to texts and authors, the series includes 'sourcebooks', which allow access to reprinted contextual and critical materials as well as annotated extracts of primary text.

Available in this series

Geoffrey Chaucer by Gillian Rudd
Ben Jonson by James Loxley
William Shakespeare's The Merchant of Venice: A Sourcebook edited by S. P. Cerasano
William Shakespeare's King Lear: A Sourcebook edited by Grace Ioppolo
William Shakespeare's Othello: A Sourcebook edited by Andrew Hadfield
John Milton by Richard Bradford
John Milton's Paradise Lost: A Sourcebook edited by Margaret Kean
Alexander Pope by Paul Baines
Mary Wollstonecraft's A Vindication of the Rights of Woman: A Sourcebook edited by Adriana Craciun
Jane Austen's Emma: A Sourcebook edited by Paula Byrne
Mary Shelley's Frankenstein: A Sourcebook edited by Timothy Morton
The Poems of John Keats: A Sourcebook edited by John Strachan
Charles Dickens's David Copperfield: A Sourcebook edited by Richard J. Dunn
Charles Dickens's Bleak House: A Sourcebook edited by Janice M. Allan
Herman Melville's Moby-Dick: A Sourcebook edited by Michael J. Davey
Harriet Beecher Stowe's Uncle Tom's Cabin: A Sourcebook edited by Debra J. Rosenthal
Walt Whitman's Song of Myself: A Sourcebook and Critical Edition edited by Ezra Greenspan
Robert Browning by Stefan Hawlin
Henrik Ibsen's Hedda Gabler: A Sourcebook edited by Christopher Innes
Thomas Hardy by Geoffrey Harvey

* Some books in this series were originally published in the Routledge Literary Sourcebooks series, edited by Duncan Wu, or the Complete Critical Guide to English Literature series, edited by Richard Bradford and Jan Jedrzejewski.

Charlotte Perkins Gilman's The Yellow Wallpaper: A Sourcebook and Critical Edition edited by Catherine J. Golden
Kate Chopin's The Awakening: A Sourcebook edited by Janet Beer and Elizabeth Nolan
D. H. Lawrence by Fiona Becket
The Poems of W. B. Yeats: A Sourcebook edited by Michael O'Neill
E. M. Forster's A Passage to India: A Sourcebook edited by Peter Childs
Samuel Beckett by David Pattie

John Milton's
Paradise Lost
A Sourcebook

Edited by Margaret Kean

Routledge
Taylor & Francis Group
LONDON AND NEW YORK

First published 2005
by Routledge
2 Park Square, Milton Park, Abingdon, Oxon, OX14 4RN

Simultaneously published in the USA and Canada
by Routledge
270 Madison Avenue, New York, NY 10016

Routledge is an imprint of the Taylor & Francis Group

Typeset in Sabon and Gill Sans by RefineCatch Ltd, Bungay, Suffolk
Printed and bound in Great Britain by
TJ International Ltd, Padstow, Cornwall

British Library Cataloguing in Publication Data
A catalogue record for this book is available from the British Library

Library of Congress Cataloging in Publication Data
John Milton's Paradise lost : a sourcebook / edited by Margaret Kean.
p. cm. – (Routledge guides to literature)
Includes bibliographical references (p.) and index.
1. Milton, John, 1608–1674. Paradise lost – Handbooks, manuals, etc. 2. Religious poetry, English – Early modern, 1500–1700 – History and criticism – Handbooks, manuals, etc. 3. Epic poetry, English – History and criticism – Handbooks, manuals, etc. 4. Fall of man in literature – Handbooks, manuals, etc. I. Kean, Margaret, 1968– II. Series.
PR3562.J64 2005
821′.4 – dc22 2004011362

ISBN 0–415–30324–9 (hbk)
ISBN 0–415–30325–7 (pbk)

Contents

2: Interpretations

4: Further Reading

Annotation and Footnotes

Annotation is a key feature of this series. Both the original notes from reprinted texts and new annotations by the editor appear at the bottom of the relevant page. The reprinted notes are prefaced by the author's name in square brackets, e.g. '[Robinson's note]'.

Acknowledgements

I wish to thank Duncan Wu, Liz Thompson, Fiona Cairns, Kate Parker and the staff at Routledge for their support. Particular thanks are due to Gordon Campbell and an anonymous reader for their careful consideration of this book in manuscript form. My thanks also go to Michael Phillips for his most generous response to my queries regarding his copy of the Bentley edition of *Paradise Lost* and to Lyndall Gordon for her tip regarding Wollstonecraft's letters.

The following publishers, institutions and individuals have kindly given permission to reprint materials:

Reprinted by permission of the publisher from 'Milton's God' in *Reviving Liberty: Radical Christian Humanism in Milton's Great Poems* by Joan S. Bennett, pp. 76–9, Cambridge, Mass.: Harvard University Press. Copyright © 1989 by the Presidents and Fellows of Harvard College.

Francis C. Blessington, *Paradise Lost and the Classical Epic*. Routledge & Kegan Paul, 1979.

Karen L. Edwards, *Milton and the Natural World: Science and Poetry in Paradise Lost*. Cambridge University Press © Karen Edwards, 1999.

Stephen M. Fallon, *Milton among the Philosophers: Poetry and Materialism in Seventeenth-century England*. © Cornell University Press, 1991. Extracts of which were previously published in Stephen M. Fallon, 'The Metaphysics of Milton's divorce tracts', chapter 3 in David Loewenstein and James Grantham Turner, *Politics, Poetics and Hermeneutics in Milton's Prose*, Cambridge University Press, 1990.

Sandra M. Gilbert and Susan Gubar, *The Madwoman in the Attic: the Woman Writer and the Nineteenth-century Literary Imagination*. © Yale University Press, 1979.

Barbara K. Lewalski, *Paradise Lost and the Rhetoric of Literary Forms*. © 1985 Princeton University Press. Reprinted by permission of Princeton University Press.

Diane McColley, *Milton's Eve*. University of Illinois Press, 1983.

Lucy Newlyn, *Paradise Lost and the Romantic Reader*. Oxford University Press, 2001, pp. 97 and 99–100.

Christopher Ricks, *Milton's Grand Style*. Oxford University Press, 1978, pp. 93–6.

James G. Turner, *One Flesh: Paradisal Marriage and Sexual Relations in the Age of Milton*. Oxford University Press, 1994, pp. 303–4.

Introduction

The epic tradition in Western poetry tackles the big questions: What is man's relationship to the divine? What is community? Is the individual's fate predetermined? Is fame a sufficient recompense for an early death on the battlefield? What constitutes a hero? What constitutes a foe? What is our destiny? *Paradise Lost* inquires into all these areas of fundamental human concern but it sets a new question of its own: What constitutes human liberty and how can it best be supported? This was a highly charged theme for Milton to explore in the mid-seventeenth century and it carried intense moral, theological and political implications. It is no less relevant to the world we live in today. What rights does the individual have in society and what obligations? What system of civic government is best and should one's fidelity to any system of social government be complete? How best should we govern our own private lives and our relations with other individuals? What does it mean to have been given sovereignty over the earth? Such questions are not purely theoretical; they have practical consequences for the way we act as individuals and for the way we interact with our fellow man.

Milton encourages us to reflect on the fundamental nature of human beings by recasting the Biblical origin-story of Adam and Eve as epic. In Milton's conception, when God created Adam and Eve, He endowed them with freedom of thought and action. Adam and Eve were expelled from Paradise for eating the forbidden fruit but Milton believes that the divine creational gift of freedom [the *imago dei* or the image of God in man] was not retracted, and that all mankind still retains the potential for right reasoning. The negation of that divine gift comes when an individual ignores the rigorous option and chooses instead to fall into the worship of false gods. Milton's view of idolatrous behaviour is comprehensive and includes ambition, tyranny, selfish or egocentric behaviour, self-indulgence of the passions, political compromise and moral slackness. It also includes any unthinking acceptance on the part of an individual of *any* system of thought, be it philosophical, political, social or religious. For Milton, both personal and civic freedom require the individual to remain alert and to exercise reasoned choice at all times. We may no longer share Milton's religious beliefs but we can nevertheless see the continuing relevance of the arguments presented in *Paradise Lost* regarding authority, gender issues, environmental concerns, the justification of war, guilt and the responsibility that each individual has to witness to the truth. The great English epic was first published in 1667 but it remains a poem for our times: a fierce *exposé* of political corruption, rhetorical spin and imperialist ambitions; a deep examination of personal relationships and of the tensions that occur in marriage; a striking presentation of the diversity of life on earth and of the essential interdependency of all life forms; and most important of all, a resounding endorsement of the individual's right to liberty of conscience.

This sourcebook is designed to assist readers who wish both to enjoy the poetry and to engage with the argument of this great poem. It consists of four main sections – Contexts, Interpretations, Key Passages and Further Reading. Each of the first three sections has its own introduction and a headnote prefaces each extract.

The first section, 'Contexts', positions Milton's personal and political commitments within the context of the ideological conflicts of his time, and it includes a chronology outlining significant events in the poet's life as well as relevant historical events. The second section, 'Interpretations', encompasses a long and varied history of responses to the poem, from the immediate reaction of Milton's contemporaries to present-day commentary. Many of these extracts are taken from the work of well-known authors rather than critics, a proof of the remarkable influence *Paradise Lost* has had on English literature. In the extracts from primary sources within both sections 1 and 2, the original spelling and grammar have been retained, except where it would lead the modern reader into undue confusion. Section 2 also includes a substantial amount of twentieth-century critical study as an aid to interpreting the poem and an indication of the range of viable critical approaches. The intention here is to encourage new readers to enter into their own dialogue with the poem, rather than to weigh them down with old critical feuds. The extracts from secondary criticism look at genre; style; the role of the narrator and of the reader within the epic; theological questions; the critical opposition to an orthodox Christian interpretation of the poem; the classical inheritance; Milton's metaphysics; life in the garden and the depiction of the Fall within the epic; reception. These extracts from secondary criticism reference the twelve book text of *Paradise Lost*, and the Yale edition of Milton's prose, unless otherwise stated.

The third section, 'Key Passages', consists of a series of annotated extracts from the poem. Footnotes provide glosses for unfamiliar terms, explain difficult phrasing, and suggest cross-connections to other moments within the epic, as well as other Miltonic, Biblical and classical references.[1] These notes are intended to be clear and crisp and are in no way definitive. A guide to further reading comprises the fourth section, giving suggestions for both modern editions of the poem and secondary criticism. Finally, a short glossary of terms used within this sourcebook has been included to assist any student undertaking his or her own critical discussion of the religious, political and stylistic aspects of Milton's epic.

1 All Biblical references are to the Authorised Version (1611) [King James Bible]. Line references and translations for classical texts are taken from the Loeb Classical Library series, in particular *Homer. Iliad*, 2 vols, trans. A. T. Murray, revised W. F. Wyatt (Cambridge, Mass.: Harvard University Press, 1999); *Virgil. Aeneid*, 2 vols, trans. H. R. Fairclough (Cambridge, Mass.: Harvard University Press, 1935); *Ovid. Metamorphoses* 2 vols, trans. F. J. Miller, revised G. P. Goold (Cambridge, Mass.: Harvard University Press, 1977).

1

Contexts

Contextual Overview

The 'desire to know' (IV 523) is one of the defining characteristics of humanity and a central theme in *Paradise Lost*. It is therefore hardly surprising to discover that Milton has drawn upon a vast range of sources in the construction of his epic. The accumulated information in the poem amounts to an encyclopaedia[1] of human knowledge, as seen, summarised, and assessed from the point of view of a mid-seventeenth century English Protestant. Milton's text offers a theological debate and an exploration of the human psyche. It explores areas of scientific interest, such as cosmology and natural history, and of diverse political interests, including gender issues and the absolute sovereignty of the divine. It can propose a radical re-assessment of the nature of the created universe at the same time as it gives respect to human emotions. It is deeply concerned with history and our understanding of historical process, as well as with the nature of individual memory or inspired prophecy and the ways in which we construct personal narratives and cultural myths. It is composed by someone who knows at least ten languages,[2] and who is interested in music, mathematics, geography and astronomy, as well as literary form. It moves us across both space and time, and takes us not only to Hell and back but to Heaven. It includes its own hexameron [a history of the Creation as found in the book of *Genesis*], a full-blown war, extended visions of the future, a parliamentary debate, numerous supernatural figures and a protracted depiction of the creational perfection of mankind. All of this is a remarkable achievement in itself and evidence of a lifetime of study on Milton's part. However, what is even more challenging is that Milton expects his reader[3] to become conscious within the reading process of the use to which knowledge and

1 Barbara K. Lewalski, *Paradise Lost and the Rhetoric of Literary Forms* (Princeton, NJ: Princeton University Press, 1985), p. 23, terms *Paradise Lost* an 'encyclopaedia' of literary forms.

2 Milton composed in English, Latin, classical Greek and Italian. He also knew French, Spanish, Dutch, Hebrew, Aramaic and Syriac. See John Hale, *Milton's Languages: the Impact of Multilingualism on Style* (Cambridge: Cambridge University Press, 1997), p. 78.

3 I shall identify the reader as male and use the term 'man' throughout my text as a generic term for mankind, male and female. I do so for convenience but trust that it will occasionally jar. The historical marginalisation of woman should in any case be admitted as part of the reading experience for *Paradise Lost*, although this does not make Milton a misogynist, just a patriarch. In fact, you may come to agree that Milton actually gives a remarkably high and meaningful status to Eve within the poem. The problem lies as much in reactionary critical interpretations of the gender differentials within the epic as in the text itself. (For more on this, see Wollstonecraft, **pp. 48–9.**)

the background materials have been put. This means not just source spotting, although that has been a critical obsession for over three hundred years now, but something much more fundamental, more radical and more modern. This is a poem that encourages us to behave as conscious beings and to be alert to the activities of reading, writing and discoursing. We are to scrutinise our own procedures as literate, rational beings and thereby to learn to apply our knowledge wisely. All human systems of thought are to be examined but particularly our narrative strategies and our religious and ideological preconceptions.

The political circumstances under which Milton lived influence the choice of subject matter for his epic and the radical revision that both the epic genre and the *Genesis* story undergo. The middle decades of the seventeenth century are the period of the most intense political upheavals and shocking constitutional changes that Britain has yet seen. Religious disputes and complaints over the royal prerogative and unjust taxation lead to the Civil Wars of the 1640s, when Parliamentary troops fight in open rebellion against the anointed Stuart monarch, King Charles I. Charles is eventually taken prisoner and tried before Parliament. He is executed on 30 January 1649, leaving England without a crowned Head of State for the next decade. Great Rebellion or English Revolution? The term that one chooses does to a large extent determine one's interpretation of these historical events. Stuart monarchy is restored in 1660 when Charles II, the son of the beheaded king, returns from exile on the continent. Charles II rides in triumph into London on 29 May 1660, his thirtieth birthday. His Restoration[4] is widely celebrated and comes as a great relief to many in the nation. It is no exaggeration to say that over the previous twenty years almost every part of the British Isles had experienced military manoeuvres, forced sequestration of goods, armed skirmishes, the violent suppression of revolt, and the murderous (and mutilating) power of both the cannon and the musket on the battlefields of the Civil Wars. It is hard to say whether the monarchy would have returned to England had Cromwell lived longer and the Protectorate become more firmly established but he dies in 1658 and his son is incapable of exerting the same authority as his father. It is hoped by many that the return of Stuart monarchy will bring stability and facilitate trade. Milton is less pragmatic. He has been a vocal proponent of the Parliamentarian cause, and in his prose writing defends the deposition of Charles I as a tyrant (*Tenure of Kings and Magistrates* 1649, see **pp. 20–1**). He becomes Latin Secretary to the Commonwealth in 1649, and continues to hold that office under Cromwell's Protectorate, publishing influential, some would say infamous, defences of the regicide (*Eikonoklastes* (1649) and the Latin *Defences* of the 1650s). Milton's deepest fear, however, was always that the English nation would not prove itself worthy of its newly won civic liberty. His awareness of what he would term an idolatrous tendency in man to settle for the familiar, to resist change and to accept compromise can be traced throughout his political writings. For Milton, the Restoration of Stuart monarchy is a form of self-enslavement by the English nation and a scandalous rejection of their God-given right to freedom. His complete disillusionment can be seen in the prose tract

4 The term 'Restoration' covers both the actual event marking the re-establishment of monarchical rule in England and the following period of Stuart rule.

published on the eve of Restoration, *The Ready and Easy Way to Establish a Free Commonwealth* (1660), see **pp. 22–3**, but, as we shall see, his later epic *Paradise Lost* (1667) would seem to offer an alternative mode of resistance and to have discovered a path out of political despair and towards spiritual election in a new covenant between God and at least one individual Englishman. It could certainly be argued that his epic poem is an attempt to re-educate the English, not as a chosen nation but as individuals, and to rebuild from the ruins of the Restoration moment an audience fit to become the 'children of reviving liberty' (see **p. 23**).

Paradise Lost is often termed an epic of defeat or an anti-epic for just these reasons. Published under restored Stuart monarchy, it is rooted in political disillusionment rather than the celebration of national supremacy. It has nothing but contempt for imperial ambitions. It has no secular patron and it promotes a narratorial voice beset with insecurity and anxiety. In effect, it interrogates the authority of the epic tradition and amounts to a radical manifesto for a revised identification of true heroism. The story is primarily one of failure to live up to an ideal. Adam and Eve will fall and be expelled from Paradise, bringing 'death into the world and all our woe' (*PL* I 3, see **p. 86**). However, the epic narrative does admit the possibility of renewal, embedding that message in its imagery: light from darkness, creative forces that are stronger than destructive ones, love that overcomes malice, the seed of hope that grows after despair. Although this compositional frame is overtly dependent upon general Christian notions of sin and salvation, it is also specifically keyed to be relevant to those contemporaries who are experiencing political defeat and religious persecution under the Restoration settlement.

The real heroes in *Paradise Lost* are those who are willing to suffer and to face persecution in the cause of truth. Amongst their number, we can name the faithful angel, Abdiel; the repentant Adam and Eve; the exemplary figures revealed to Adam by the archangel Michael in Books XI and XII; and the narrator. This is crucial to the Miltonic revision of epic. Individual fortitude, inner strength and the courage shown by the solitary individual who keeps faith against the odds are the only achievements deemed worthy of praise in the new world order. This new world order is on the one hand the universal postlapsarian experience [i.e., the common destiny of mankind in an imperfect, fallen world]. On the other hand, it speaks directly to the contemporary political situation and the state-endorsed persecution of Puritans and members of the more radical religious sects (e.g., Quakers) that took place after the Restoration. Following the accession of Charles II, a number of Acts of Parliament are passed which repress all religious observance not conforming to the liturgy of the Church of England [i.e., Anglicanism]. Milton, of course, considers this to be spiritual coercion and he would encourage the godly minority [dissenters] to hold firm in these times of repression.[5] His most bold analogy is made by the angel, Abdiel, who stands alone

5 We should remember here that Milton's own religious beliefs and observances are far from orthodox. He distrusts ritual and standardised forms of prayer and opposes episcopacy [bishops]. He denies the doctrine of the Trinity and believes instead in Subordinationism or Arianism, which views the Son as a separate, subordinate entity, and not eternally co-existent with the Father.

against his persecutors at the end of Book V (see **pp. 119–22**), but later returns triumphant at the head of a vast angelic army, declaring

> . . . I alone
> Seemed in thy world erroneous to dissent
> From all. My sect thou seest, now learn too late
> How few sometimes may know, when thousands err (VI 145–8)

A totally contrasting political response to the events of the 1660s can be found in John Dryden's heroic poem, *Annus Mirabilis*. This, like *Paradise Lost*, was first published in 1667. Dryden's text is strongly pro-Stuart in its argument and deeply suspicious of Puritans and dissenters. It goes as far as to suggest that the ghosts of Cromwell and the other regicides dance and 'sing their Sabbath notes' (line 892) while the Great Fire of London rages through the city. Dryden accesses the Virgilian epic tradition to compliment his Stuart patrons and produces a text which endorses both monarchy and empire. The final stanzas of *Annus Mirabilis* appropriate the prophetic mode for royalist propaganda, anticipating bright times ahead in the future trading success of London and the nation, united under Stuart rule. This is the antithesis of *Paradise Lost*'s apocalyptic perspective. For Milton, it will require the Second Coming of the Son and the destruction by fire of 'Satan with his perverted World' (XII 547) before true prosperity will return to man, 'New Heavens, new Earth, Ages of endless date/Founded in righteousness and peace and love/ To bring forth fruits Joy and eternal Bliss' (XII 549–51).

Paradise Lost plays off its readership's assumptions about classical epic. Satan's journey to Paradise to wreak revenge upon the Godhead by destroying His latest Creation is the central theme for what we might term the internal dynamic of a Satanic epic within *Paradise Lost*. Satan styles himself as an indomitable champion and a brave adventurer, though we may see him more as a profiteer and colonial exploiter of a new world. The Satanic epic began fittingly enough in the emptiness of Hell, where Satan's voice first gained our attention. It is in Satan's vocabulary that we recognise the values most closely associated with the pagan hero of Homeric epic – strength, courage, audacity, arrogance, pride, charisma, embitteredness, rhetorical skill and mendaciousness, and above all else prestige and reputation and fame. Satan combines the strength and pride of Achilles with the linguistic skill of Odysseus. Yet, his rhetoric remains obsessed with the founding of an empire and it is this aspect, taken from the later Virgilian model for epic, that carries the greater and more insidious threat in *Paradise Lost*. In effect it would be far better to consider the figure of Satan as an embodiment of such epic ambition rather than as an embodiment of that rather notional term, 'evil'. Within Satan's version of events, he is the champion of choice and freedom and God is the tyrant, a repressive and envious force (e.g., I 242–63, see **pp. 91–2**). This view of the Thunderer is dependent upon a pagan notion of Jupiter, and is based on the epic depictions of a pantheon of unjust and fractious figures, who impose their whims upon mere mortals for their own capricious reasons. Despite his rhetoric of freedom, Satan is truly obsessed with being himself one of the gods, to be glorified by his followers and to torment ill-fated victims of his own.

A counterbalance to such idolatrous projections is made within *Paradise Lost* through an alternative presentation of Homeric motifs. The story of the War in

Heaven told by Raphael in Books V and VI is, stylistically, the most epic section of the poem, with descriptions of military prowess and skill in arms, of individual combatants and their moment of domination on the battlefield [*aristeia*]. Yet, when we look back on the narration of the War in Heaven, what we are most likely to remember is the destructive and futile escalation of aggression, the illogicality of immortals engaging in mortal conflict, and the diabolical invention of gunpowder. Such belligerence is contrasted with the solitary courage of the loyal angel, Abdiel (V 877–907, see **pp. 121–2**) and the concluding revelation of God's overwhelming power as the Son rides out in the chariot of paternal deity not to engage with the rebels but to see them flee before him thunderstruck (VI 749–66, see **pp. 122–3**). From the perspective of Heaven, Homeric war is sterile and destructive and not even the obedient angels manage to keep their dignity as they face cannon shot or throw mountains around. The only thing that can be proven from this experience is the surpassing power of the Almighty. It is the theophany [revelation] of divine power that finally exposes Satan's ridiculous pretension in attempting to fight not against other created entities but against God. It seems likely that Milton's presentation of the destructive futility of war owes something to the contemporary experience of Civil War conflicts but Milton is no pacifist. The faithful angels must continue the fight despite its stalemate, until the revelation of the Son brings victory; the 'godly' Restoration reader must continue to oppose secular tyranny and moral wickedness even although no lasting improvements can be assured, until the Second Coming of the Son brings about the ultimate victory of the saints.

Milton's contemporary readership would have had a detailed knowledge of the Bible and a respect for the authority of Scripture. *Genesis* 2–3 is the story of Adam and Eve in the garden. It tells of their Creation, their temptation and fall, and the resulting expulsion of the couple from Paradise. It is a short but puzzling text, full of puns and conflicting emotions, where an anthropomorphic [i.e., displaying human attributes] God expels man from Paradise out of a mixture of spite and suspicion. It sits oddly against the abstract description of divinity as the creative force in *Genesis* 1. We know now that in fact there are two separate texts here, written hundreds of years apart: *Genesis* 2–3 is a much older text than *Genesis* 1. However, that information was not available to seventeenth-century Biblical commentators and many found real difficulty in equating the abstract narrative of the opening chapter with the amplified plot of events taking place in the garden, told in chapters two and three. Milton's version actually makes more sense of the 'story' than *Genesis*, by allowing different narrators to provide distinct perspectives upon events. In fact, we have come to take Milton rather for granted. You may be surprised to find when you reread the *Genesis* account that Adam and Eve are not tempted by Satan but just by a serpent.[6] Nor is Eve on her own when the temptation takes place, instead she gives the fruit 'also unto her husband with her' (*Genesis* 3.6). The fruit is not specified to be an apple in *Genesis* and Adam certainly does not warrant a completely separate temptation where he is allowed to fall from love rather than from a weakness in his logic.

6 A link between the *Genesis* serpent and the devil is found in the apocrypha [i.e. those texts of the Old Testament considered to be of doubtful authenticity by the Jews and excluded from the canon at the Reformation].

What Milton has done in reworking this basic myth on man's origins, and its exegesis in generations of Biblical commentary,[7] is to produce a text of remarkable subtlety and psychological depth. It is not a novel, and these are representative human figures rather than developed characters, but nonetheless the range of experiences and emotions displayed is impressive. As important as the intellectually satisfying dramatic rendition of temptation produced in Book IX of the epic, is the epic's wider presentation of the condition of Edenic innocence. The significance which is now being placed on this story will only really work if the reader can be persuaded that mature adult human beings could really have continued to exist in a state of innocence. Many commentators thought Adam and Eve fell on the day that they were created; Milton gives them a whole two weeks in Paradise. He has them work, gives them a full sex life, and shows them to be rationally monotheistic creatures. He has them scrutinise their own situation, assess a troubling dream, converse with an angelic messenger in an extended educative episode and debate between themselves the appropriate way to tend the garden. He makes us sympathise with both individuals at their moment of trial and traces the complexity of their motivation. Most important of all, he uses the Edenic experience as a means of discussing human nature and free will. Each of these aspects of *Paradise Lost* is a Miltonic addition to his Scriptural source.

The fact that man was created free is repeated over and over in the poem: by Adam to Eve; by the angelic messenger Raphael to the human couple; by the archangel Michael to Adam; by God the Father within the theodicy of Book III; and most significantly of all, by God in direct conversation with the newly created Adam (VIII 437–41). It is the freedom inherent within the individual to give consent, or otherwise, to God's plan which defines the rational creature. In Book III, God explains why he has given the gift of free will to the angels and to humanity,

> Not free, what proof could they have given sincere
> Of true allegiance, constant faith or love,
> Where only what they needs must do, appeared,
> Not what they would? (III 103–6, see **p. 102**)

Without freedom of choice, there is little value to such terms as 'faith', 'love' or 'loyalty'. They are not proofs of an individual's willing commitment but of forced submission. In the speech cited here, God explains that there must be freedom of choice for rational creatures (and he quotes Milton's *Areopagitica* in doing so, see **pp. 19–20**), but also that this emancipation brings with it responsibility for one's own actions. The divine gift of free will necessarily involves the possibility that one might make the *wrong* decision, not by mistake but by choice. It is therefore a defining factor in man's naked perfection that he maintains the potential for

7 It is Paul who defines the story of the Fall of man as central to our understanding of the Christian narrative, by identifying it as the source of all our sins and the crime which makes the sacrifice of Christ necessary. Within the Old Testament, the *Genesis* story of the Fall is less influential a way of thinking about man's condition (suggesting as it does that man has been expelled from an ideal environment) than is the narrative of Exodus (suggesting that man is on a journey to a promised land).

imperfection, placed alongside his sufficiency to stand. Equally, after the Fall, although the perfection of the human condition has been lost, man retains the potential for independent reasoned choice.

Responsibility for one's actions and beliefs always lies with the individual. It is startling to realise just how rigorously Milton believes this. In *Areopagitica* (1644), he goes as far as to argue that it is a form of heresy [here meaning a false opinion] to believe in something just because others do, even if those other people are respected leaders within the community. He writes that 'A man may be a heretic in the truth; and if he believe things only because his Pastor says so, or the Assembly so determines, without knowing any other reason, though his belief is true, yet the very truth he holds, becomes his heresy'.[8] It is not enough for Milton that you have got the right answer, each individual has ultimately to be able to show their working. It is therefore significant that, within the epic, revelation is shown to be an unfolding process and one that admits interrogation by rational creatures. Indeed, questioning is actively encouraged. Before the Fall, Adam asks God directly for further clarification of his role (e.g., VIII 379–92, see **pp. 128–9**) and he can quiz Raphael about angelic sex (VIII 614–29). After the Fall, man is more likely to make mistakes as his reasoning powers are diminished but he is still thought worthy of the archangel Michael's tutelage. Michael goes so far as to warn Adam quite categorically that, after the death of Jesus and the passing of the first generation of eye-witnesses, all forms of religious worship on earth will become corrupted (XII 504–51). The godly must not put their trust in orthodoxy or any set of established doctrines but must rely on the Scriptures alone, and even there, as error will have crept into the textual transmission, only one's conscience and the inner spirit can be a true guide to interpretation. That spirit is freely available to all men through God's grace. Salvation is neither arbitrary nor pre-selective for Milton. It lies in the active choice of the individual to accept or deny God's grace (III 194–202, see **p. 104**). Within the seventeenth-century theological debates over grace and salvation, we can identify this view as Arminian (because of its admission of free will) as opposed to a Calvinist doctrine of absolute predestination, but God's term in Milton's poem is 'free'.

> Man shall not quite be lost, but saved who will,
> Yet not of will in him, but grace in me
> Freely vouchsafed (III 173–5)

God gives His grace freely but there is also a responsibility lying with the individual to respond voluntarily to God's providential plan. Mankind's free will has not been taken away after the Fall and nor has the ability to apply one's individual reason to the question of faith. Interrogative education is essential in Milton's epic, not just for the figures within the narrative but for the reader. It is a central process in the poem's justification of the 'ways of God to men' (I 26, see **p. 86**) but a system of belief based upon the testing of ideas and the scrutinising of narrative form is one that even the most secular of modern readers can appreciate.

8 Milton, John, *Areopagitica* (1644), p. 26. [I have modernised the spelling.]

Chronology

Bullet points are used to denote events in the life of John Milton, and asterisks to denote historical and literary events.

1608

- Milton born (9 December) in Bread Street, London. His father, also named John Milton, was a talented amateur musician and a successful scrivener [i.e., a notary, financial investor and money lender]

1620

- Milton enters St Paul's School in London

1625

- Milton is admitted to Christ's College, Cambridge

* Death of James I (1603–25) and accession of his son Charles I (1625–49). King Charles marries the Catholic French princess, Henrietta Maria

1629

- Milton takes his B.A. degree. He composes his first major English poem, *On the Morning of Christ's Nativity*

1632

- Milton receives his M.A. degree. He now begins a programme of rigorous private study, concentrating on historical, political and theological topics. This will continue until his continental tour in 1638

1634

- Milton's *A Maske* (now better known as *Comus*), with music by his friend Henry Lawes, is performed at Ludlow Castle (29 September)

1637

- Death of Milton's mother
- Milton composes *Lycidas* (published 1638). This is ostensibly an elegy for a drowned university friend, Edward King, but it is also a confident public statement regarding Milton's own poetic ambitions

1638–9

- Continental tour through France, Italy and Switzerland. Milton meets and discourses with numerous European scholars and intellectuals, including the lawyer/theologian Hugo Grotius and the scientist Galileo. In July of 1639 Milton returns to England in order to take part in political life

1640–2

- Milton lives in London and tutors pupils, including his nephews John and Edward Phillips. He writes a number of polemic pamphlets advocating reform in church government and the abolition of episcopacy

1642

- Milton marries Mary Powell, who comes from a Royalist Oxfordshire family. She leaves him about a month later (August) and returns to her parents' home
- The name of Milton's younger brother Christopher appears in the Reading muster-roll (October) as a supporter of the Royalist cause

* Start of the English Civil War (August). The first major battle is at Edgehill (October), where both sides claim a victory

1643–5

- Milton publishes a number of prose tracts in defence of divorce

1644

- Milton publishes *Of Education* (June); *Areopagitica* (November)
- Milton notes in a letter that his eyesight is beginning to fail (September)

* Victory for Parliament at the Battle of Marston Moor (July)

1645

- Mary Powell returns to her husband in London (July/August?). Milton's first collection of poems, *Poems of Mr. John Milton, Both English and Latin*, is registered for publication (actual publication January 1646)

1646

- Milton's daughter Anne born (29 July)

* King Charles I surrenders to the Scots at Newark (5 May). The Scots hand the King over to the English Parliament early in 1647

1647

- Deaths of Milton's father-in-law Richard Powell (January) and of his own father (March). Milton gains property from both

* The Putney debates take place between representatives of the army and of Parliament over the future government of England and the extension of the franchise

1648

- Milton's daughter Mary born

* Second English Civil War (May–August)

- * Colonel Pride's purge of the Long Parliament removes Presbyterians from the House of Commons (December). Parliament subsequently votes to bring the King to trial

1649

- • Milton's *On the Tenure of Kings and Magistrates* is published in February. On 15 March, he is appointed as Secretary for Foreign Tongues to the Council of State. *Eikonoklastes* is published in October
- * The trial of King Charles I takes place; he is executed on 30 January
- * Parliament abolishes the House of Lords and the monarchy (March). The Commonwealth is declared on 19 May

1651

- • Milton's *Defensio Pro Populo Anglicano* [First Defence] is published in February
- • Milton's son John is born on 16 March but dies in 1652
- * Cromwell defeats Charles II at the Battle of Worcester (3 September)

1652

- • Milton now totally blind
- • Milton's daughter Deborah born (2 May). Death of his wife, Mary Powell, a few days later and of infant son John in June.

1653

- * Cromwell declared Lord Protector (December).

1654

- • Milton's *Pro Populo Anglicano Defensio Secunda* [Second Defence] is published in May

1655

- • Milton's *Pro Se Defensio* [Defence of Himself] is published in August

1656

- • Milton marries Katherine Woodcock (November)

1658

- • Death of Milton's second wife, Katherine Woodcock, and of their infant daughter Katherine (born October, 1657)
- • Milton probably begins to compose *Paradise Lost*
- * Death of Cromwell, 3 September. His son, Richard Cromwell, becomes Protector but resigns in May 1659

1660

- • Milton's *The Ready and Easie Way to Establish a Free Commonwealth* is published (1st edn February; 2nd edn April)
- • Copies of Milton's political prose texts are publicly burnt in both June and

August. He goes into hiding and is briefly imprisoned but set free in December

* Restoration of the Stuart monarchy. Charles II accedes (1660–85)

* Act of Indemnity (29 August). Milton is not one of the 102 persons exempt by name from the general pardon. Others who signed the death warrant for King Charles I, or who were notable supporters of regicide, are singled out for capital punishment

1661

* The bodies of Cromwell, Bradshaw and Ireton are disinterred and publicly disparaged on the anniversary of King Charles I's execution (January 30). The heads of the three regicides are then put on display on poles at Westminster Hall

1663

- Milton marries Elizabeth Minshull

1665

- Plague in London. Milton moves out of London in early summer to Chalfont St Giles where a Quaker friend, Thomas Ellwood, has taken a house for him. Milton gives Ellwood a manuscript copy of *Paradise Lost* to read

1666

* Great Fire of London (September)

1667

- The first edition of *Paradise Lost: A Poem in Ten Books* is published

1671

- Two new major poems by Milton are published together, *Paradise Regained* and *Samson Agonistes*

1673

- Milton publishes a second edition of his minor poetry, expanding *Poems 1645*

1674

- Milton's revised second edition of *Paradise Lost* is published. This edition in twelve books is the standard text used by most modern editions
- Death of Milton (8 ? November). Buried on 12 November in St Giles, Cripplegate, London

Contemporary Documents

From ***Facsimile of the Manuscript of Milton's Minor Poems***
(Cambridge: Cambridge University Press, 1899)

Milton held ambitions to produce an epic poem in English from an early stage and he put much thought into finding an appropriate subject. Notes made in the early 1640s listing possible themes (mainly episodes from Old Testament or British history) are still extant in a manuscript now held by Trinity College in Cambridge. That manuscript also contains drafts of early poems and initial plans for a sacred tragedy based on the *Genesis* story of man's Fall.

Milton's first outline suggests a morality play structure and it is rewarding to contrast his first 'cast lists' with the epic as we now have it. It is uncertain how far Milton developed his ideas at this point but, according to Edward Phillips (see **pp. 28–9**), Satan's striking soliloquy as he approaches the new world (*PL* IV 32–113, see **pp. 105–7**), was composed around this time. Milton retains interest in the dramatic mode and employs it within his epic as a means of providing psychological depth. The invocation to Book IX specifically identifies a need to change the generic mode to 'tragic' (IX 6, see **p. 132**) now that the actual events of Adam and Eve's Fall are to be presented. Moreover, the unfolding transitions within the couple's emotional state [*peripeteia* and *anagnorisis*] that run throughout Books IX and X of the epic owe much to Milton's knowledge of classical tragedy.

From **John Milton, *Of Education, To Master Samuel Hartlib*** (1644), p. 2

This short treatise is addressed to Samuel Hartlib, a major educational reformer of the time. Milton argues that the youth of England must be properly educated if they are to act as future civic and military guardians of the fledging Protestant republic. He suggests a curriculum that will train both body and

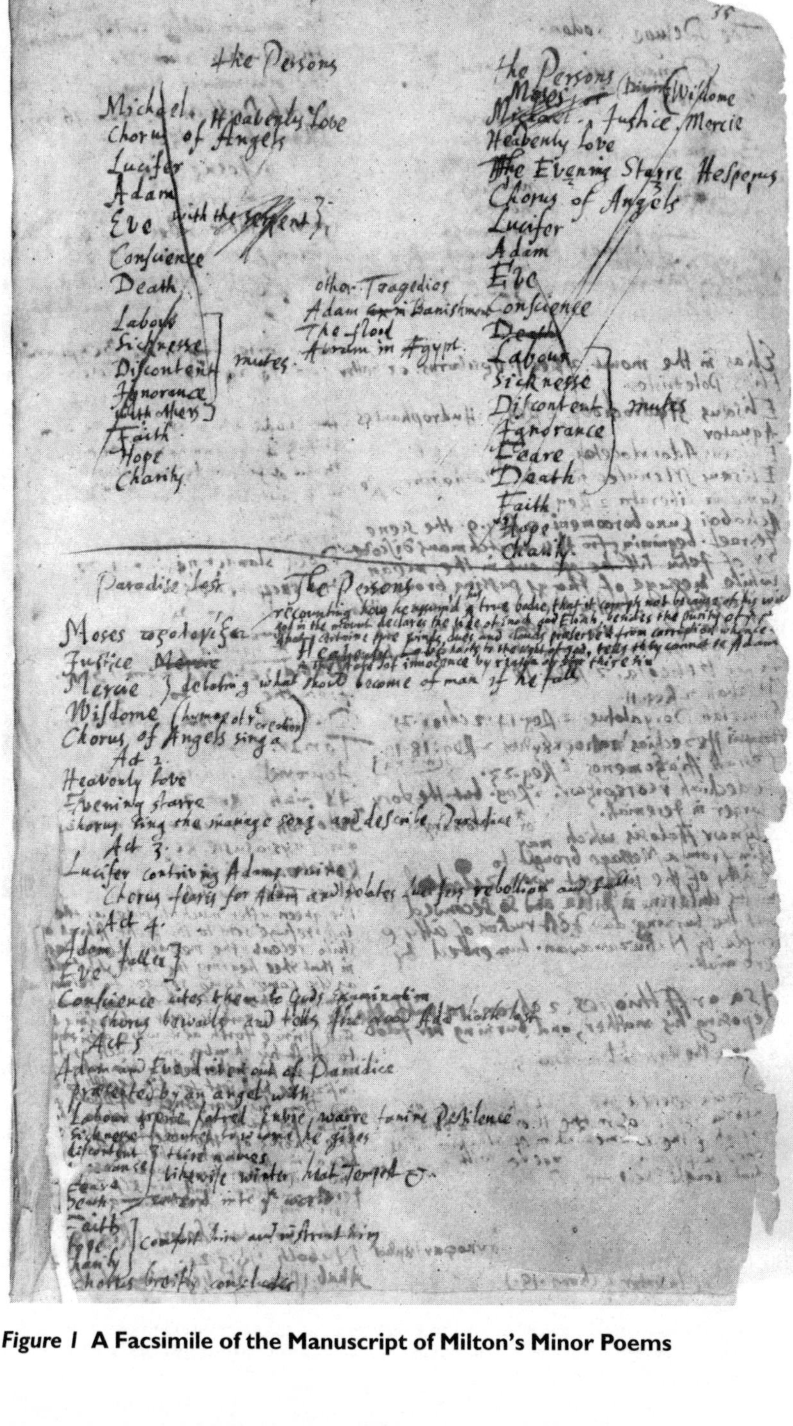

Figure 1 **A Facsimile of the Manuscript of Milton's Minor Poems**

mind in preparation for public service in times of both peace and war. The usual lessons on Latin grammar, arithmetic and geometry are to be supplemented by knowledge of agriculture, moral philosophy and cosmology. Music and classical literature are important elements in the educational process, as is the discipline of military drill. As this extract makes clear, there is also always a religious imperative behind the training of the mind.

. . . The end then of learning is to repair the ruins of our first parents by regaining to know God aright, and out of that knowledge to love him, to imitate him, to be like him, as we may the neerest by possessing our souls of true vertue, which being united to the heavenly grace of faith makes up the highest perfection.

From **John Milton, *Areopagitica; A Speech of Mr. John Milton for the Liberty of Unlicenc'd Printing, To the Parlament of England*** (1644), pp. 12–13, 17

Areopagitica, the most famous of Milton's prose tracts, is a printed 'speech' addressed directly to Parliament. Its title refers to the Areopagus, the famous hill in republican Athens where the Court of Athens met. The Court of Athens was addressed by numerous famous orators, such as Demosthenes, Isocrates and the apostle, Paul. So Milton's choice of title both flatters the English Parliament and indicates its weighty responsibility in judging this new oration. The tract makes high claims for the freedom of the author and the reader (albeit an educated Protestant reader) to engage with each other through the medium of print and has been seen as a prescient call for freedom of the press. Milton argues strongly in this tract that censorship does not strengthen the state but rather weakens it. What is of real value to the state is a citizenry capable of reasoned argument in times of crisis. It is only by the constant testing of ideas through reading and thinking that an individual can further both his knowledge and his virtue. This thesis is itself tested by its incorporation into Eve's argument before the separation of our first parents in Book IX of the epic, (see **pp. 133–5**).

Good and evill we know in the field of this World grow up together almost inseparably; and the knowledge of good is so involv'd and interwoven with the knowledge of evill, and in so many cunning resemblances hardly to be discern'd, that those confused seeds which were impos'd on *Psyche* as an incessant labour to cull out, and sort asunder, were not more intermixt.[1] It was from out the rinde of one apple tasted, that the knowledge of good and evill as two twins cleaving together leapt forth into the World. And perhaps this is that doom which *Adam*

1 Venus sets Psyche the impossible task of sorting a vast quantity of mixed grains and seeds out into separate piles before nightfall. Psyche succeeds, with the help of ants. See Apuleius, *The Golden Ass* IV–VI.

fell into of knowing good and evill, that is to say of knowing good by evill. As therefore the state of man now is; what wisdome can there be to choose, what continence to forbeare without the knowledge of evill? He that can apprehend and consider vice with all her baits and seeming pleasures, and yet abstain, and yet distinguish, and yet prefer that which is truly better, he is the true wayfaring Christian. I cannot praise a fugitive and cloister'd vertue, unexercis'd & unbreath'd, that never sallies out and sees her adversary, but slinks out of the race, where that immortall garland is to be run for, not without dust and heat.[2] Assuredly we bring not innocence into the world, we bring impurity much rather: that which purifies us is triall, and triall is by what is contrary. That vertue therefore which is but a youngling in the contemplation of evill, and knows not the utmost that vice promises to her followers, and rejects it, is but a blank virtue, not a pure; her whiteness is but an excrementall[3] whitenesse; Which was the reason why our sage and serious Poet *Spencer*, whom I dare be known to think a better teacher then *Scotus* or *Aquinas*,[4] describing true temperance under the person of *Guion*, brings him in with his palmer through the cave of Mammon, and the bowr of earthly blisse that he might see and know, and yet abstain.[5] Since therefore the knowledge and survay of vice is in this world so necessary to the constituting of human vertue, and the scanning of error to the confirmation of truth, how can we more safely, and with lesse danger scout into the regions of sin and falsity then by reading all manner of tractats, and hearing all manner of reason?

The premise behind this enthusiastic endorsement of intellectual training is that each individual retains the ability to make a morally correct choice. God gave reason to mankind at the time of the Creation and Milton insists on our continued freedom to choose. It is not God's fault that Adam fell, rather it is an indication of God's goodness that He did not attempt to coerce Adam or limit man's options. Milton would not wish it to be thought that trial predicates failure but rather that it presents an opportunity to win approval for one's volitional obedience and continued self-regulation. The key argument here, 'reason is but choosing', will be put forward by God the Father in Book III of *Paradise Lost*, (see **pp. 101–3**).

2 The idea of the Christian life as a race that must be run is to be found in *Hebrews* 12.1 and *1 Corinthians* 9.24. However, the most likely reference here is to Paul's encouragement of those who will continue the ministry after his death. 'I have fought a good fight, I have finished my course, I have kept the faith: Henceforth there is laid up for me a crown of righteousness, which the Lord, the righteous judge, shall give me at that day: and not to me only, but unto all them also that love his appearing' (*Second Letter to Timothy* 4.7–8).

3 A neologism, meaning surface or superficial. The term strongly suggests that such a veneer of whiteness is no better than refuse.

4 The Franciscan, Duns Scotus, and the Dominican, Thomas Aquinas, become seminal figures in the late sixteenth-century dispute between the two orders on the nature of divine grace.

5 In Book II of Edmund Spenser's *The Faerie Queene* (1596), Guyon, the Knight of Temperance, journeys through the Cave of Mammon and then destroys the Bower of Bliss. The Palmer (a representative of reason) assists the Knight when he encounters the erotic temptations of the Bower but Milton is mistaken when he says that the Palmer is Guyon's guide through the Cave of Mammon. As Milton would maintain that reason should always be active, it is easy to see why he has made this mistake.

. . . [M]any there be that complain of divin Providence for suffering *Adam* to transgresse, foolish tongues! when God gave him reason, he gave him freedom to choose, for reason is but choosing; he had bin else a meer artificiall *Adam*, such an *Adam* as he is in the motions.[6] We our selves esteem not of that obedience, or love, or gift, which is of force: God therefore left him free, set before him a provoking object, ever almost in his eyes; herein consisted his merit, herein the right of his reward, the praise of his abstinence. Wherefore did he creat passions within us, pleasures round about us, but that these rightly temper'd[7] are the very ingredients of vertu?

From **John Milton, *The Tenure of Kings and Magistrates*** (1649), pp. 1–2

Milton completed this text of political theory before the execution of the King and published it less than a month later. It argues that kings derive their authority solely from the people and therefore that any legitimate government is contractual. This means that a king who does not govern according to the law is no king but a tyrant, and may be legitimately deposed. The full title of Milton's tract says it all: *The Tenure of Kings and Magistrates: proving, that it is Lawfull, and hath been held so through all Ages, for any, who have the Power, to call to account a Tyrant, or wicked King, and after due conviction, to depose, and put him to death; if the ordinary Magistrate have neglected or deny'd to doe it.* The argument is necessary in order to justify Parliament's treatment of King Charles but, in addition, Milton wants to criticise the Presbyterians for their continued opposition to regicide and to introduce the idea that promotion of an English republic will be a means toward millennial reform and the reign of Christ. Within a few weeks of this text's publication, Milton is offered the post of Secretary for Foreign Tongues to the new Council of State.

This extract gives the opening lines of the tract. It employs characteristic Miltonic phrasing and makes clear once again his endorsement of man's reasoning powers.

If men within themselves would be govern'd by reason, and not generally give up thir understanding to a double tyrannie, of Custom from without, and blind affections within,[1] they would discerne better, what it is to favour and uphold the Tyrant of a Nation.[2] But being slaves within doors, no wonder that they strive so much to have the public State conformably govern'd to the inward vitious[3] rule, by which they govern themselves. For indeed none can love freedom heartilie, but good men; the rest love not freedom, but licence;[4] which never hath more scope or

6 Puppet shows.
7 Regulated, balanced.

1 i.e., of tradition or personal sentiment.
2 i.e. King Charles I.
3 i.e., vicious.
4 By licence, Milton means lax behaviour. True liberty for the individual requires him to maintain a reasoned, disciplined and virtuous stance. The opposite of liberty is complacency or self-indulgence.

more indulgence then under Tyrants. Hence is it that Tyrants are not oft offended, nor stand much in doubt of bad men, as being all naturally servile; but in whom vertue and true worth most is eminent, them they feare in earnest, as by right thir Maisters, against them lies all thir hatred and suspicion. Consequentlie neither doe bad men hate Tyrants, but have been always readiest with the falsifi'd names of *Loyalty*, and *Obedience*, to colour over thir base compliances.

From ***King Charls His Speech Made upon the Scaffold at Whitehal-Gate immediately before his Execution***. A facsimile of this pamphlet is to be found in *The Trial and Execution of King Charles* I (Leeds: Scholar Press, 1966)

Charles I was publicly executed outside the Banqueting Hall on Whitehall in London on 30 January 1649. Many believed such violence against God's anointed representative to be an act of sacrilege, despite the attempts made to impose a legal frame upon the proceedings. The event itself became a disputed spectacle of power as the King, having previously refused to take part in his trial, made use of his final moments to justify his position and claim martyr status. The struggle to win hearts was linked to the control of certain key terms. It is significant that even on the scaffold the King claims that he has always fought for the liberty and freedom of the people. He would define their freedom as having its source in monarchical government, as opposed to the argument in texts such as Milton's *Tenure* (see **pp. 20–1**) that the authority of the King has its source in the people.

Within days of Charles's execution a publication entitled *Eikon Basilike. The Portraiture of his Sacred Majesty in his Solitudes and Sufferings* was in circulation. This purported to be Charles's own thoughts and prayers and included a striking engraved frontispiece with Charles on the right looking up to Heaven and holding in his hand a crown of thorns. The emotional appeal of *Eikon Basilike* [the image of the King] was enormous and Milton was commissioned by the new Commonwealth to respond. His *Eikonoklastes* [the breaking of the image] appeared in October. Milton argued that the English people were prone to 'a civil kinde of Idolatry in idolizing their kings' but his attack could not cancel the popular success of *Eikon Basilike*.

For the people: and truly I desire their Liberty and Freedom as much as any body whomsoever, but I must tell you, That their Liberty and their Freedom consists in having of Government; those Laws, by which their Life and their Goods may be most their own. It is not for having share in Government (Sir) that is nothing pertaining to them; A Subject and a Soveraign are clean different things, and therefore until they do that, I mean, that you do put the People in that Liberty as I say, certainly they will never enjoy themselves.

Sirs, It was for this that now I am come here: If I would have given way to an Arbitrary way, for to have all Laws changed according to the power of the Sword, I needed not to have come here, and therefore I tell you (and I pray God it be not laid to your charge) that I am the Martyr of the People.

From **John Milton, *The Readie & Easie Way to Establish A Free Commonwealth***, 2nd Edition (1660), pp. 104–8

As the Restoration of Charles II became a certainty in 1659/60, numerous panegyrics [a public speech or articulation in praise of someone] and celebratory pamphlets were printed. Milton however kept openly to his anti-monarchical principles. He published two editions of *The Readie and Easie Way* in quick succession in 1660. The first was a last-ditch effort to sustain England as a republic; the second an obdurate protest made despite the imminent return of the Stuarts. In both editions, Milton stands alone in vindication of the truth. He adopts the voice of the prophet Jeremiah, a prophet of doom and lamentation who *must* speak out even though his words fall on deaf ears.

This extract is from the final paragraph of the second edition. Milton begs his readers to consider the dire consequences of sliding back into debased modes of governance – or as he puts it here in intentionally clumsy phrasing, 'monarchizing our government' – and he heightens his political argument by introducing weighty religious parallels. God's chosen people, the English, are turning their backs on freedom and this is as shocking a *volte face* as if, when facing hardships, the Jews had actually chosen to return to slavery in Egypt. Overtly then, Milton equates monarchical government and enslavement. Moreover, he says that the death of English liberty is a double affront to God, as man's freedom was a gift given by the Creator and then later redeemed by Christ's sacrifice. The peroration [conclusion] describes the people as an unthinking, irrational multitude and likens them to a river in flood. The phrases come tumbling forth in mimetic fashion as the sentence depicts the nation being carried towards an imminent catastrophe, even though Milton can still conceive of a remnant of honourable individuals who might see reason and quell this 'epidemic madness' at the eleventh hour. The intransigent nature of his argument here reflects his long-standing belief that the rights of an educated minority to liberty of conscience outweigh the wishes of an ignorant majority.

. . . if lastly, after all this light among us, the same reason shall pass for current to put our necks again under kingship, as was made use of by the *Jews* to returne back to *Egypt* and to the worship of thir idol queen,[1] because they falsly imagind that they then livd in more plentie and prosperitie, our condition is not sound but rotten, both in religion and all civil prudence; and will bring us soon, the way we are marching, to those calamities which attend alwaies and unavoidably on luxurie, all national judgments under forein or domestic slaverie: so far we shall be from mending our condition by monarchizing our government, whatever new conceit now possesses us. However with all hazard I have ventur'd what I thought my duty to speak in season, and to forewarne my countrey in time: [. . .] What I have spoken, is the language of that which is not call'd amiss the *good Old Cause*:[2] if it

1 Stuart monarchy and Old Testament Egyptian idolatry are to be regarded as synonymous.
2 i.e., English republicanism.

seem strange to any, it will not seem more strange, I hope, then convincing to backsliders.[3] Thus much I should perhaps have said though I were sure I should have spoken only to trees and stones; and had none to cry to, but with the Prophet, O *earth, earth, earth!* to tell the very soil itself, what her perverse inhabitants are deaf to.[4] Nay though what I have spoke, should happ'n (which Thou suffer not, who didst create mankinde free; nor Thou next, who didst redeem us from being servants of men!) to be the last words of our expiring libertie. But I trust I shall have spoken perswasion to abundance of sensible and ingenuous[5] men: to som perhaps whom God may raise of these stones to become children of reviving libertie;[6] and may reclaim, though they seem now chusing them a captain back for *Egypt*,[7] to bethink themselves a little and consider whither they are rushing; to exhort this torrent also of the people, not to be so impetuos, but to keep thir due channell;[8] and at length recovering and uniting thir better resolutions, now that they see alreadie how open and unbounded the insolence and rage is of our common enemies, to stay[9] these ruinous proceedings; justly and timely fearing to what a precipice of destruction the deluge of this epidemic madness would burrie us through the general defection of a misguided and abus'd multitude.[10]

From **Edmund Waller, 'To The King, Upon His Majesties Happy Return'**, 1–18. *Poems, etc/Written Upon Several Occasions by Edmond Waller* (1664), pp. 171–2

The Royalist Edmund Waller wrote poetry under the reigns of both Charles I and II and his eloquence and polished style were much admired. Indeed, the publisher's Preface to Milton's *Poems 1645* went so far as to hope that Milton would prove to be as popular a poet as Waller. This extract gives only the opening lines of a Waller poem but it is enough to give a taste of the standard approach to the Restoration of Stuart monarchy in 1660. The employment of sun imagery to express the absolute sovereignty of Charles II, and the life-giving

3 People who have fallen away from religion; apostates.
4 *Jeremiah* 22.29. A wider context (22.24–9) was pertinent in the first edition as it affirmed that the sinful kings of Judah would not return. However, as the Stuart Restoration became a certainty, such an allusion is less apt. In the second edition the emphasis shifts to the prophet's heroic vindication of the truth, even though his message is falling on deaf ears.
5 Free-born, of an honourable disposition.
6 Milton is warning his audience that God may create a new chosen nation (breathe life into the very stones if need be) if the English abandon liberty. The term 'reviving' was added in the second edition. The Biblical reference is to *Luke* 3.8, 'begin not to say within yourselves, We have Abraham to our father: for I say unto you, That God is able of these stones to raise up children unto Abraham'.
7 Added in the second edition, perhaps a reference to General Monck's part in arranging the return of Charles II.
8 i.e., to advise the people not to be so rash. The people are being compared to a river which should not break its banks but keep in its due channel.
9 Put a halt to.
10 The first edition of the tract had 'the misguided and abus'd multitude'. The use of the indefinite article softens the point somewhat.

vigour that he brings to a benighted England, is commonplace. In a rather over-complicated conceit, Waller suggests that it is only the knowledge of their guilt during the Interregnum that saves the English people from being completely overwhelmed by the joy of the moment. A familiarity with such Royalist imagery can help us appreciate how careful Milton is to centre his epic on the unique sovereignty of the Son and the truly indescribable power of the divine (see **pp. 122–3**). It also helps to explain why the Restoration Licenser for the Press picked out the reference to an eclipse of the sun that 'Perplexes monarchs' (*PL* I 594–9) as politically subversive (see **pp. 92–3**).

The rising Sun complies with our weak sight,
First gilds the Clouds, then shews his globe of light
At such a distance from our eyes, as though
He knew what harm his hasty Beams would do.
But your full MAJESTY at once breaks forth
In the Meridian[1] of your Reign. Your worth,
Your youth, and all the splendor of Your State,
Wrapt up, till now, in clouds of adverse fate
With such a floud of light invade our eyes,
And our spread Hearts with so great joy surprise,
That, if Your Grace incline that we should live,
You must not, (SIR) too hastily forgive.
Our guilt preserves us from th'excess of joy,
Which scatter spirits, and would life destroy.
All are obnoxious, and this faulty Land,
Like fainting Hester,[2] does before you stand,
Watching Your Sceptre, the revolted Sea
Trembles to think she did Your Foes obey.

From **John Milton [?], *De Doctrina Christiana***, eds J. H. Hanford and W. H. Dunn, trans. Charles R. Sumner, Ch I.XI, 'Of the Fall of Our First Parents and of Sin', in *The Works of John Milton*, ed. F. A. Patterson *et al.*, 18 vols, (Columbia: Columbia University Press, 1931–40) Vol. 15, pp. 181, 183

The Latin manuscript of this long theological treatise was found amongst Milton's papers. It was given the title *De Doctrina Christiana* [*Of Christian Doctrine*] and first published in 1825. Recently, some critics have questioned whether it can be proven to be the work of Milton but its unorthodox stance on subjects such as Creation and the Trinity certainly accords with Milton's epic articulations.

1 Midday; the moment of highest elevation. Charles II celebrated his thirtieth birthday in the year 1660 and he is also being flattered for his comparative youth and vigour.

2 Esther is one of the seven female prophets of Israel. She remained faithful to her king and husband but also secured the deliverance of her people from persecution.

In any case, the extract given here is not at all controversial but it does give a sobering exposition of how one might logically consider the full repercussions of man's first disobedience, as told in *Genesis* 2–3. Milton provides an equally inclusive depiction of Adam and Eve's original transgression in *Paradise Lost*.

If the circumstances of his crime are duly considered, it will be acknowledged to have been a most heinous offence, and a transgression of the whole law. For what sin can be named, which was not included in this one act? It comprised at once distrust in the divine veracity, and a proportionate credulity in the assurances of Satan; unbelief; ingratitude; disobedience; gluttony; in the man excessive uxoriousness, in the woman a want of proper regard for her husband, in both an insensibility to the welfare of their offspring, and that offspring the whole human race; parricide, theft, invasion of the rights of others, sacrilege, deceit, presumption in aspiring to divine attributes, fraud in the means employed to attain the object, pride, and arrogance. Whence it is said, Eccles.vii.29. "God hath made man upright, but they have sought out many inventions." James ii.10. "whosoever shall keep the whole law, and yet offend in one point, he is guilty of all."

John Milton, 'The Verse', *Paradise Lost* (1674), A4

This prose preface was added to later issues of the first edition of *Paradise Lost* (1667) on the request of the printer. The first readers of the poem, more used to the rhyming couplets of Dryden or Waller, must have found Milton's blank verse daunting. The note explains how best to approach the verse paragraph, where the meaning flows from 'one verse into another' rather than forming tight two-line rhymed segments. Although the subject matter here is ostensibly aesthetic, Milton's underlying argument has political resonance. He refutes rhyme as the 'invention of a barbarous age' and a 'modern bondage'. He is in fact attacking the Restoration establishment by condemning its literary taste. Style is a political activity for Milton and he claims that his blank verse has classical precedent on its side and stands as a model of what can be achieved by those Englishmen who continue to champion liberty. Milton does not reject all prosody, however. His metrical composition remains excellent and the verse paragraph relies on his skill with half rhyme, alliteration, assonance, repetition, inversion and many other tropes.

The Measure is English Heroic Verse without Rime, as that of Homer in Greek, and of Virgil in Latin; Rime being no necessary adjunct or true Ornament of Poem or good Verse, in longer Works especially, but the Invention of a barbarous Age, to set off wretched matter and lame Meeter; grace't indeed since by the use of some famous modern Poets, carried away by Custom, but much to thir own vexation, hindrance, and constraint to express many things otherwise, and for the most part worse then else they would have exprest them. Not without cause therefore some both Italian and Spanish Poets of prime note have rejected Rime both in longer and shorter Works, as have also long since our best English Tragedies, as a thing of it self, to all judicious ears, triveal and of no true musical delight; which consists onely in apt Numbers, fit quantity of Syllables, and the sense variously drawn out from one Verse into another, not in the jingling sound of like endings, a fault avoyded by the learned Ancients both in Poetry and all good Oratory. This neglect then of Rime so little is to be taken for a defect, though it may seem so perhaps to vulgar Readers, that it rather is to be esteem'd an example set, the first in English, of ancient liberty recover'd to Heroic Poem from the troublesom and modern bondage of Rimeing.

From **John Dryden, *Virgil's Æneis***, Book I, 1–18. *The Works of Virgil in English* (1697), pp. 251–2.

John Dryden's career-long interest in Virgil offers certain helpful comparisons to our study of Milton. As a young man in 1658, Dryden walked with Milton and Marvell in the funeral procession for Cromwell but his political and poetic temperament soon drew him to the service of the restored Stuart monarchy. He was ambitious to play a role in England's cultural renewal and hoped to act as a Virgil for a new Augustus Caesar (i.e., he hoped to be the pre-eminent poet of his age and to produce a great national poem under the patronage of Charles II). He never did write an epic but towards the end of his life he translated *The Aeneid*. Ironically, Dryden undertook this project after the exile of King James II in 1688, an event which had brought about the effective collapse of his own political ambitions. There are numerous embedded allusions within Dryden's translation to his continued adherence to James II, e.g., the added terms 'Expelled and exiled' (line 3) refer boldly to James II's situation, while lines 7–8 expand the Latin into a Stuart compliment that fits the life of Charles II (banished-restored-settled) and also presumably maps Dryden's hopes for the return of James. However, we are more interested in the fact that this near-contemporary English rhymed translation of the opening lines of Virgil's epic makes a useful comparison to the opening of *Paradise Lost*. We note the primacy of the invocation to the Muse but also the distinct difference in the way Milton's narrator identifies and Christianises his source of inspiration; the importance of imperial ambitions and lineage within the Virgilian model and the total rejection of such aspirations within Milton's epic; the impassioned nature of the classical gods and their unjust imposition of cruel fates upon human individuals as opposed to Milton's foregrounding of his theme of divine redemption.

Arms, and the Man I sing, who, forc'd by Fate,
And haughty *Juno*'s unrelenting Hate;
Expell'd and exil'd, left the *Trojan* Shoar:
Long Labours, both by Sea and Land he bore;

And in the doubtful War, before he won
The *Latian*[1] Realm, and built the destin'd Town:
His banish'd Gods restor'd to Rites Divine,
And settl'd sure Succession in his Line:
From whence the Race of Alban[2] Fathers come,
And the long Glories of Majestick *Rome*.

O Muse! the Causes and the Crimes relate,
What Goddess was provok'd, and whence her hate:
For what Offence the Queen of Heav'n began
To persecute so brave, so just a Man!
Involv'd his anxious Life in endless Cares,
Expos'd to Wants, and hurry'd into Wars!
Can Heav'nly Minds such high resentment show,
Or exercise their Spight[3] in Human Woe?

From **Helen Darbishire, ed., *The Early Lives of Milton*** (London: Constable & Co. Ltd, 1932), pp. 32–3, 72–3

This volume collects together the early biographical work on Milton. The best available evidence on how *Paradise Lost* was actually composed comes from two separate early *Lives*, prepared by individuals close to the poet. Darbishire attributes these biographies to Milton's two nephews, John Phillips and Edward Phillips. However, one of the texts is anonymous. Current critical opinion follows the work of William Riley Parker in identifying Milton's student and friend Cyriack Skinner (and not John Phillips) as its author. In these extracts we learn of the importance of the amanuensis [secretary] for the blind poet and something of the frustration inherent in such an unwieldy editorial method. First, the anonymous account gives us a thumbnail sketch of Milton the man, a summary of his financial affairs at the time of the Restoration and an account of his daily routine and favourite authors. Next, Edward Phillips offers us intriguing information on the composition dates for the epic. He claims to have been given at least part of Satan's address to the sun (see Book IV 32–41) to read in the 1640s. We usually consider the epic to have been composed between 1658 and 1663 but this eye-witness account does fit with what we know of Milton's early drafts for a drama on the Fall (see **pp. 16–17**).

1 Latium. The 'destined town' is a reference to Aeneas's role in establishing a homeland for the Trojans and founding a new empire in the west.

2 Alba Longa is the city founded by Aeneas's son Ascanius near the site of modern Rome.

3 Spite. The Latin term *irae* has already been translated in the line above as resentment. Dryden expands the thought in order to form a couplet balancing heavenly anger against the suffering it causes to man. The power of the term 'woe' and its placement at the end of the line is the first of many echoes of Miltonic diction to be found in Dryden's translation of Virgil, (*PL* I 3, see **p. 86**).

From ***The Life of Mr John Milton by John Phillips***, pp. 32–3 [i.e., Cyriack Skinner's Account]

Hee was of a moderate Stature, and well proportion'd, of a ruddy Complexion, light brown Hair, & handsom Features; save that his Eyes were none of the quickest. But his blindness, which proceeded from a Gutta Serena,[1] added no further blemish to them, His deportment was sweet and affable; and his Gate erect & Manly, bespeaking Courage and undauntedness (or a Nil conscire) On which account hee wore a Sword while hee had his Sight, and was skill'd in using it. Hee had an excellent Ear, and could bear a part both in Vocal & Instrumental Music. His moderate Estate left him by his Father was through his good Oeconomy[2] sufficient to maintain him. Out of his Secretary's Salary hee had sav'd two thousand pounds, which being logd'd in the Excise, and that Bank failing upon the Restoration, hee utterly lost; Beside which, and the ceasing of his Imploiment hee had no damage by that change of Affairs.[3] For hee early sued out his Pardon; and by means of that, when the Serjeant of the house of Commons had officiously seisd him, was quickly set at liberty. [. . .] By the great fire in 1666 hee had a house in Bread street burnt: w[ch] was all the Real Estate hee had. Hee rendered his Studies and various Works more easy & pleasant by allotting them thir several portions of the day. Of these the time friendly to the Muses fell to his Poetry; And hee waking early (as is the use of temperate men) had commonly a good Stock of Verses ready against his Amanuensis[4] came; which if it happened to bee later than ordinary, hee would complain, Saying *hee wanted to bee milkd*. The Evenings hee likewise spent in reading some choice Poets, by way of refreshment after the days toyl, and to store his Fancy against Morning. Besides his ordinary lectures out of the Bible and the best Commentators on the week day, That was his sole subject on Sundays. And Davids Psalms were in esteem with him above all Poetry.

From ***The Life of Mr John Milton by Edward Phillips*** (1694), pp. 72–3

But the Heighth of his Noble Fancy and Invention began now to be seriously and mainly imployed in a Subject worthy of such a Muse, *viz*. A Heroick Poem, Entituled, *Paradise Lost*; the Noblest in the general Esteem of Learned and Judicious Persons, of any yet written by any either Ancient or Modern: This Subject was first designed a Tragedy, and in the Fourth Book of the Poem there are Ten Verses, which several Years before the Poem was begun, were shewn to me, and some others, as designed for the very beginning of the said Tragedy. The Verses are these;

> O Thou that with surpassing Glory Crown'd!
> Look'st from thy sole Dominion, like the God

1 It is now thought that Milton suffered from glaucoma. See note to *PL* III 25–6, see **p. 100**.
2 Household management.
3 i.e, Beside losing his savings and his job, he did not suffer by the change in government.
4 A number of educated younger men were willing to read to, and act as scribe for, the blind Milton. This suggests that the accepted stories of Milton's misogynistic exploitation of his daughters for such tasks are probably much exaggerated.

Of this New World; at whose sight all the Stars
Hide their diminish'd Heads; to thee I call,
But with no friendly Voice; and add thy Name,
O Sun! to tell thee how I hate thy Beams
That bring to my remembrance, from what State
I fell; how Glorious once above thy Sphere;
Till Pride and worse Ambition threw me down,
Warring in Heaven, against Heaven's Glorious King.

[. . .] I had the perusal of it from the very beginning; for some years, as I went from time to time, to Visit him, in a Parcel of Ten, Twenty, or Thirty Verses at a Time, which being Written by whatever hand came next, might possibly want Correction as to the Orthography and Pointing;[1] having as the Summer came on, not been shewed any for a considerable while, and desiring the reason thereof, was answered, That his Vein never happily flow'd, but from the *Autumnal Equinoctial* to the *Vernal*,[2] and that whatever he attempted was never to his satisfaction, though he courted his fancy never so much; so that in all the years he was about this Poem, he may be said to have spent but half his time therein.

1 Spelling and punctuation.
2 The equinoxes are the two days of the year when day and night are of equal length. The autumnal equinox occurs in late September, the vernal [spring] equinox in late March. Phillips is saying that Milton worked most productively from autumn to spring.

2

Interpretations

Critical History

Paradise lost, a Poem in tenne Bookes was published late in 1667. Milton received five pounds from the printer Samuel Simmons. He was to have another five pounds once 1,300 copies from the first impression were sold but it looks as if Simmons had to work hard to market the poem.[1] A number of issues appear in 1668 with variant title pages and additions by Milton of a note on 'The Verse' (see **pp. 25–6**) and prose 'Arguments' [plot summaries] to head each book. Perhaps, reading between the lines, we can deduce that from the very beginning, readers of *Paradise Lost* have required some assistance in assimilating its materials. If *Paradise Lost* was not an immediate best-seller, we should perhaps remind ourselves how surprising it is that the work of such an infamous regicide was being published at all. Thomas Ellwood, a Quaker friend of Milton, records reading the manuscript of *Paradise Lost* in 1665 but it seems likely that the political climate was not then favourable for publication. That changed with the calamitous events of 1666 and 1667, which saw the economy rocked by costly naval encounters, plague in London, the Great Fire and then the affront to national honour when the Dutch sailed up the Medway and set fire to the English ships in dock. Public discontent at government corruption and incompetence spread and the first major upheaval in English domestic politics since the Restoration occurred with the Fall of Clarendon, the Lord Chancellor, from office. Many publications responded to events by urging spiritual renewal on a nation that seemed to be experiencing divine displeasure and, accordingly, the theme of Milton's epic may now have made it seem admissible for licensing and publication.[2] Even so, the earliest extant comments upon the poem show a sharp awareness of its author's politics and his reputation. Praise for the stylistic achievement or worthy subject matter is leavened by a sensitivity towards Milton's republican tendencies in, for example, the correspondence between Beale and Evelyn (see **p. 41**) and the practice of

1 The second five pounds was paid in April 1669, meaning that it took just under eighteen months for the first impression to sell out.

2 Nicholas von Maltzahn gives a much more nuanced discussion of the circumstances of publication in his excellent essay, 'The First Reception of *Paradise Lost* (1667)' *RES* 47 (1996), 479–99. He traces a shift in 1667 from apocalyptic foreboding to an incisive debate over toleration and growing hopes of freedom for dissenters. He thinks *Paradise Lost* was not published until October or early November 1667, though it had been licensed in April, and therefore argues that the first readers would have encountered the poem against the specific backdrop of a debate over toleration.

reading Milton's poem with an eye to his biography is a more-or-less constant factor in the history of Milton studies.[3]

Most readers' experience of *Paradise Lost* is actually based not on the first edition of the poem but the second. This was published in 1674, just a few months before Milton's death, and it offers a significantly different reading experience because it restructures the poem as a twelve-book epic. The question of why Milton reshapes his epic has exercised many critics. The new shape allows Milton to foreground certain internal symmetries and structural arguments but, more importantly, a twelve-book structure follows the standard set in Virgil's *Aeneid*. This would seem to suggest a growing confidence in the standing of this poem as an epic in English. Recently, David Norbrook has argued persuasively that the original ten-book structure was a republican statement, based on the Roman anti-epic by Lucan, *Pharsalia*, and a conscious refutation of the Augustan ambitions of the Restoration moment (see headnote, **pp. 25–6**).[4] If so, then the immediate oppositional context for Milton's composition is here giving way to a longer-term campaign to reach and shape a readership 'fit' (*PL* VII 31, see **p. 125**) to discover the poem's embedded message of liberty.

The twelve-book epic looks like a literary classic should look, though in a modest and inexpensive format. Certain prefatory materials to the poem are now included: two commendatory poems, one in Latin by S.B. [Samuel Barrow], one in English rhyming couplets by A.M. [Andrew Marvell]; Milton's note on 'The Verse'; and prose 'Arguments' to head each book. The education of the 'fit' reader is underway before the poem begins. Barrow indicates the salient points as he compares Milton's War in Heaven favourably with the work of both Homer and Virgil, and picks out the depiction of cosmic zeal in the Son riding forth in the Chariot of Paternal Deity for particular praise. Marvell's poem, 'On Mr Milton's *Paradise Lost*', goes even further (see **pp. 42–3**). It is a remarkable piece of writing and it could be said to have launched what is now well over three centuries of sustained critical debate on the epic. The tone of Marvell's poem is both dialectic and competitive. It is in conversation with Milton, voicing doubts in order to dismiss them and presenting its 'fit' reading in contradistinction to other responses.[5] This kind of multivalency – defending, refuting, revising, debating, echoing, and resisting – can be found in numerous subsequent creative responses to Milton's work and the ploy of using one's reading of Milton as a weapon with which to fight other battles will continue. Olaudah Equiano, for example, exposes

3 There has been more interest in Milton's biography than in that of any other English poet and we now have a remarkably detailed picture of his life and times. The most recent biography is a modest 777 pages, B. K. Lewalski, *The Life of John Milton* (Oxford: Blackwell, 2000).

4 David Norbrook, *Writing the English Revolution: Poetry, Rhetoric and Politics 1627–1660*. (Cambridge: Cambridge University Press, 1999), pp. 433–67.

5 Marvell is personally interested in attacking the poet laureate, John Dryden, and he uses Dryden's approach to Milton's epic to do it. Dryden's rhymed drama, *The Fall of Angells and man in innocence: An heroick opera*, is based on *Paradise Lost*. It is entered in the Stationers' Register in April 1674 and probably circulates in manuscript thereafter. It was not published until 1677, under the new title *The State of Innocence and Fall of Man: an Opera*, and with an obsequious dedication to Mary of Modena, the Catholic wife of James, Duke of York. Marvell is outraged that Milton's sacred Protestant poem dedicated to the ancient liberties should be turned into verse couplets to flatter the Stuarts and entertain the court. However, looked at from Dryden's point of view, the work is an astute revision of Milton's story line and philosophical inquiry to conform to a Restoration aesthetic.

the inhumanity of the slave trade to his English readers by employing their canonical poem against them (see **pp. 47–8**); in the 1790s, the proto-feminist Mary Wollstonecraft demolishes extant banal patriarchal readings of Eve and calls Milton to account for his internal contradictions (see **pp. 48–9**); in the 1930s and 1940s, T. S. Eliot and F. R. Leavis promote their struggle against Victorian versification and in favour of modernist forms through an attack on Milton's style (see **p. 55**).

The year 1688 is both a historical milestone and an important date in the reception history for *Paradise Lost*. The 'Glorious Revolution' sees the Catholic Stuart King, James II, leaving England for exile and the Protestant, William of Orange, being invited to take the throne. Parliament's power is now in the ascendancy, and questions of constitutional reform and a limited monarchy are once again openly debated. More than a decade after his death, Milton's political prose is republished for its arguments regarding religious toleration, a contract theory of government, and freedom of the press. Also in 1688, the publisher Jacob Tonson produces a grand folio edition of *Paradise Lost*, complete with illustrations and a commendatory epigram by Dryden.[6] This is the first example of subscription publication, meaning that it was financed in advance by payments made by over 500 individuals. Whig politics[7] but more importantly cultural pride and entrepreneurial business sense unite in the production of this edition.[8] The cultural status of Milton's poem is increased when, in 1695, the first supplementary notes to the epic are published by P.H. [Patrick Hume]. They could be bought separately or bound with the Tonson edition of the poetry. This meant that what we would identify as a modern edition, complete with notes and commentary, now existed. After this, the Milton industry really begins to churn and, quite staggeringly, only fifty years later, a variorum[9] edition is made available, namely *John Milton: Paradise Lost, A Poem in Twelve Books, with Notes of Various Authors*, compiled by Thomas Newton in 1749.

A real boost to the epic poem's fortunes may be said to have come in the first half of 1712 when Joseph Addison publishes a series of eighteen essays on the poem in *The Spectator*. This was a daily periodical with an extremely wide circulation, particularly amongst the new middle class, and its influence on social manners and literary taste was considerable. By recommending *Paradise Lost* for detailed consideration across a number of months, the periodical assumes *Paradise Lost* to be a poem already known by its readership and one which they would agree to be worthy of extended coverage and consideration. The result is an expanded and well-briefed audience for Milton's poem, and a sustained critical appraisal of Milton's work which is often republished. Addison's own preference

6 This is the fourth edition of Milton's epic. The third was published in 1678.

7 By 'Whig politics' I mean the opposition to James II on the grounds of his Catholicism and also the introduction in 1688 of a Bill of Rights limiting monarchical powers. The illustrations to Books I and II in Tonson's edition are specifically antagonistic towards James II, e.g., the figure of Satan at Hell's gates has the face of James II. See John King, *Milton and Religious Controversy: Satire and Polemic in Paradise Lost* (Cambridge: Cambridge University Press, 2000), pp. 60–8.

8 It is worth noting that Tonson also publishes Dryden's translation of the *Works of Virgil* in 1697, and again employs the subscription method.

9 A variorum edition compiles the scholarly notes of various previous commentators. It is an approach usually reserved for Biblical or classical texts.

is for the War in Heaven and, like most of his contemporary commentators, he also deeply admires the Edenic sections. His approach is to examine Milton by the 'Rules of Epic Poetry' (No. 267) and he compares Milton with both Virgil and Homer in some detail. This sets the framework for reading the epic as classical and stylistic rather than theological and political. Addison also poses the question, 'Who is the hero?' He dismisses Dryden's view that it is Satan (see **p. 44**) and proposes Messiah (No. 297).[10] Since then, almost every figure within the poem, and even the reader of the poem, has been nominated as 'hero'. Many critics would now say that this is not the right question to ask but we must still admit that Addison's 'rules' have had an abiding influence.

The eighteenth century also sees intense editorial interest in *Paradise Lost*,[11] much of it stimulated by the publication of Richard Bentley's *Milton's Paradise Lost: A New Edition* (1732) (see **pp. 45–6**). Many of Bentley's proposals were controversial but his work certainly encouraged a closer scrutiny of Milton's poetry than ever before. By the later eighteenth century, Milton has been adopted, alongside Shakespeare, as the mainstay of an English literary canon. The poet of radical republican tendencies has become a figure of established literary authority. The inherent contradiction is one that distresses Samuel Johnson (see **pp. 44–5**) but to which many of the Romantic writers respond creatively. It is no exaggeration to say that Milton's work, particularly *Paradise Lost* with its subversive potential and incisive exploration of the experience of alienation, is a touchstone for all the Romantic writers (see below Blake, **p. 50**, Coleridge, **pp. 50–1**, P. B. Shelley, **p. 51**, Mary Shelley, **pp. 52–3**). Later, there is some surprise to find, on the discovery of the manuscript of *De Doctrina Christiana* (see **pp. 24–5**) in 1823, that the national poet and inspired Christian bard had in fact been extremely unorthodox in his beliefs but ultimately the niceties of Milton's theological heterodoxies do not interest the nineteenth century much.[12] Thomas Macaulay, for example, sets out to write a review of the theological thesis but actually produces the long essay, 'Milton' (1825), a general survey of the statesman-poet as a 'champion' of principled thought and high-mindedness very much in keeping with Macaulay's own values. Victorian poets such as Matthew Arnold and Alfred, Lord Tennyson, concentrate on Milton's style, and any doctrinal ambivalences are in the main allowed to lie undisturbed while the national epic becomes a cornerstone of the British Empire and its education system.

The sheer volume of Milton scholarship over the course of the twentieth

10 For support of this claim, see *PL* III 410–15. Kenneth Borris makes the case for the Son as 'hero' in *Allegory and Epic in English Renaissance Literature: Heroic Form in Sidney, Spenser, and Milton* (Cambridge: Cambridge University Press, 2000).

11 There are over a hundred editions of Milton's poetry by the end of the eighteenth century according to Kay G. Stevenson, 'Reading Milton, 1674–1800' in *A Companion to Milton*, ed. Thomas N. Corns (Oxford: Blackwell, 2001), pp. 447–62.

12 We have to wait some time for Maurice Kelley's, *This Great Argument: a Study of Milton's De Doctrina Christiana as a gloss upon Paradise Lost* (Princeton, NJ: Princeton University Press, 1941). This monograph remains the most significant reading of the theology of *Paradise Lost* against the doctrinal issues raised in *De Doctrina Christiana*. However, the authorship of *De Doctrina Christiana* is now disputed. For a useful summary of the present controversy, see Michael Lieb, '*De Doctrina Christiana* and the Question of Authorship', *Milton Studies*, 41 (2002), pp. 172–230.

century is staggering[13] and the wide range of theoretical approaches and critical interests involved is equally daunting. We can, however, identify the 1960s as a watershed, and focus our discussions accordingly. The early twentieth century inherits a favourable impression of Milton's work, based in general on the Christian principles extractable from his epic theme, and specifically on his stylistic achievements in the development in *Paradise Lost* of non-dramatic blank verse. Each of these assumptions is soon to be challenged in heated exchanges between critics. The first attack is on Milton's style and it is made by the poet, T. S. Eliot. His essay, 'Milton' (1936), claims that the stylistic effect of Milton's text appeals only to the ear and does not carry the sense of the argument or the rhythm of a speech act.[14] According to T. S. Eliot, soon ably supported by the academic, F. R. Leavis (see **p. 55**), Milton was a bad influence for all later poets. They would see his work consigned to obscurity but in the event their offensive against the 'Grand Style' backfires in so far as it stimulates close readings of *Paradise Lost*, thereby bringing ever more attention to the poetry. The controversy over Milton's style runs until the early 1960s, when a new page is turned with the appearance of a collection of essays, *The Living Milton* (1960), edited by Frank Kermode, and the publication of Christopher Ricks's, *Milton's Grand Style* (1963), (see **pp. 57–9**). Ricks offers a close analysis of Milton's syntax, proposing that the epic has been consciously designed to exploit ambiguity and to offer a range of different stylistic effects. The method employed by Ricks is rather old-fashioned, in that he uses close reading to disclose Milton's authorial intention, but he is remarkably open to the dynamic play of language. By contrast, Stanley Fish in *Surprised by Sin* (1967) employs a new theoretical approach (reader-response or reception theory) to place the responsibility for the construction of meaning with each individual *reader* (and not the author) but he ends up encouraging the reader to learn to constrain his exegetical activities (see **pp. 59–60**).[15]

The second great clash of the earlier twentieth century is between C. S. Lewis and William Empson (see **pp. 60–1**), over whether the epic should be read as an orthodox Christian poem or not. C. S. Lewis publishes *A Preface to Paradise Lost* in 1942 in order to defend and revitalise the experience of reading *Paradise Lost* as a Christian epic on the Fall of Man. For Lewis, it is a mistake (originating in Romantic misreadings of the poem) to find rebellion admirable in its own right: Satan is not a heroic figure and Eve's transgression is lamentable.[16] William Empson categorically disagrees. His book, *Milton's God* (see **pp. 60–1**), published in 1961, is an abrasive attack on such conformity. Empson privileges the role of the rebel who dares to question imposed authorities. Under his reading, the epic endorses a humane rather than a Christian heroism in its championing of the courage required to question restrictive obedience to a 'God'.

We might claim Empson as *the* great apostate of twentieth-century Milton

13 A conservative estimate for the number of studies and essays published since 1970 would be over 6,000.

14 T. S. Eliot, 'Milton I (1936)', in *On Poetry and Poets* (London and Boston: Faber & Faber, 1957), pp. 138–45.

15 J. P. Rumrich refutes Fish's reading of Milton in *Milton Unbound* (Cambridge: Cambridge University Press, 1996).

16 It should be noted that Lewis is reading Milton squarely from his own viewpoint as a twentieth-century Anglican.

studies were it not that the rise of critical theory in the 1960s has opened the floodgates to so many diverse and heterodox [unorthodox] readings of *Paradise Lost*. But before we turn to the modern state of Milton studies, there is one final legacy of the controversy over Milton's style which needs to be addressed. T. S. Eliot said that Milton 'made a great epic impossible for succeeding generations'.[17] Great poets are few and far between in any culture but it should be stated quite categorically that the epic tradition did not die out after Milton, it simply did as it has always done and re-created itself anew for later generations. Alexander Pope's *The Dunciad* (1743) must stand as one of the most significant works in the English canon and it is now being appreciated less as mock-epic than as a modern kind of classic.[18] William Wordsworth's *The Prelude* (1805) repeatedly acknowledges Milton as a mainstay of its cultural inheritance but with less of a sense of rivalry than a conscious awareness of a necessary transition occurring as Milton's Christian quest is secularised and internalised. Walt Whitman in *Leaves of Grass* (1855, 1860) outdoes both Milton and Wordsworth in his democratic celebration of self.

It is in any case myopic to expect that every generation and every group should turn to epic poetry as the only appropriate medium for discussion of the core human concerns. With the rise of the novel, we find a new world for responses to Milton. From Defoe onwards, the novelists have read Milton. Mary Shelley's haunting revision of the Creation myth in *Frankenstein* (1818) deserves special note (see **pp. 52–3**), as do Herman Melville's *Moby Dick* (1851), George Eliot's portrayal of Casaubon in *Middlemarch* (1871–2) and Philip Pullman's recent trilogy, *His Dark Materials* (2001) (see **p. 56**), which includes the death of God, but not, it should be said, of narratorial omniscience.

Since the 1960s, academics have been applying critical theories to the study of *Paradise Lost*. Our understanding of the poem as a cultural product, both of the mid-seventeenth century and of each subsequent reading thereafter, is benefiting greatly from such theoretical focus. There are now numerous Marxist, feminist, psycho-analytical[19] and poststructuralist[20] responses to the epic. Christopher Hill, a Marxist historian, publishes his seminal study, *Milton and the English Revolution*, in 1977. Hill's knowledge of mid-seventeenth century politics leads him to identify Milton as a radical, in regard to both his religious and political beliefs. He

17 See T. S. Eliot, 'Milton II (1947)', in *On Poetry and Poets* (London and Boston: Faber & Faber, 1957), pp. 146–61, quoting p. 150. The suggestion that Miltonic achievement stifles subsequent creativity returns in expanded form in Bloom's thesis that an anxiety of influence was felt by all post-Renaissance writers. Harold Bloom, *The Anxiety of Influence* (New York: Oxford University Press, 1973).

18 Valerie Rumbold makes this point convincingly in her edition, *Alexander Pope. The Dunciad in Four Books* (Harlow, Essex: Pearson Education Ltd, 1999), pp.16–17.

19 Psychoanalytical approaches to the epic are best approached via either Northrop Frye's (Jungian) work on archetypal myths and the collective unconscious or William Kerrigan's (Freudian) assessment of Miltonic creativity and religious authority in terms of oedipal desire. See Northrop Frye, 'The Revelation to Eve' in Balachandra Rajan, ed., *Paradise Lost: a Tercentenary Tribute* (Toronto: University of Toronto Press, 1969), pp. 18–47; William Kerrigan, *The Sacred Complex: on the Psychogenesis of Paradise Lost* (Cambridge, Mass.: Harvard University Press, 1983).

20 The most assured poststructuralist reading is Catherine Belsey, *John Milton: Language, Gender, Power* (Oxford: Blackwell, 1988). Belsey takes Jacques Derrida's theory on indeterminacy and the deferral of meaning and applies it to the problem of representing God through language, arguing that there can be no such thing as a single truth or a fixed meaning within the poem.

therefore reads against the established figure of Milton as high-culture poet, and instead links him to popular revolutionary groups, such as the Levellers, Ranters and Fifth Monarchists. This interest in popular culture and the English radical tradition has revitalised academic research on the politics of the mid-seventeenth century and Hill's influence continues to be felt – although Andrew Milner, *John Milton and the English Revolution* (1981) has now clarified Milton's allegiance as Independent [a grouping associated with Cromwell's leadership] rather than Leveller. Current scholarship is building on an ever-increasing understanding of the language of political engagement in the middle decades of the seventeenth century. One recent product of this is David Norbrook's detailed study of republican discourse in the period, *Writing the English Revolution* (1999). A clearer understanding of the radical philosophical thought of the mid-seventeenth century is also emerging and our view of Milton's ontology and his concept of matter is changing as a result (see Fallon, **pp. 64–6**).

Much of the best recent criticism engages with feminist theory and gender studies. In the 1970s, the feminist critic, Sandra Gilbert, argued that Milton's endorsement of the Biblical narrative of woman's 'secondariness' [i.e., that she was created after man and as a 'helpmeet' to him] had proved crippling to the creative spirit of later women writers (see Gilbert, **pp. 74–6**). Since then, David Aers and Bob Hodge have disputed any simple assumption that Milton is misogynist but their Marxist understanding of historical and cultural preconditions leads them to conclude that, despite the radical potential of his divorce tracts, Milton remains a product of his class and gender. Christine Froula traces the patriarchal discourses embedded in the epic's retelling of *Genesis* and her work is much cited.[21] For Froula, the full weight of western culture lies behind the identification of Eve as subordinate to Adam. She argues that Eve's narrative in Book IV of the epic (see **pp. 110–12**) shapes a scene where the first woman learns about gender roles and accedes to patriarchal authority. James Turner's monograph, *One Flesh: Paradisal Marriage and Sexual Relations in the Age of Milton* (1987) is more discursive, providing a detailed consideration of the contemporary gender relations and contradictory theories regarding prelapsarian sexuality prevalent in the seventeenth century (see Turner, **pp. 71–2**). Mary Nyquist has produced some of the most stimulating feminist criticism to date. Her essay, 'The genesis of gendered subjectivity in the divorce tracts and in *Paradise Lost*',[22] includes a sophisticated textual analysis of the two *Genesis* texts, before it turns to Eve's narrative. Nyquist reads the structural placement of Eve's narrative as a significant construction of a private, domestic, space within the epic, and she contends that Adam and Eve's marital relations reflect the bourgeois society emerging in the mid-seventeenth century. Maureen Quilligan is equally interested in reading *Paradise Lost* as a poem presaging modernity. Her recent consideration of human labour, both before and after the Fall, combines the problem of gender roles with an examination of another historical form of subjection, namely the emerging

21 David Aers and Bob Hodge, ' "Rational Burning": Milton on Sex and Marriage', *Milton Studies* 13 (1979), pp. 3–33; Christine Froula, 'When Eve reads Milton: Undoing the Canonical Economy', *Critical Inquiry* 10 (1983), pp. 321–47.

22 See Mary Nyquist and Margaret W. Ferguson, eds, *Re-membering Milton: Essays on the Texts and Traditions* (New York and London: Methuen, 1987, repr. 1988), pp. 99–127.

slave economy of the later seventeenth century.[23] It is work of this kind, drawing on feminist, historical and Marxist approaches, which continues to enhance our critical understanding of the English epic and its ideological implications.

23 Maureen Quilligan, 'Freedom, Service, and the Trade in Slaves: The Problem of Labour in *Paradise Lost*' in Maureen Quilligan, *et al.*, eds, *Subject and Object in Renaissance Culture* (Cambridge: Cambridge University Press, 1996), pp. 213–34. Reprinted in William Zunder, ed., *Paradise Lost* (Basingstoke: Macmillan, 1999), pp. 170–94.

Early Critical Reception

From **John Beale. Letters to John Evelyn, 18 November 1668; 18 December 1669**. Taken from the *Evelyn Collection* in the British Library [MS Letters 68, 18 November 1668; MS Letters 93, f 1°, 18 December 1669]. Quoted (p. 189) by Nicholas von Maltzahn, 'Laureate, Republican, Calvinist: An Early Response to Milton and *Paradise Lost*,' *Milton Studies* 29 (1992), pp. 181–98

Two letters from John Beale to John Evelyn. Both correspondents have strong Royalist connections. The first extract is a somewhat barbed comment, whereby Beale admits Milton's poetic power but cannot forgive the political prose. The second extract is brief and looks rather cryptic on the page. Beale is discussing the Nimrod passage which is now to be found in Book XII (see **pp. 151–3**). but, as Beale is reading the first edition, he has given line references accordingly. Milton explicitly yokes monarchy with tyranny in the person of Nimrod. This anti-monarchical intention does not escape Beale, and so Milton's 'old Principle' is a reference to his republicanism.

You will Joyne with mee to whisper in a smile, that he writes so good verse, that tis pity he ever wrote in prose, & wee wish he had alwayes wanted[1] prose as much as Cicero wanted verse.

Milton holds to his old Principle. Lib 10 verse 918 & 927, 954, 972 &c.

1 'Wanted' means lacked. Beale is wryly comparing Cicero, a great Latin stylist of political prose who never attempted to write poetry, with Milton. He wishes that Milton, a great poet, had followed the example of Cicero by sticking to what he was good at rather than by entering politics.

From **Andrew Marvell, 'On *Paradise Lost*'**, in John Milton, *Paradise Lost* (1674), A3. Lines 1–12, 41–54

Andrew Marvell's respect for Milton dates from his first reading of *Poems 1645*. The two later became friends despite the age gap, and late in the 1650s Marvell worked in the same office as Milton. Marvell went on to serve as MP for Hull, but always remained critical of arbitrary royal power. It is thought that Marvell may have been one of those instrumental not only in securing Milton's release from prison in 1660 but also in keeping Milton's name from appearing on the list of those to be executed for their part in the regicide of Charles I.

'On Mr Milton's *Paradise Lost*' was first published as one of the commendatory verses in the 1674 edition of *Paradise Lost*. It is an intelligent piece of writing, bold in its own opinions and subtle in its reading of the epic. Marvell voices his doubts that the subject is inappropriate for verse and then that the poet will prove unable to complete such an onerous task successfully, before lauding Milton's great achievement. 'Pardon me, mighty Poet' he says in line 23 and goes on to call Milton a prophet (line 43). The partisan nature of these compliments may be missed unless we are aware firstly of Marvell's earlier phrasing of an address to Cromwell, 'Pardon, great Prince,' (see 'The First Anniversary of the Government under O.C.', line 395), and secondly that Milton's blindness was presumed by Royalists to be a just punishment on him for his support of regicide rather than a mark of divine favour. The final quatrain [four lines] is beautifully calibrated and delightfully witty, particularly as Marvell must have known that it would sit right by Milton's attack on the 'bondage' of modern rhyme (see **pp. 25–6**). Marvell admits that his couplet form requires him to replace his praise with the rhyming end word 'commend'. However, by drawing attention to his ability to work successfully within such formal restrictions, Marvell compels us to appreciate just how much *he* can do with a couplet in praise of an epic!

When I beheld the Poet blind, yet bold,[1]
In slender Book his vast Design unfold,
Messiah Crown'd, Gods Reconcil'd Decree,
Rebelling Angels, the Forbidden Tree,
Heav'n, Hell, Earth, Chaos, All;[2] the Argument
Held me a while misdoubting his Intent,
That he would ruine (for I saw him strong)
The sacred Truths to Fable and old Song
(So *Sampson* groap'd the Temples Posts in spight)[3]
The World o'rewhelming to revenge his sight.

1 Audacious; courageous; confident.
2 An audacious summary of the epic in less than three lines. It is interesting to see what this early reader has picked out as the crucial themes and incidents. His awareness of the significance of the word 'All' for Milton is particularly noteworthy.
3 Milton's poem *Samson Agonistes* was published in 1671. The Old Testament Samson brought the temple of the Philistines down around their heads out of revenge for their having blinded and enslaved him. He killed himself in the process (*Judges* 16.28–31). Marvell both suggests a link between Milton and the blind Samson who acted out of bitterness and dismisses that fear as unfounded. He also wittily restrains his own allusion within the 'pillars' of a bracket.

Yet as I read, soon growing less severe,
I lik'd his Project, the success did fear; . . .
Where couldst thou words of such a compas find?
Whence furnish such a vast expence[4] of Mind?
Just Heav'n Thee, like *Tiresias*,[5] to requite,
Rewards with Prophesie thy loss of sight.
Well mightest thou scorn thy Readers to allure
With tinkling Rhime, of thy own sense secure;
While the Town-Bayes writes all the while and spells,
And like a Pack-horse tires without his Bells.[6]
Their Fancies like our Bushy-points appear,
The Poets tag them, we for fashion wear.[7]
I too transported by the Mode offend,
And while I meant to Praise thee, must Commend.
Thy Verse created like thy Theme sublime,
In *Number*, Weight, and Measure, needs not Rhime.

From **John Dryden, *Dedication of the Aeneis in The Works of Virgil: containing his Pastorals, Georgics and Æneis***. Translated by Mr Dryden (1697), pp. 208–9

John Dryden's achievements as a literary critic are now underrated, though his considerations of literary practice and his projection of an English literary canon helped develop both the scope and technical vocabulary of our discipline. Comments on Milton are scattered widely through Dryden's texts, suggesting both a persistent interest and a competitive edge. In the opening remarks to his translation of Virgil's epic, Dryden proposes Homer's *Iliad*, Virgil's *Aeneid* and the sixteenth-century work, *Gerusalemme liberata* [Jerusalem Delivered], by Torquato Tasso, as the greatest poems of all time. No other poets have come near this level of achievement he says, though he considers a number of claims in order to dismiss them. Within the English tradition, he thinks only Spenser and Milton merit consideration – though both fail to come up to the mark.

As an early response to Milton's status as a writer of epic, this extract is certainly double-edged. It reads Milton through Spenser, a strategy which

4 Expenditure of time, effort.

5 Tiresias was blinded by Juno but given the gift of prophecy by Jupiter. See also *PL* III 36, **p. 100**.

6 Dryden was satirised as the dramatist, Bayes, in *The Rehearsal* (1672) by the Duke of Buckingham. 'Bay', meaning laurel, would be used to crown the poet and Dryden was the first poet laureate. However, a 'bay' is also a type of horse and Marvell is saying that Dryden's use of rhyme reminds him of the gait of a trotting workhorse which moves in time with the bells jangling on its harness.

7 A complicated joke suggesting that rhyme is no more than a current fashion. 'Points' were the laces which attached the hose to the doublet, they were said to be 'bushy' if tied in tassels. One might also attach metal tags to the ends of the laces but 'to tag' also means to translate blank verse into rhyme. This is a personal joke at Dryden's expense. John Aubrey records that Dryden visited Milton to ask permission to rework *Paradise Lost* as a drama in rhyme and Milton 'told him he would give him leave to tagge his verses'. See Darbishire, *Early Lives*, p. 7.

admits the strongly Protestant connection between the two writers, but which also injects a slight tone of ridicule by transferring the allegorical and romance terminology pertinent to the earlier poet on to a reading of Milton. Dryden also posits the Devil (i.e. Satan) to be the hero of the epic and does so well before Blake's famous claim (see **p. 50**). That Dryden would be alive to the subversive energy of the Satanic figure is fascinating but his comments remain at a remove from the later Romantic readings of moral ambivalence and courageous resistance. Instead, Dryden intends a political jibe at Milton when he suggests an affiliation with the Devil.

There have been but one great *Ilias* and one Æneis in so many ages. The next, but the next with a long Interval betwixt, was the *Jerusalem*: I mean not so much in distance of Time, as, in Excellency. After these three are entred, some Lord Chamberlain should be appointed, some Critick of Authority shou'd be set before the Door, to keep out a Crowd of little Poets, who press for Admission, and are not of Quality. [. . .] *Spencer* has a better plea for his *Fairy-Queen*, had his Action been finish'd, or had been one: And *Milton*, if the Devil had not been his Heroe, instead of *Adam*; if the Gyant had not foil'd the Knight, and driven him out of his strong hold, to wander through the World with his Lady Errant: and if there had not been more Machining Persons[1] than Humane, in his Poem. After these, the rest of our English Poets shall not be mention'd. I have that Honour for them which I ought to have: but if they are Worthies, they are not to be rank'd amongst the three whom I have nam'd, and who are establish'd in their Reputation.

From **Samuel Johnson, *Lives of the English Poets* [Life of Milton]**, (1779), ed. George Birkbeck Hill (Oxford: Clarendon Press, 1905), 3 Vols, Vol i, pp. 183–4

Dr Johnson was an influential neoclassical literary critic and a famous English literary figure in the eighteenth century. His *Prefaces Biographical and Critical to the Works of the English Poets* was first published in 1779–81. Johnson is no friend to Milton the republican but he strives to appear fair and objective when assessing *Paradise Lost*. He admires the poet's technical ability but nevertheless makes two particularly telling criticisms. He finds that the epic cannot engage our human sympathies because it deals with experiences so far beyond our understanding and he considers Milton's diction to be 'so far removed from common usage that an unlearned reader when he first opens his book finds himself surprised by a new language' (pp. 189–90). Both of these criticisms will recur in early twentieth-century criticism of Milton's epic (see **p. 55**). Johnson's overall opinion is evident from this pithy extract.

1 Supernatural figures.

The want of human interest is always felt. *Paradise Lost* is one of the books which the reader admires and lays down, and forgets to take up again. None ever wished it longer than it is. Its perusal is a duty rather than a pleasure. We read Milton for instruction, retire harassed and overburdened, and look elsewhere for recreation; we desert our master, and seek for companions.

From **Richard Bentley, *Milton's Paradise Lost. A New Edition*.** (London, 1732), pp. 4, 299

Richard Bentley was a well-respected classical scholar and editor in his day but his edition of *Paradise Lost* is now something of a curiosity. Working on the premise that errors crept into the blind poet's text because of his reliance on amanuenses and an editor, Bentley suggests over 800 emendations to the 1674 printed text. His 'perfecting' of the text often exposes his own literal mindedness but it is striking that he should have been interested at all in employing his scholarly skills on such a recent poem. His endeavours are proof of the high regard in which *Paradise Lost* was now being held. Within a couple of generations, it had to all extents and purposes become a classic, worthy of detailed scholarly consideration and analysis. However, despite his good intentions, Bentley's emendations infuriated many poetry lovers and attracted much critical response. Included alongside the two extracts from Bentley's edition therefore are the exasperated outbursts of two other readers (Jonathan Swift and W.B.) who would always wish to defend their Milton from the Bentleys of this world. The first example is Bentley's note for Book I, 63, 'No light but rather darkness visible'. This is one of the best known, and most hauntingly indefinite, phrases in the entire poem. Bentley however will attempt to explicate it thoroughly. The second extract is Bentley's reading of the very final lines of the epic.

Darkness visible and *darkness palpable* are in due place very good Expressions: but the next Line makes *visible* here a flat Contradiction. *Darkness visible* will not serve to *discover Sights of Woe* through it, but to cover and hide them. Nothing is visible to the Eye, but so far as it is Opake,[1] and not seen through; not by transmitting the Rays, but by reflecting them back. To come up to the Author's Idea, we may say thus, *No Light, but rather* A TRANSPICUOUS[2] GLOOM.

Why then does this Distich[3] dismiss our first Parents in Anguish, and the Reader in Melancholy? And how can the Expression be justified, *with wand'ring Steps and slow? Why wand'ring?* Erratic Steps? Very improper: when in the Line before, they were *guided by Providence*. And why *Slow*? when even *Eve* profess'd her Readiness and Alacrity for the Journey, 614; *But now lead on : In Me is no delay*. And why *their solitary Way*? All Words to represent a sorrowful Parting? When even their former Walks in Paradise were as solitary, as their Way now:

1 Opaque.
2 A Latinate term meaning something that can be seen through.
3 Two lines of verse.

there being no Body besides Them Two, both here and there. Shall I therefore, after so many prior Presumptions, presume at last to offer a Distich, as close as may be to the Author's Words, and entirely agreeable to his Scheme ?

> THEN *hand in hand with* SOCIAL *steps their Way*
> *Through* Eden *took*, WITH HEAV'NLY COMFORT CHEER'D.

From **Jonathan Swift, *Milton Restor'd and Bentley Depos'd*** (London, 1732), p. 26

A lesser-known publication by the famous Augustan satirist, author of *Gulliver's Travels* (1726). The pamphlet goes through listing Bentley's emendations and making 'remarks' upon them. Sadly, Swift only works through Book I but one can feel the righteous indignation fuelling his pen in this trouncing of Bentley's clodden scholarship. Rather amusingly, Swift set a pseudo-Miltonic epigraph on his titlepage, 'Sing Heav'nly Muse, from Pedantry be free'.

If there were really any Darkness in this Passage, I am sure the Doctor has not rendred it visible by his Note upon it [. . .] I believe the Poet's Meaning, however bold his Expression may be, will be readily apprehended by his Readers but for *transpicuous Gloom*, equivalent to Darkness, and yet *transparent*. I confess it is to me much more obscure than any thing I have yet met with in *Milton*.

From **marginalia in a copy of Richard Bentley, *Milton's Paradise Lost*** (1732), pp. 398–9. Collection of Michael Phillips. (The relevant pages are reproduced in Michael Phillips, *William Blake. The Creation of the Songs. From Manuscript to Illuminated Printing.* (London: The British Library, 2000), pp. 56–7)

This example of a reader's response to the Bentley edition of *Paradise Lost* comes from the marginal comments written into one copy of the edition. Printed materials cannot tell the full story of *Paradise Lost's* readership and it is in evidence such as marginalia that we may discover more about the general reader and perhaps the 'fit' audience. The comment quoted here is one of two in the volume signed with the initials, W.B. It is possible that W.B. is William Blake. In any case, the annotator is showing frustration at Bentley's crass audacity. The emendation made by Bentley to the last lines of the poem is simply crossed out, along with Bentley's note to those lines, and in the margin we have a repost by the reader stating that he admires Bentley's 'hardiness'.

. . . who would expunge these last two Lines, as proper and surely as beautiful as any! in the whole Poem, and substitute cold expressions foreign to the Author's ~~Judgement~~ probable and natural meaning, *viz.* 'that they left Paradise with regret' if any one thinks otherwise I desire no better proof of the state of his feelings

From **Edmund Burke, *A Philosophical Enquiry into the Origin of Our Ideas of the Sublime and Beautiful*** (1757)

Burke's treatise on the distinction between the beautiful and the sublime remains extremely influential. He identifies uncertainty, intensity and terror as central qualities in heightening the aesthetic experience to the level of sublimity and takes a number of his examples from *Paradise Lost* (see **pp. 92–3**). The Romantic poets are greatly influenced by Burke's theory of the sublime.

Here is a very noble picture; and in what does this poetical picture consist? In images of a tower, an archangel, the sun rising through mists, or in an eclipse, the ruin of monarchs, and the revolution of kingdoms. The mind is hurried out of itself, by a croud of great and confused images; which affect because they are crouded and confused.

From **Olaudah Equiano, *The Interesting Narrative of the Life of Olaudah Equiano, or Gustavus Vassa, The African*** (1789), vol i, pp. 189–90

Olaudah Equiano's *Interesting Narrative* is the autobiography of a freed slave and it was an immediate bestseller on its publication in 1789. Equiano tells us that he was kidnapped in Africa at the age of ten, enslaved and transported to the Caribbean. He had many adventures before being bought by a British naval officer and taken to London. He then served in the Royal Navy for a number of years but was denied his promised freedom in 1762. Instead, the officer resold him and he found himself embarked once again for the West Indies without any knowledge of his ultimate fate. This extract comes from that moment in Equiano's story as he describes his voyage to the island of Monserrat. It recounts his shock at the English officer's perfidy and his psychological terror at discovering that not only is he to remain a slave but that he will be returning to the physical cruelties of life in the West Indies. His desperation leads Equiano to quote from *Paradise Lost* the lines that first describe to us the experience of Hell (see **pp. 86–7**). Equiano finally succeeded in buying his freedom in 1766. He then worked as a supervisor on plantations and later settled in England, becoming a leading figure in the anti-slavery movement.

The turbulence of my emotions, however, naturally gave way to calmer thoughts, and I soon perceived what fate had decreed no mortal on earth could prevent. The convoy sailed on without any accident, with a pleasant gale and smooth sea, for six weeks, till February, when one morning the OEolus ran down a brig,[1] one of the convoy, and she instantly went down and was ingulfed in the dark recesses of

1 The Aeolus is the name of a navy frigate that is escorting the convoy across the Atlantic. Unfortunately, it collides with one of the merchant ships and that vessel is sunk.

the ocean. The convoy was immediately thrown into great confusion till it was day-light; and the OEolus was illuminated with lights to prevent any farther mischief. On the 13th of February 1763, from the mast-head, we descried our destined island Montserrat; and soon after I beheld those

> Regions of sorrow, doleful shades, where peace
> And rest can rarely dwell.[2] Hope never comes
> That comes to all, but torture without end
> Still urges.

At the sight of this land of bondage, a fresh horror ran through all my frame, and chilled me to the heart. My former slavery now rose in dreadful review to my mind, and displayed nothing but misery, stripes, and chains; and, in the first paroxysm of my grief, I called upon God's thunder, and his avenging power, to direct the stroke of death to me, rather than permit me to become a slave, and to be sold from lord to lord.

From **Mary Wollstonecraft, *A Vindication of the Rights of Woman: with Strictures on Political and Moral Subjects*** (London, 1792), pp. 33, 114

Wollstonecraft offers a stringent critique of Milton's depiction of prelapsarian Eve within *A Vindication of the Rights of Woman* (1792). This radical tract encourages female education as the best means of achieving social equality between the sexes. Wollstonecraft wants to expose the tyranny of patriarchal conventions and to bring about a revolution in female manners through education. Her approach combines both literary criticism and social comment. She needs to counter stereotypes of female character and she understands clearly that literary texts make up part of our cultural conditioning. In part it is because Wollstonecraft knows and esteems Milton's work that she exposes the inconsistencies in his thought (e.g., she considers the childlike innocence of Eve depicted in Book IV to contradict Adam's wish in Book VIII for an equal and rational mate, see **pp. 128–9**) but she is also responding directly to the anodyne application of Milton's Eve in conduct books such as James Fordyce's *Sermons to Young Women* (1766). *Rights of Woman* is a rallying cry to all women and a rhetorical *tour de force* intended for wide circulation. Elsewhere, in her personal letters, we can find Wollstonecraft acknowledging the erotic within Milton's exploration of Edenic relations most positively. For example, in a letter to William Godwin of 15 September 1796, Wollstonecraft suggests that she would follow Eve's example in preferring information to be intermixed with kisses (compare *PL* VIII 52–7): 'You are to give me a lesson this evening – And, a word in your ear, I shall not be very angry if you sweeten grammatical disquisitions after the Miltonic mode'.

2 Poignantly, Equiano's version emends the line very slightly from 'rest can never dwell' to 'rarely dwell'.

Women are told from their infancy, and taught by the example of their mothers, that a little knowledge of human weakness, justly termed cunning, softness of temper, *outward* obedience, and a scrupulous attention to a puerile kind of propriety, will obtain for them the protection of man; and should they be beautiful, every thing else is needless, for, at least, twenty years of their lives.

Thus Milton describes our first frail mother; though when he tells us that women are formed for softness and sweet attractive grace,[1] I cannot comprehend his meaning, unless, in the true Mahometan strain,[2] he meant to deprive us of souls, and insinuate that we were beings only designed by sweet attractive grace, and docile blind obedience, to gratify the senses of man when he can no longer soar on the wing of contemplation.

How grossly do they insult us who thus advise us only to render ourselves gentle, domestic brutes ! [. . .]

Let not men then in the pride of power, use the same arguments that tyrannic kings and venal ministers have used, and fallaciously assert that woman ought to be subjected because she has always been so. – But, when man, governed by reasonable laws, enjoys his natural freedom, let him despise woman; if she do not share it with him; and, till that glorious period arrives, in descanting on the folly of the sex, let him not overlook his own.

Women, it is true, obtaining power by unjust means, by practising or fostering vice, evidently lose the rank which reason would assign them, and they become either abject slaves or capricious tyrants. They lose all simplicity, all dignity of mind, in acquiring power, and act as men are observed to act when they have been exalted by the same means.

It is time to effect a revolution in female manners – time to restore to them their lost dignity – and make them, as a part of the human species, labour by reforming themselves to reform the world. It is time to separate unchangeable morals from local manners. – If men be demi-gods – why let us serve them! And if the dignity of the female soul be as disputable as that of animals – if their reason does not afford sufficient light to direct their conduct whilst unerring instinct is denied – they are surely of all creatures the most miserable! and, bent beneath the iron hand of destiny, must submit to be a *fair defect* in Creation.[3] But to justify the ways of Providence respecting them, by pointing out some irrefragable[4] reason for thus making such a large portion of mankind accountable and not accountable, would puzzle the subtilest casuist.[5]

1 *PL* IV 298.
2 Mohammedan. Wollstonecraft is in full rhetorical flow but it is, of course, not true to say that Islam deprives women of souls.
3 *PL* X 891–2. The next sentence echoes *PL* I 26 (see **p. 86**).
4 Undeniable, indisputable.
5 One who resolves difficult cases of conscience. Often employed (as here) in a negative sense to imply that the individual is capable of sophistry or excessive quibbling.

From **William Blake, *The Marriage of Heaven and Hell***, Plates 5 and 6 (1790–3) in *William Blake's Writing*, 2 vols, ed. G. E. Bentley (Oxford: Clarendon Press, 1978), vol. i, pp. 79–80

William Blake, the radical poet and visionary, disagreed profoundly with orthodox religion and patriarchal authority. Yet he had an abiding admiration for Milton. In fact, his principles of opposition are in part developed through his reading of *Paradise Lost*. This extract, a conscious inversion of the orthodox Christian interpretation of the epic's theology, is often quoted. It comes from *The Marriage of Heaven and Hell* (engraved 1790–3). In this text, constructed out of axiomatic paradoxes, Blake aimed to embody the fact, as he saw it, that opposition is a vital part of the human condition.

Those who restrain desire do so because theirs is weak enough to be restrained; and the restrainer or reason usurps its place & governs the unwilling.

And, being restraind, it by degrees becomes passive till it is only the shadow of desire.

The history of this is written in Paradise Lost, & the Governor or Reason is call'd Messiah. [. . .]

Note. The reason Milton wrote in fetters[1] when he wrote of Angels & God, and at liberty when of Devils & Hell, is because he was a true Poet and of the Devils party without knowing it.

From **Samuel Taylor Coleridge, *Lectures 1808–19 On Literature***, ed. R. A. Foakes (London and Princeton, NJ: Routledge & Kegan Paul/Princeton University Press, 1987), p. 496 in Volume 5.ii of *The Collected Works of Samuel Taylor Coleridge*, 16 Vols, General ed. Kathleen Coburn (London & Princeton, NJ: Routledge & Kegan Paul/Princeton University Press, 1971–2001)

Coleridge's most famous poems, *Kubla Khan* and *The Rime of the Ancient Mariner*, reveal an interest in such Miltonic themes as paradisal gardens and the Fall of man but his reading of *Paradise Lost* was also important to his developing theory of the imagination. Coleridge, like Burke before him, seems to have been particularly taken by the passage in Book II on Death (see **pp. 96–8**). He refers to its thrillingly apposite indefinition on a number of occasions and quotes it in chapter 13, 'On the Imagination', in *Biographia Literaria*. This quotation comes from John Payne Collier's account of one of Coleridge's many public lectures.

The grandest efforts of poetry are where the imagination is called forth, not to produce a distinct form, but a strong working of the mind, still offering what is still repelled, and again creating what is again rejected; the result being what the

1 Chains or shackles. Blake wishes forcefully to suggest an imposed impediment to free movement.

poet wishes to impress, namely, the substitution of a sublime feeling of the unimaginable for a mere image. I have sometimes thought that the passage just read[1] might be quoted as exhibiting the narrow limit of painting, as compared with the boundless power of poetry: *painting cannot go beyond a certain point; poetry rejects all control, all confinement*. Yet we know that sundry painters have attempted pictures of the meeting between Satan and Death at the gates of Hell; and how was Death represented? Not as Milton has described him, but by the most defined thing that can be imagined – a skeleton, the dryest and hardest image that it is possible to discover; . . .

From **P. B. Shelley, *A Defence of Poetry*** (1821), ed. Albert S. Cook (Boston: Ginn & Company, 1891), pp. 30–1

Shelley's prose *Defence*, written in 1821, is a political manifesto. Responding to the contention that poetry had become an obsolete art, Shelley proudly counters with his claim that poets are the 'unacknowledged legislators of the world' (p. 46). Such a prominent role for the poet as prophet or legislator helps to explain the social critique that underpins Shelley's own work and his reading of *Paradise Lost*. In this extract from the *Defence*, Shelley contends that the wrongs perpetrated against Satan and his indefatigable resistance make him a 'superior being' (even though he is ambitious, etc.). The conclusion that God is a tyrant is a remarkably strong counter-current in Milton studies, traceable from Blake and Godwin, through Shelley to Empson and now on to Pullman.

Nothing can exceed the energy and magnificence of Satan as expressed in *Paradise Lost*. It is a mistake to suppose that he could ever have been intended for the popular personification of evil. Implacable hate, patient cunning, and a sleepless refinement of device to inflict the extremest anguish on an enemy – these things are evil; and, although venial in a slave are not to be forgiven in a tyrant; although redeemed by much that ennobles his defeat in one subdued, are marked by all that dishonours his conquest in the victor. Milton's Devil as a moral being is as far superior to his God as one who perseveres in some purpose which he has conceived to be excellent, in spite of adversity and torture, is to one who in the cold security of undoubted triumph inflicts the most horrible revenge upon his enemy, not from any mistaken notion of inducing him to repent of a perseverance in enmity, but with the alleged design of exasperating him to deserve new torments. Milton has so far violated the popular creed (if this shall be judged to be a violation) as to have alleged no superiority of moral virtue to his God over his Devil. And this bold neglect of a direct moral purpose is the most decisive proof of the supremacy of Milton's genius.

1 *PL* II 666–73. See p. 98.

From **Mary Shelley, *Frankenstein or the Modern Prometheus*** (1818), Book II, Ch. 7

First published in 1818, the novel *Frankenstein* offers a far-reaching critique of human audacity and ambition. Its male protagonist is a young scientist who brings to life a being from inanimate materials. The creature is deemed monstrous by all that behold it and is rejected even by its creator. The denial of all human sympathy, and a growing conscious understanding of his enforced alienation, leads the monster to undertake a protracted and horrific revenge upon his creator. The story has been variously interpreted as a Gothic novel, a critique of modern science, an archetypal moral tale, and a feminist expression of the woman's writer's alienation (see **p. 75**). The importance of the Miltonic connection is acknowledged on the novel's title page with its epigraph, 'Did I request thee, Maker, from my clay / To mould Me man? Did I solicit thee / From darkness to promote me?' This quotation comes from Book X 743–5 of *Paradise Lost* and is part of Adam's impassioned lament as he begins to realise the full implications of his disobedience. Adam will conclude that he cannot blame his Creator for what has happened but must accept responsibility for his own actions (see **pp. 144–7**). Shelley, shrewdly, lets the Miltonic question stand unanswered on her title page. She does so in the face of the male Romantic tradition, including her knowledge of the question posed and answered by her father, William Godwin, in his *Enquiry Concerning Political Justice* (1793), 'Why did Satan rebel against his maker? . . . because he saw no sufficient reason for that extreme inequality of rank and power which the creator assumed' (p. 309).

This extract comes from the monster's personal narration of his earliest impressions of the world and his experiences of rejection. The monster's conscious self (like that of his ultimate 'creator' the author Mary Shelley) is constructed in part through social contact and in part through self-education. He is provided with a small but pertinent library by Shelley – Milton for theology and morality, Plutarch for public and civic virtues, Goethe for private sentiment, and finally the personal journal of Frankenstein which gives the monster an insight into the callous ambition and prejudice of his author.

But *Paradise Lost* excited different and far deeper emotions. I read it, as I had read the other volumes which had fallen into my hands, as a true history. It moved every feeling of wonder and awe, that the picture of an omnipotent God warring with his creatures was capable of exciting. I often referred the several situations, as their similarity struck me, to my own. Like Adam, I was apparently united by no link to any other being in existence; but his state was far different from mine in every other respect. He had come forth from the hands of God a perfect creature, happy and prosperous, guarded by the especial care of his Creator; he was allowed to converse with and acquire knowledge from beings of a superior nature: but I was wretched, helpless, and alone. Many times I considered Satan as the fitter emblem of my condition; for often, like him, when I viewed the bliss of my protectors, the bitter gall of envy rose within me.

Another circumstance strengthened and confirmed these feelings. Soon after my arrival in the hovel, I discovered some papers in the pocket of the dress which I had taken from your laboratory. At first I had neglected them; but now that I was able to decypher the characters in which they were written, I began to study them with diligence. It was your journal of the four months that preceded my Creation. You minutely described in these papers every step you took in the progress of your work; this history was mingled with accounts of domestic occurrences. You, doubtless, recollect these papers. Here they are. Every thing is related in them which bears reference to my accursed origin; the whole detail of that series of disgusting circumstances which produced it is set in view; the minutest description of my odious and loathsome person is given, in language which painted your own horrors and rendered mine ineffacable.[1] I sickened as I read. 'Hateful day when I received life!' I exclaimed in agony. 'Cursed creator! Why did you form a monster so hideous that even you turned from me in disgust? God, in pity, made man beautiful and alluring, after his own image; but my form is a filthy type of yours, more horrid from its very resemblance. Satan had his companions, fellow-devils, to admire and encourage him; but I am solitary and detested.'

1 i.e., unable to be erased.

Modern Criticism

From **Karl Marx, *Theories of Surplus Value***, Part I (Moscow, n.d.), p. 389 in Christopher Hill, *Milton and the English Revolution* (London: Faber & Faber, 1977), p. 354

Karl Marx did not himself develop a systematic aesthetic theory but he did include comments on literature and the arts within his texts. Here, although he judges *Paradise Lost* as an economic product, relating it to the historical and ideological conditions of production possible in its time, he also retains some acceptance of an individual imperative. Marxist criticism insists that the literary work be studied as a product of historical and ideological conditions. This refers not only to the moment of composition or publication of a material product but also to the conditions under which later audiences have encountered and responded to it. The approach has been extremely influential within Milton studies.

The same kind of labour may be *productive* or *unproductive*. For example Milton, who wrote *Paradise Lost* for £5, was an *unproductive labourer*. On the other hand, the writer who turns out stuff for his publisher in factory style, is a *productive labourer*. Milton produced *Paradise Lost* for the same reason that a silk worm produces silk. It was an activity of *his* nature.

From **Sigmund Freud, Letter to Martha Bernays** (16 August 1882) in Ernest Jones, *Sigmund Freud. Life and Works*, 2 Vols (London: Hogarth Press, 1980), Vol. i., p. 195

Paradise Lost was one of Freud's favourite books but it is nonetheless a little bizarre to find this reference in a love letter, particularly as he goes on to cite lines relating to Hell! Freud is known as the father of psychoanalysis for his work on the unconscious mind at the beginning of the twentieth century. Many of his theories have been readily applied as tools in literary criticism, and those regarding repression, the interpretation of dreams and the Oedipal complex [the repressed or unconscious desire of the (male) child for the mother's love, in rivalry to the Father] have been particularly stimulating in criticism on Milton's epic. It is therefore rather satisfying to know that Freud had read Milton, though Milton never had the opportunity to read Freud.

I am taking up again the history of the island, the works of the men who were my real teachers – all of them English or Scotch; and I am recalling what is for me the most interesting historical period, the reign of the Puritans and Oliver Cromwell with its lofty monument of that time – *Paradise Lost*, where only recently, when I did not feel sure of your love, I found consolation and comfort.

From **F. R. Leavis, 'Milton's Verse'** in *Revaluation: Tradition and Development in English Poetry* (London: Chatto & Windus, 1936), pp. 43–4

Leavis was one of the most influential literary critics and teachers of the twentieth century. His work brought a new vigour and seriousness to English Studies, though his opinions were often controversial. He championed T. S. Eliot and Ezra Pound over Tennyson and Swinburne in *New Bearings in English Poetry* (1932), co-founded the review *Scrutiny* which he then edited from 1932–53, and drew up a new canon of novelists in *The Great Tradition* (1948). His views on Milton chime with those of T. S. Eliot.

Even in the first two books of *Paradise Lost*, where the myth has vigorous life and one can admire the magnificent invention that Milton's verse is, we feel, after a few hundred lines, our sense of dissatisfaction growing into something stronger. In the end we find ourselves protesting – protesting against the routine gesture, the heavy fall, of the verse, flinching from the unforeseen thud that comes so inevitably, and, at last, so irresistibly: for reading *Paradise Lost* is a matter of resisting, of standing up against, the verse-movement, of subduing it into something tolerably like sensitiveness, and in the end our resistance is worn down; we surrender at last to the monotony of the ritual.

From ***The Autobiography of Malcolm X*** ([Hutchison 1966], Penguin, 2001), pp. 281–2. Copyright Alex Haley and Malcolm X, 1964; Alex Haley and Betty Shabazz, 1965

Malcolm X was a controversial figure and a militant spokesman for minority rights in the US. He completed his autobiography shortly before his assassination in 1965. It was intended as a platform from which to continue the fight against oppression and racism, showing the importance of education for self-determination and as a tool to combat the Western imperialist indifference to the sufferings of minorities. This extract comes midway through Malcolm X's testimony. In prison, having recently converted to Islam, he discovers the power of education and the importance of debate as a weapon in the fight for freedom and equality. Reading the Western classics allows him to challenge many of the presumptions of a white 'civilised' superiority (e.g., Homer may well have been a black man). *Paradise Lost* in Malcolm X's eyes is a warning against European imperialist ambitions.

In either volume 43 or 44 of The Harvard Classics, I read Milton's *Paradise Lost*. The devil, kicked out of Paradise, was trying to regain possession. He was using the forces of Europe, personified by the Popes, Charlemagne, Richard the Lion-hearted, and other knights. I interpreted this to show that the Europeans were motivated and led by the devil, or the personification of the devil. So Milton and Mr Elijah Muhammad were actually saying the same thing.[1]

From **A BBC Profile interview with Philip Pullman** (First Broadcast Date: Thursday, 28 February 2002)

Pullman is a respected children's writer and the author of the acclaimed prose fiction trilogy, *His Dark Materials* (Scholastic, 2001). This new epic of innocence versus experience acknowledges a debt to Milton in its very title (*PL* II 916), though Pullman has also been strongly influenced by Blake's reading of Milton. In this television interview, Pullman recalls his encounter with the epic as a schoolboy. He remembers experiencing an immediate rapport with the poetry itself – an adrenalin rush that did not rely on the study of footnotes but on an immersion in the flow of the language.

We did Books I & II of *Paradise Lost* for 'A' Level and I just remember the sense of going through this extraordinary stuff and it having a physical effect on me. I mean it made my skin bristle, it made my heart go faster, it made me almost tremble physically – the power of this language.

From **Barbara K. Lewalski, *Paradise Lost and the Rhetoric of Literary Forms*** (Princeton, NJ: Princeton University Press, 1985), pp. 19–20

Lewalski's book explains Renaissance genre theory and shows how various literary modes and genres are fitted to different moments within Milton's epic. As students of the poem, we need to be aware of such formal strategies if we are to appreciate both Milton's technical ambition and his artistic mastery.

1 Elijah Muhammad was a founder of the sect, The Nation of Islam, and a major influence upon Malcolm X.

Milton employs specific literary modes in *Paradise Lost* to characterize the various orders of being: the heroic mode for Satan and his damned society; mixed for the celestial order; pastoral (opening out to georgic and comedic) for prelapsarian life in Eden; tragic (encompassing at length postlapsarian georgic, pastoral, and heroic) for human life in the fallen world. These modes are made to govern the relevant segments of the poem through the use of appropriate subject matter, topoi,[1] tone, and language. Also, each mode is introduced by explicit signals. As the narrative begins, the epic question and its answer (1.27–54) present Satan and hell in heroic terms. The Edenic pastoral mode is introduced by reference to the garden as "A happy rural seat of various view" (4.247). The forthright announcement "I now must change / These Notes to Tragic" (9.5–6) heralds the Fall sequence. And the affirmation that a tragic subject may be more heroic than traditional epic themes leads into the mixed modes of postlapsarian but regenerate human life.

These several modes import into the poem the values traditionally associated with them: great deeds, battle courage, glory (*aristeia*) for the heroic mode; love and song, *otium*, the carefree life for pastoral; responsibility, discipline, and the labor of husbandry for georgic; the easy resolution of difficulties through dialogue and intellect for the comedic; the pity and terror of the human condition for the tragic. These contrasting modes and their modulations, together with the mixed modes that present the celestial order, engage us in an ongoing critique of the various perspectives on human life that they provide.

From **Christopher Ricks, *Milton's Grand Style*** (Oxford: Oxford University Press, 1963), pp. 93–6

Milton's Grand Style is one of the most rewarding guides to Milton's epic and a classic within Milton criticism. When it was first published in the 1960s, Ricks was bravely contradicting the received critical wisdom that Milton's style was deficient. He did so by producing a stimulating close appreciation of the subtleties in Milton's language and syntax. In this extract Ricks gives us the memorable phrase 'fluidity of syntax' for the poetic expression of harmonious correspondence and sensory interplay to be found in the Edenic state.

Milton uses such fluidity of syntax so that it both makes clear sense and also is suggestive. Sometimes the suggestion is of a hyperbolical beauty which it would be indecorous to state as fact – particularly in the epic. To show this at work, it is best to take one of the most powerful and consistent of the Paradisal images: the mingled beauties of sight and of scent (and of sound too). The image itself is a lovely one, but it is the mingling syntax which brings it to life, which both suggests the magically pre-lapsarian and states the matter of fact. [. . .]

When we see Eve as she

> strews the ground
> With Rose and Odours from the shrub unfum'd (v. 348–9)

1 Traditional themes.

we know perfectly well what is meant and find no unseemly violence of syntax. But the actual sequence – 'strews the ground with odours' – makes the scents magically visible and physical. So, too, does the superb word-order in these lines:

So to the Silvan Lodge
They came, that like Pomona's Arbour smil'd
With flourets deck't and fragrant smells; but Eve
Undeckt . . . (v. 377–80)

If we want simple sense, then 'deck't' goes only with 'flourets' and not with 'smells' – 'deck't with smells' might be too boldly metaphorical if baldly stated. But the lines do obliquely state it, and the encircling of 'fragrant smells' by *deck't* and *undeckt* ensures that the metaphor is not so obliquely presented as to be itself invisible. The imagination once again treats scents as if they were as solid and visible as flowers. And there is also a perfectly intelligible non-metaphorical syntax ('smil'd with fragrant smells and deck't with flourets'). The lines combine the virtues of both poetry and prose. Moreover, they achieve through syntax the mingling of the senses which Keats achieves through diction: 'Nor what soft incense hangs upon the boughs.'

This particular image for the beauty of Paradise can take simpler forms. There is the syntactical stroke of describing 'Cassia, Nard, and Balme' not – as we would expect – as 'odorous flowers', but as 'flouring Odours'. Bentley found the phrase 'Affectation extravagant'; Pearce paltered; and it was left to Richardson to maintain that the phrase was a fine one.[1] And the beautifully unexpected substantiality of the scents here is skilfully introduced by 'field' and 'Groves':

and now is come
Into the blissful field, through Groves of Myrrhe,
And flouring Odours, Cassia, Nard, and Balme. (v. 291–3)

Or the syntactical imagination can juxtapose 'Rose' and 'Odours' as if they were of equal substantiality, and then apply to them both a verb that, in its vigour, insists on the substantial

fresh Gales and gentle Aires
Whisper'd it to the Woods, and from thir wings
Flung Rose, flung Odours from the spicie Shrub. (viii. 515–17)

The close parallel there with the first passage quoted above (v. 348–9) brings out how important to Milton is this image of Paradise. (The biographical critic would justifiably make at once for Milton's blindness.) And the poet invests Eve with this image as Satan fatally finds her:

1 Ricks is referencing three eighteenth-century commentators. Jonathan Richardson, *Explanatory Notes on Paradise Lost* (1734), p. 218; Richard Bentley, *Paradise Lost* (1732), p. 157; Zachery Pearce, *A Review of the Text of Milton's Paradise Lost* (1732), p. 169.

Eve separate he spies,
Veil'd in a Cloud of Fragrance, where she stood,
Half spi'd . . . (ix. 424–6)

The veil and the cloud make the roses' scent beautifully visible – does 'Half spi'd' even perhaps suggest that the scent was so thick that it almost hid her? Not really, because I have cut short the sentence:

Half spi'd, so thick the Roses bushing round
About her glowd.

Reasonably, it is not the scent but the roses which hide her. But the other instances of Milton's seeing a scent, and the general fluidity of his syntax, persuade me that we are meant for a moment to believe that 'Half spi'd' follows the *Fragrance*, just as it follows 'he spies'. Of course it in fact anticipates the roses, but the deliberate 'flicker of hesitation' which Dr. Davie finds elsewhere in Milton is perhaps being used here with characteristic subtlety.[2] Like a skilful advocate, Milton says something which would be impermissibly far-fetched, and then has it struck from the record. But his skill has lodged it in our minds or feelings.

From **Stanley Fish, *Surprised by Sin: the Reader in Paradise Lost*** (Macmillan, 1967; [paperback] Berkeley, Cal. & London: University of California Press, 1971), p. 38

Stanley Fish's reader-response approach to *Paradise Lost* has been both remarkably influential and markedly controversial. His contention is that the reading experience of *Paradise Lost* mirrors its doctrinal message. Each reader immediately falls into error by listening to the rhetoric of Satan. This error is pointed out to us by the morally superior narrator and, in order to rectify our fault, we must humbly admit our fallen deficiencies, learn to be distrustful of rhetoric, and submit to the guidance of the narrator. This short extract more or less sums up Fish's position. His reading-as-trial-of-virtue thesis is presumably to be associated with that delineated by Milton in his prose tract, *Areopagitica* (see **pp. 18–20**). However, Fish's insistence on the discovery of a single orthodox reading position frustrates many more liberal-minded literary critics who continue to enjoy the free play of metaphor within poetry.

Most poets write for an audience assumed fit.[1] Why is the fitness of Milton's audience a concern of the poem itself? One answer to this question has been given in the preceding pages: only by forcing upon his reader an awareness of his limited

2 Donald Davie, 'Syntax and Music in *Paradise Lost*' in *The Living Milton*, ed. Frank Kermode (London: Routledge & Kegan Paul, 1960), pp. 70–84, quoting p. 73. Davie is commentating on the phrase 'that voluntary move/ Harmonious numbers' (III 37–8), see **pp. 99–100**.

1 Cf., VII 31, see **p. 125**.

perspective can Milton provide even a negative intuition of what another would be like; it is a brilliant solution to the impossible demands of his subject, enabling him to avoid the falsification of anthropomorphism and the ineffectiveness of abstraction. Another answer follows from this one: the reader who fails repeatedly before the pressures of the poem soon realizes that his difficulty proves its major assertions – the fact of the Fall, and his own (that is Adam's) responsibility for it, and the subsequent woes of the human situation. The reasoning is circular, but the circularity is appropriate to the uniqueness of the poem's subject matter; for while in most poems effects are achieved through the manipulation of reader response, this poet is telling the story that *created* and still creates the responses of its reader and of all readers. The reader who falls before the lures of Satanic rhetoric displays again the weakness of Adam, and his inability to avoid repeating that fall throughout indicates the extent to which Adam's lapse has made the reassertion of right reason impossible. Rhetoric is thus simultaneously the sign of the reader's infirmity and the means by which he is brought first to self-knowledge, and then to contrition, and finally, perhaps, to grace and everlasting bliss.

From **William Empson, *Milton's God*** (London: Chatto & Windus, 1961), pp. 261–2

Empson's approach lies squarely within a liberal humanist tradition but his tone is intentionally controversial. Amongst his own contemporaries, he has the critic C. S. Lewis in his sights, but he is infuriated in general by what he sees as Christian complacency and therefore chooses to combine his reading of Milton with wider social comment. Empson is an atheist and he finds Christianity to be a seriously flawed system of belief (his word is 'evil'). As this extract opens he has just posited the case that Christians, by their obsession with suffering and torture, actually worship the Devil. His wider thesis is akin to Blake's in that he identifies the strength of Milton's poem to lie in its subversive implications, specifically for Empson the championing of human courage and emotion over restrictive obedience. In Empson's reading, the poem far from justifying the ways of God to man actually amounts to an indictment of the injustices inherent in the Christian belief system.

A Christian is likely to find this idea evidently wrong, by definition; because it is a basic belief of Christians that their God is the origin and sanction of all goodness. There is no harm in the dogma itself, so long as we are allowed to recognize that our own consciences must decide whether what other people tell us about God is really good. Our own consciences are therefore the final judges even of truths vouchsafed to us by Revelation; there are seventeenth-century Anglicans who use this important doctrine, but it was not standard and I do not know its earlier history. The curious moral impudence of the neo-Christian literary critic comes from presuming that he has already been told the only correct moral answers. Maybe this is a fair enough reaction when confronted with much of our current literary output, but it is professionally bad for him, because the central function of imaginative literature is to make you realize that other people act on moral convictions different from your own. This indeed is why I think it makes an important difference to one's reading of Milton if he can be found good at such acts of imagination. What is more, it has been thought from Aeschylus to Ibsen[1] that a literary work may present a current moral problem, and to some extent alter the judgement of those who appreciate it by making them see the case as a whole. I was startled to realize that Professor W. K. Wimsatt, in his essay 'Poetry and Morals' (*The Verbal Icon*, 1954), in effect rejects this whole conception as romantic, since he already knows moral truth from a better source than the records of human experience. How about Huck Finn saying "All right, I'll go to Hell then" rather than betray Jim? Surely a lot of characters in fiction, not only Milton's Satan, must become pretty dull if the orthodoxy is always right. I do not mean to deny, of course, that the critic ought to express what moral convictions he has, and ought often to say that the author is wrong; but the idea that there actually couldn't be a moral debate in a literary work amounts to a collapse of the Western mind, quite unforeseen when I was young.

From **Dennis R. Danielson, *Milton's Good God: a Study in Literary Theodicy*** (Cambridge: Cambridge University Press, 1982), pp. 92–3

Danielson has produced one of the best introductions available to the theology in *Paradise Lost*. It is required reading for anyone who wishes to know how the Christian position might be defended against such critics as Empson. This extract clarifies both the doctrine of free will and the dilemma faced by most readers when they try to balance divine foreknowledge with human autonomy. It should be read alongside the lengthy conversation between God the Father and the Son in *Paradise Lost* Book III (see **pp. 101–4**) and Milton's defence of free will in *Areopagitica* (see **pp. 18–20**).

The Free Will Defense is a traditional model to explain how God's omnipotence and goodness might indeed both be asserted, even given the fact that this world contains evil, particularly moral evil. The argument is one that continues to provoke a great deal of interest in philosophical circles; put simplistically, it runs as follows: Evil, at least a great deal of it, is caused by the misuse of free will by angels and humans. However, it is a very great good that there be angels and humans, and that they be free creatures rather than some sort of automata. Furthermore, angels and humans cannot be both free and fully automatic. Not being fully automatic, their choices cannot be wholly controlled by God. Hence it may be that God had no choice but to make no free creatures at all, or else to make ones who could cause evil. Given such a choice, God was justified in creating humans and angels as he did. And yet the fact that he faced a dilemma in so doing is no slur on his omnipotence, because omnipotence does not include the power to

1 Aeschylus is the earliest of the great Greek tragic dramatists; Ibsen is an innovative late nineteenth-century dramatist.

actualize two incompossibles [*sic*], such as a person's being both fully automatic and free. Therefore, the argument concludes, the claims that God is omnipotent and wholly good and that evil exists in the world need imply no contradiction.

Clearly, each of this argument's constituent assertions needs clarification and support; but, in general, its plausibility as a whole will depend on the plausibility of the claims (1) that free creatures indeed cannot be wholly determined, (2) that the freedom of those creatures is finally 'worth it,' given the amount of evil they cause, and (3) that omnipotence cannot guarantee that what it creates will be the best of all possible worlds.

From **Francis C. Blessington, *Paradise Lost and the Classical Epic*** (London: Routledge & Kegan Paul, 1979), pp. 46–9

Blessington offers an accessible and thought-provoking introduction to the classical influence on *Paradise Lost*, and to Milton's ongoing dialogue with his epic precursors. He compares, for example, the character of Satan to that of Achilles in *The Iliad* and reveals surprising connections between the roles of Patroklos and Eve. It may surprise many modern readers to discover that the epic tradition remains relevant even to a discussion of Milton's theodicy, as this extract proves.

What the classical tradition invoked by Milton shows is that the relationship between man and god has changed as well as continued from the earlier epics. The Greeks and the Romans feared but did not love their gods. Man and god seldom confer in the classical epics, and the father of the gods and man never, but Adam actually argues with God for a mate. The distancing of the relationship of God and man is the legacy of the fall and is exemplified in the classical epics, but in *Paradise Lost*, the pristine relationship between God and man is momentarily restored.

The justice and mercy of God are the principal defenses of the ways of God to man. The first rests upon the assumption that man has free will, a claim that the Father makes: 'I made him just and right,/ Sufficient to have stood, though free to fall' (III, 98–9). The background of the three classical epics helps prove man's free will, if we accept Milton's reading of them, and I think we can. In his prose, Milton claims that the *Iliad* and the *Odyssey* were proof for the free will of man that existed '*besides fate*' (*Prose*, II, 294). Further, Milton found in the *Aeneid* (I, 39–41) an example of divine justice (*Prose*, VI, 387), where the sins of one sinner require expiation by a whole race. In his reading of the classical epics, Milton emphasizes that these epics are all partially theodicies: latent in the epic tradition is a defense of God's ways to man. The *Iliad* shows us a philosophically vague but poetically vivid picture of the relationship between god and man, between fate and free will, and between god and fate. A similar series of relationships inform the *Aeneid*, but it is to the *Odyssey* that we must turn in order to see the key passage that influenced Milton's conception of his God. The passage that Milton referred to in his prose and that Northrop Frye suggests in passing as a source for the speeches of the Father in Book III[1] gave the plaintive tone, the pure style, and the basis of defense for the God of *Paradise Lost*:

Blessington here quotes *The Odyssey* I, 26–43 in Greek before offering his own translation.

> (The other gods were together in the halls of Olympian Zeus, and the father of gods and men began to speak to them, for he remembered in his heart splendid Aigisthos, whom the far-famed son of Agamemnon, Orestes, killed. Remembering him, he spoke to the immortal gods: 'Alas, how men now find fault with the gods. They say evil comes from us, but they themselves have suffering due to their wicked deeds besides fate; as now besides his fate, Aigisthos married the wife of the son of Atreus and killed him returning home, Aigisthos knowing full well of [his own] utter destruction, since sending Hermes, sharp-sighted Argeiphontes, we told him before not to kill him nor to woo his wife. "For revenge will come from Orestes for the son of Atreus, when he comes of age and wants his land." Thus Hermes spoke, but these good intentions did not persuade the heart of Aigisthos; now he has atoned for all.')

This speech is the *locus classicus* of classical theodicy in epic poetry. Readers who remember this speech are likely to see in the Father's defensiveness a classical precedent:

> . . . So will fall
> Hee and his faithless Progeny: whose fault?
> Whose but his own? ingrate, he had of mee
> All he could have; I made him just and right,
> Sufficient to have stood, though free to fall (III, 95–9).

Readers are also likely to recollect that Hermes corresponds to Raphael and Abdiel, the two divine warners, who warn man and the rebellious angels, respectively, of their false steps. As Milton reminds us by using this parallel, the *Odyssey* is an epic of trial and fall: the suitors, the crew of Odysseus, Melanthios, and the twelve maidservants are all tested, judged guilty, and destroyed; on the other hand, Penelope, Telemachos, Laertes, Eumaeus, and Phemios are tested, judged innocent, and saved. The action of the poem proves the justice claimed by Zeus in the opening speech, just as the action of *Paradise Lost* makes good the Father's claim for the free will of His creatures. [. . .]

Milton's God goes beyond Zeus, of course. He has endowed man with reason, so that He need not rely upon force alone, and His greater power enables Him to do what Zeus often wanted to do but could not: save man's life. The Son's offer of His life for man's has no classical parallel and so it stands out all the more.

1 [Blessington's note.] Northrop Frye, *The Return of Eden* (University of Toronto Press, 1965), p. 99.

From **Stephen M. Fallon, *Milton among the Philosophers: Poetry and Materialism in Seventeenth-century England*** (Ithaca, NY: Cornell University Press, 1991), pp. 79, 80, 99–100, 102, 105–6

The discussion of seventeenth-century philosophy undertaken by Fallon is exacting but his argument is extremely important for furthering our critical awareness of Milton's radical thought. Fallon's careful study traces Milton's gradual development of heterodox views, arguing that by the 1650s Milton had come to believe in a holistic view of man and creation. This belief that matter and spirit are manifestations of one substance is a highly unorthodox position. It will affect our reading of the creational books of the epic profoundly and also our understanding of Chaos.

The young Milton's poetry is dualist, that is to say it presupposes a relation of body and soul traceable to Plato and Renaissance Neoplatonists. Embodied souls, having descended from the immaterial and supercelestial realm of the immutable forms, are trapped in alien matter. Properly directed souls aspire to escape the body and to reascend to their natural home; depraved souls descend into grosser bodies, either while alive or after death in reincarnation as brutes. [. . .]

By the time he came to write the Latin prose *Christian Doctrine* and *Paradise Lost* in the late 1650s and after, Milton had unequivocally repudiated the dualism of the early poems and thus separated himself from the Neoplatonism then reigning at Christ's, his undergraduate college at Cambridge. Instead of being trapped in an ontologically alien body, the soul is one with the body. Spirit and matter become for Milton two modes of the same substance: spirit is rarefied matter, and matter is dense spirit. All things, from insensate objects through souls are manifestations of this one substance. [. . .]

Milton's monistic conception of the relationship between body and soul is an affront to any of the available dualist conceptions, including the Platonic, the Christianized Aristotelian, and the Cartesian. "Unless we prefer to be instructed about the nature of the soul by heathen authors," Milton argues, we must conclude that "Man is a living being [*animal*], intrinsically and properly one and individual. He is not double or separable: not, as is commonly thought, produced from and composed of two different and distinct elements, soul and body. On the contrary, the whole man is the soul, and the soul the man [*totum hominem esse animam, et animam hominem*]: a body, in other words, an individual substance, animated, sensitive, and rational" (*CP* 6:317–18; *Works* 15:40). While Milton points to the Bible for authority and claims explicitly to shun "heathen authors," his conception here stems from Aristotle's hylomorphism: for Aristotle the form is the organization of body, not a superadded entity, and the soul is the form of a living body. Significantly though, Milton insists, unlike the great Christian Aristotelian Thomas Aquinas, that the rational soul is not different in kind from the sensitive and vegetative souls. Where Thomas thought that the vital and sensitive souls are transmitted in the semen while the rational or intellectual soul is incorporeal and infused by God, Milton agrees with Aristotle that the semen contains the entire soul (*CP* 6:319–22).[1] Milton claims disingenuously that "Nearly everyone agrees that all form – and the human soul is a kind of form – is produced by the power of matter [*ex potentia materiae produci*]" (*CP* 6:322; *Works* 15:48).[2] In fact, Christian Aristotelians followed Aquinas in excluding the production of the soul from the power of matter. [. . .]

Milton's materialist monism treats spirit and matter as manifestations, differing in degree and not qualitatively, of the one corporeal substance. Milton's spirit does not coexist with an alien matter; it contains matter: "Spirit, being the more excellent substance, virtually, as they say, and eminently contains within itself what is clearly the inferior substance [matter]; in the same way as the spiritual and rational faculty contains the corporeal, that is, the sentient and vegetative faculty" (*CP* 6:309). Milton struggles here to articulate monism with a vocabulary tempered by centuries of dualism. The inferiority of matter is neither moral nor dependent on an ontological gulf separating it from spirit; matter is merely more gross and less vital spirit. [. . .]

In Raphael's speech the plant begins as a metaphor for the steps of the hierarchy of matter only to become a synecdoche for the process by which creatures ascend the hierarchy. The focus shifts from synchronic image to diachronic process. The spiritous nature of the matter closer to God is analogized progressively in flower, fruit, and perfume (the "spirits odorous," a later version of the intellect preserved in a vial in *Areopagitica*?),[3] but these phenomena, present all at once to our senses, are themselves serial products of metabolism. The flowers and fruit, then, become man's food and are progressively metabolized into the faculties and, apparently, the soul itself. At the end of the process of digestion, the tenuously corporeal takes over the role normally reserved for the incorporeal by Platonists and scholastic Aristotelians. The tenuous intellectual spirits give rise to life, sense, fancy (or imagination), and understanding, and through them to reason, the being of the soul. Human discursive reason and angel intuitive reason differ "but in degree, of kind the same." This relation continues the principle of organization of the one first matter. When Milton has Raphael say,

> Wonder not then, what God for you saw good
> If I refuse not, but convert, as you,
> To proper substance; time may come when men
> With Angels may participate, and find
> No inconvenient Diet, nor too light Fare:
> And from these corporal nutriments perhaps
> Your bodies may at last turn all to spirit,
> Improv'd by tract of time, and wing'd ascend
> Ethereal, as wee, or may at choice
> Here or in Heav'nly Paradises dwell, (5.491–500)

1 [Fallon's note.] See *Summa theologiae* I, Q.118.

2 [Fallon's note.] Following William Hunter, I have modified the Yale translation. See "Milton's Power of Matter," *Journal of the History of Ideas* 13 (1952), pp. 551–62. My discussion of Milton and Aristotelian hylomorphism is indebted to this brief article, which contains a lucid discussion of Milton's conception of *potentia materiae*.

3 'For Books are not absolutely dead things, but do contain a potency of life in them to be as active as that soul was whose progeny they are: nay they do preserve as in a vial the purest efficacy and extraction of that living intellect that bred them', *Areopagitica* (1644), p. 4. [modernised spelling]

the roles of digester and digested are interchanged. The refined spirits in the plant are a product of the digestion of crude materials. The logic of the plant simile asks us to see man as digested by the world. From crude material to odorous spirits in the metabolism of the plant, from human being to angel in the metabolism of the animate world.

From **Diane K. McColley, *Milton's Eve*** (Champaign, Ill.: University of Illinois Press, 1983), pp. 110–11

Feminist responses to Milton's epic multiplied rapidly in the 1970s and 1980s. They offered a necessary corrective to (male) critical presumptions of woman's inherent weakness and susceptibility but sometimes rejected Milton out of hand as a misogynistic and authoritarian figure. McColley's work did not adopt such a polemic position but rather quietly built up the case for a more nuanced discussion of gender politics within the epic and beyond. She argues that it is Eve who asks the difficult questions first; Eve who is more thoroughly tested; and Eve who first conceives of a redemptive possibility (when she offers to take Adam's punishment upon herself in Book X). McColley also focuses our attention on life in the garden state, arguing that Eve is even more attuned to the Edenic environment than Adam. She has taken these insights further in her most recent work on the ecological implications of the poem.

When Milton shows Adam and Eve engaged in the art of gardening, he departs radically from the iconographic and literary traditions he inherited and provides the world its first demonstration of what a productive and responsible active life before the Fall might be. Cultivating one's garden is an activity of such universal application that there is scarcely any art, science, emotion, virtue, or ethic for which it cannot stand; and Milton's mimesis[1] of it is his pattern for a regenerate response to one's calling to do the work of this world, including his own work of poesie, in response to the divine voice. It is curious, therefore, that so many readers have seen the gardening of Adam and Eve as an inconsequential pastime, or a simple allegory of emotional order, and in particular have thought Eve's suggestion to Adam that they separate for a while to concentrate on their work a mere whim, a bit of feminine dabbling, or an excuse for willful roving. On the contrary, Milton's Eve is distinguished from all other Eves by the fact that she takes her work seriously.

A possible reason for the failure to take Eve's seriousness seriously is that modern psychology, and perhaps a pervasive subjectivity in moral life,[2] lead us in questions of motive to look for desires, appetites, "emotions" (as distinguished from the seventeenth-century "motions"), inward needs, and self-assertions. Nothing could be farther from the seventeenth-century conviction that one is

1 Representation.
2 [McColley's note.] For an excellent account of the habit of objective intellectual analysis of moral choices in Milton's age see Camille Wells Slights, *The Casuistical Tradition in Shakespeare, Donne, Herbert and Milton* (Princeton, 1981).

called by God and empowered by his Spirit to do her or his work in the world, and that this delegation of creativity and providence is the fount of human dignity and right relation and a major source of joy. The prelapsarian conscience as Milton represents it is *called* (and so grows) by what is outside itself: by God, by other beings, by needs and beauties and glories one's talents fit and move one to serve. The Garden is not only, as it is so often seen, a mirror of Adam's and Eve's emotional states, though it is affected by them. It is an organic community of interconnected lives to which their healthy minds delightedly respond. Eve's suggestion that she work on her own for a bit is a part of her response to her callings. God has called her, and the Garden calls her. Her motives or "motions" are not merely the devices and desires of her own heart. They are objective tasks to which her heart responds, and above all the voice of God commending all "kinds" to the care of humankind who are images of his generous love.

From **Karen L. Edwards, *Milton and the Natural World: Science and Poetry in Paradise Lost*** (Cambridge: Cambridge University Press, 1999), pp. 124–6

Edwards is interested in the development of natural history during the seventeenth century and she looks to see how Milton's poem engages with the new science and its methods of genus classification. This extract relates Raphael's metaphors in Book V to the extended description within Book VII of *Paradise Lost* of the six days of Creation (see **pp. 125–8**). Edwards's core argument is that Adam's understanding of life on earth is non-competitive and non-hierarchical. The lion may appear first amongst the mammals but it is not inherently superior. This is a crucial point to set against Satanic ambition and the rejection of imperialism within the poem. It should also be remembered if you encounter over-subtle critical discussions of an inequality between Adam and Eve before the Fall. Book VII encourages diversity and multiplicity, celebrating the life-force and the perfection of each created entity.

The work of Creation in *Paradise Lost* is represented as a balance between two impulses: dividing and distinguishing, and integrating into wholeness. The Son's initial creative act demonstrates that balance. The circumference he draws around the universe simultaneously separates it from Chaos and forms it into a discrete whole. Just so, Raphael's representation of the Fifth and Sixth Days' work sets distinctions among the creatures within an integrating order. We may call that order the scale of nature, or with Lovejoy call it the Great Chain of Being,[1] as long as we remember that to name it is not necessarily to understand its workings in *Paradise Lost*. Allusions to the *scala naturae* occur throughout the poem, most explicitly in book V, when Raphael compares the structure of the universe to a

1 Edwards is referring to Arthur O. Lovejoy's seminal work, *The Great Chain of Being: a Study of the History of an Idea* (Cambridge, Mass.: Harvard University Press, 1964).

plant. In conventional form, the Great Chain of Being is static. Because it assumes that each creature has an ordained place, it reinforces established political and social hierarchies. As scholars have frequently observed, however, Milton's construing of "the scale of nature" is dynamic – "as dynamic as any evolutionary system of more recent times" remarks Alastair Fowler (*PL*, v.469–90n).[2] A number of studies have demonstrated that this dynamic scale of being has important consequences for Milton's political and theological views. It has important consequences, too, for Milton's natural history; as Adam's response to Raphael's plant metaphor suggests:

> Well hast thou taught the way that might direct
> Our knowledge, and the scale of nature set.
> From centre to circumference, whereon
> In contemplation of created things
> By steps we may ascend to God. (*PL*, v.508–12)

Two images are juxtaposed here, the scale and the circle. If we identify Adam's *circumference* with the Son's (*PL*, vii.231), it will be clear that Adam understands from Raphael's words that there is not one scale of nature but many, perhaps an infinite number. He seems to picture them radiating out from God's throne as ribbons stream out from a maypole. The contemplator of created things can start at any point (i.e., any creature) on the "circumference" and ascend from there to God.

The difficulty with even the dynamic scale of nature perceived by Fowler and others is that it remains linear and there is only one line. Because creatures occupy a "lower" or "higher" place in relation to other creatures, comparisons of worth are inevitable, though usually disguised. The debate about whether Adam should have insisted that Eve stay by his side in book IX is of course a question about whether Adam's authority is higher than Eve's. To assume that Raphael has much to teach Adam and little to learn from him is to assume that angels are superior to human beings. Such comparisons assess the "inferior" in terms of the "superior," which means that they do not fully see either. The inadequacy of using comparisons for knowing a creature's worth becomes clear in the animal realm. Is an elephant superior to a whale? Is a crocodile superior to a butterfly? The questions are nonsensical. Adam's response to Raphael draws a new picture of the scale of nature, one which assigns absolute rather than relative worth to each creature and which strips away the worst implications of "knowing one's place." As Raphael's plant does, so each creature *in itself* offers the contemplator the means to ascend step by step to God.

2 Edwards references the first edition of Fowler (1968).

From **Joan S. Bennett, *Reviving Liberty: Radical Christian Humanism in Milton's Great Poems*** (Cambridge, Mass.: Harvard University Press, 1989), pp. 77–9

In this extract, Bennett offers an astute close reading of the errors in logic made by Eve during her temptation in Book IX of *Paradise Lost* (see **pp. 137–41**). Bennett identifies this scene as a fine dramatisation of serious doctrinal issues and she reads it against the standard articulations set by the Elizabethan divine and legal thinker, Richard Hooker, in his *Of the Laws of Ecclesiastical Polity* (1593). Bennett's wider thesis positions Milton's later poetry as representative of a radicalisation of the Christian humanist tradition.

Before the Fall, Adam and Eve are like the unfallen angels, aware that "His Laws" are "our Laws." When Adam sins, he falls as Abdiel stood, still aware, "not deceiv'd." It is Eve, separated from Adam, who becomes confused by Satan's claims about the relation between God's goodness and his power, about the connections between natural and positive law. "God therefore cannot hurt ye, and be just: / Not just, not God; not fear'd then, nor obey'd" (9.700–01). Satan's aim, as with the angels he has corrupted, is to use the subject's belief that only a just ruler should be obeyed as his means to wrench the subject's loyalty from God, whose justice he impugns.

Eve's response upon seeing that the serpent has led her to "the Tree / Of prohibition" is to rehearse the laws, positive and natural, which she and Adam had discussed at their parting.

> But of this Tree we may not taste nor touch;
> God so commanded, and left that Command
> Sole daughter of his voice; the rest, we live
> Law to ourselves, our Reason is our Law. (9.651–54)

Satan's plan in light of this faith in reason is – as it was in seducing the angels – to pervert the sense in which humans live "law to themselves" by making a positive command of God, a letter of the law, appear unreasonable and thus to seem to open up a whole new reality with no, or as yet unknown, laws; or, as Adam fears, "by some fair appearing good" to "dictate false, and misinform the Will / To do what God expressly hath forbid" (9.354–56). Satan paints for Eve a vision of a world in which God's revelation is no longer the measure of all things, and Eve allows herself to believe she is "ignorant":

> What fear I then, rather what know to fear
> Under this ignorance of Good and Evil,
> Of God or Death, of Law or Penalty? (9.773–75)

Eve's ignorance is, of course, an illusion, penetrable by reason. Apart from intuition, knowledge is attained in only two ways: by the intellect contemplatively and by experience actively. Thus, one may know good by experience and by understanding at the same time as one may know evil intellectually: this is the condition of Adam and Eve before their fall. Or one may know evil by experience and then good only intellectually: this is Satan's condition. But the experience of pure good and the experience of evil are mutually exclusive. Evil is the absence of good; and therefore the tree is, as Adam afterward acknowledges, the tree of the knowledge of good lost and evil gained.

At the moment before her fall, given her intellectual confusion, Eve has open to her two morally valid courses of action. She can, with no further thought, dismiss the amazing serpent as mistaken, once he suggests the betrayal of the "sole daughter of God's voice," or she can try to understand how the many twisting confusions that the serpent raises are to be deciphered without betraying the command. A fideistic belief[1] in God's divine right to be obeyed would underlie a choice of the first alternative. But however much latitude Milton's unfaltering commitment to religious freedom allowed his tolerance of the many versions of faith possible to fallen humanity, we should never expect to see fideism in his free Eden, as his Satan is well aware.

Satan defends his "great cause" (9.672) first with echoes of Eden's theology. A command from the governor of the universe, the serpent implies, must be just to be obeyed – "Not just, not God" (9.701). His temptation finally, however, is to atheism – "The Gods are first, and that advantage use / On our belief, that all from them proceeds" (9.718–19) – and *simultaneously* to a fideistic emphasis on God's omnipotence – "What can your knowledge hurt him, or this Tree / Impart against his will if all be his?" (9.727–28). The reasoning of Milton's serpent is so devilishly brilliant that even its conjunction of the blind disbelief of atheism with the blind faith of fideism has not stopped some readers from yielding to a "fideistic" reading of Eve's temptation and fall: Milton must have meant that though she cannot understand why, she should unquestioningly obey the letter of the law. Such blind obedience, though, is not commanded by Milton's God. In the "divine order," as Hooker explains the humanist position, "the prominence of chiefest acceptation is by the best things worthily challenged" (*Laws* 80; 1.7.7).[2] Satan will challenge Eve's "chiefest acceptation," and she is not wrong – in Milton's prelapsarian world – to let her mind engage the serpent's claim to represent "the best thing," however surprising it seems.

"There is not that good which concerneth us, but it hath evidence enough for it selfe, if reason were diligent to search it out. Through neglect thereof, abused wee are with the shew of that which is not, sometimes the subtilty of Satan inveagling us as it did Eve" (*Laws* 81; 1.7.7). Eve's failure comes in not reasoning long or hard enough, and in not calling upon the collaboration of another reasoner. Her rational sin lies not primarily in her faulty logic, but in her failure to persevere until logic and evidence yield an understanding of God's consistency: "In doing evill, we prefer a less good before a greater, the greatness whereof is by reason investigable, and may be known" (*Laws* 81; 1.7.7).

The tree, as she has known, is a sign of human free will; and free will is the

1 Fideism considers knowledge to be based on a basic act of faith.
2 Bennett is using *The Folger Library Edition of the Works of Richard Hooker*, ed. W. Speed Hill, 3 vols. (Cambridge, Mass.: Harvard University Press, 1977–81). Her references are to volume 1. She gives the page number in the edition, followed by the book, chapter and section number in Hooker.

necessary condition for the existence of goodness and evil in the experience of a rational being. Now, at the fall, if God *is* just, the vehicle appointed for the "knowledge of good and evil" must yield what its name and command promise: that knowledge by experience of evil's relation to good which is the experience of death.

Had Eve persevered, she would have to have seen that the "wisdom" which Satan offers brings with it a whole new and unknown world. Once her reason admits Satan's position as possible, then everything in the old order should become suspect – including those parts of it which Satan wants her still to assume (as that she shall be as a god, since the snake has become as a human, is "but proportion meet") and including the validity, the "rightness" of her reason. For what reason until now has been right about is the same truth that every known thing in creation has existed in proportion to: the absolute fidelity to law of the God who forbids the fruit of this tree. It is indeed a "rash" hand that, in the face either of moral wrong or of a reality whose principles are as yet completely unknown, plucks the fruit.

From **James G. Turner, *One Flesh: Paradisal Marriage and Sexual Relations in the Age of Milton*** (Oxford: Clarendon Press, 1987), pp. 303–4

This extract offers an excellent discussion of the shift in sexual relations that occurs as a result of the Fall. Turner shows by means of close reading how the prelapsarian system of love and mutual respect is disrupted and perverted. The linguistic changes seem minor but their impact is intense. Fallen sexuality develops its own erotic language based on the previous personal history of the couple but easily recognisable for the fallen reader – the linguistic shift is very much one small step for man but one resounding loss for mankind.

Turner's wider interest is in our cultural conditioning as regards human sexuality and gender. His research reveals the many (contradictory) ways in which the *Genesis* story was understood in the seventeenth century. In this context, his study of Milton's divorce tracts is extremely illuminating.

Fallen sexuality for Milton is not an entirely new experience, something visited on humanity or thrown in as a solace for the pains of expulsion – as it is in other retellings of the *Genesis* story. It is a version of Adam and Eve's established pattern, a cracked and hectic transcription of familiar music. It is not exactly 'the generalised and mechanical expression of the lust of a man for a woman, the woman being Eve because she is the only woman within reach' (Frye, p. 69);[1] this is to underestimate the wicked accuracy of the allusions which tie both Adam's speech and Milton's narration to the *personal* history of the innocent couple. Nor can it adequately be explained as a reversion to animal lust in the absence of reason, as many critics assert; the fallen couple's sexual life is actually 'founded in

1 Northrop Frye, *The Return of Eden: Five Essays on Milton's Epics* (Toronto and Buffalo: University of Toronto Press, 1965).

Reason', like Wedded Love itself, though in a perverted way. Eve's sensory perception is heightened, and her heart made more 'ample', because she anticipates divine knowledge, the apotheosis of reason; Adam's desire for Eve is increased by appreciating her 'taste', 'sapience', and 'judicious palate', and by dwelling on the stimulus of prohibition. This libertine connoisseurship is obviously corrupt, but even in the state of innocence, Milton reminds us, love is 'judicious' and 'enlarges' the heart, and reason could be devoted to the art of enhancing the pleasures of the senses. The meal prepared for Raphael is a good example; Eve concentrates her mind on an 'elegant', selective, and well-structured combination of fruits, so as to 'bring / Taste after taste upheld with kindliest change'. It is no accident that Adam evokes that episode in his first speech of fallen seduction.[2]

Just as their eating habits pass from judicious 'delicacie' to corrupt gourmandise, so their erotic life passes from 'rationall burning' to the cerebral complications of libertinism. Fallen eroticism is not 'Sex' in the sense that Satan uses it when he pretends to speak as an animal – perhaps the first example of the modern usage of the word: 'I was at first as other Beasts . . . nor aught but food discern'd / Or Sex.' Adam and Eve are not 'coupled in the rites of nature by the meer compulsion of lust', or forced by appetite as Eve was in her dream; they adopt instead a pose of voluntary epicurism and sensual 'elegance'. The hand that 'seizes' Eve's is not now given the epithet 'gentle', but Adam's gentleness has been changed not into roughness but into the *genteel* mannerisms of the Court Amorist. This new eroticism is not at all like the debased sexuality so often denounced in the divorce tracts; theirs is not an animal 'mute kindlyness', but is rather 'cherisht and reincited' by speech. Sexual desire, far from acting 'what the soul complies not with', is urged on by the excited mind. A bad marriage was defined in the divorce tracts as a 'fleshly accustoming without the soul's union and commixture of intellectuall delight'; in the newly corrupted relationship of Adam and Eve, however, there is too much intellectual delight.[3]

Paradisal sexuality moved to a calm, full rhythm, orderly, 'seasonal', and passionate at the same time. The dynamics of fallen sexuality, in contrast, are at once too slack and too tense. Satanic desire is 'pent' up and 'bursts' forth, and even in its social form, revealed to Adam in his vision of the future, lust displays an ugly tension at the heart of its apparent ease.

From **Lucy Newlyn, *Paradise Lost and the Romantic Reader*** (Oxford: Oxford University Press, 1993), pp. 97, 99–100

Newlyn offers a careful exploration of the plurality of Romantic responses to *Paradise Lost*. It is clear from her study that many Romantic writers found

2 Turner cites *PL* IV 755; IX 875, 1017–26; VIII 332–6 in this paragraph.
3 Turner cites *PL* IX 573–4, 1037; *Yale Prose* II 251, 739–40, 609, 339 in this paragraph.

recourse to Milton a positive stimulus for their own work.[1] In this extract on Satan, Newlyn clearly notes the diversity and subtleties of both Romantic readings and Miltonic influence.

Satan need not and should not be assimilated into a single consistent reading of Milton's political standpoint; he must instead be allowed the troubling ambiguity which for three centuries has so excited, and divided, readers of *Paradise Lost*. [. . .]

It would seem simplistic, then, in the face of the text's multiple indeterminacies, to argue either that Milton made Satan heroic by aligning him with republican ideals or that he wished to 'frame' republicanism by making Satan its mouthpiece. It is more likely that, in choosing the Fall as his subject, he wished to trace the process whereby good turned gradually from potential to actual evil – wished, in other words, to come to terms with the fallibility of human beings, which his own political experience had taught. Read in this way, the study of motivation in *Paradise Lost* suggests a forward-looking possibility: if what is good may be the origin of what is evil, then what is evil may none the less still have access to what is good. The moral ambiguity of Satan allows Milton to go on believing that, however far the Commonwealth had failed, there was still the chance of a political outcome which might genuinely implement the divine plan.

What the radical poets of the 1790s found in the character of Satan was a treatment of the origin of evil which reflected their own moral and political concerns. They too sought an explanation for the disappointing outcome of the French Revolution – an explanation that might leave intact the ideals out of which it had grown, and in which so much had been invested. Satan provided the focus for what turned out to be a sequence of psychological studies in motivation – Falkland, Rivers, Frankenstein, Beatrice Cenci, Cain, Manfred, to name only the most obvious.[2] Each of these studies raises the question asked by Milton in *Paradise Lost*: if the miscarriage of revolutionary ideals lies in the transition from good to bad motivation, who is finally to be held responsible – the individuals who wield earthly power, the circumstances which act upon their characters, or the divinity which shapes their ends? [. . .]

Milton's study of the origin of evil provided the ideal starting-point for writers who were deeply preoccupied with moral philosophy, and who wished to explore its political implications. The Fall narrative could be adapted to this end by the use of two different modes of Miltonic allusion: straightforwardly, and by metaphorical extension, it could suggest the way in which individual lapses explained themselves in terms of the social pressures acting on development. Writers using this mode – we might consider the fall of Falkland, or Rivers, as examples – are doing little more than translating Milton's account of the Fall into the arena of

1 Her scholarship effectively contradicts Harold Bloom's contention of an anxiety of influence, see footnote 17, p. 38.

2 Characters from William Godwin, *Caleb Williams* (1794); William Wordsworth, *The Borderers* (composed 1796–7); Mary Shelley, *Frankenstein* (1818); P. B. Shelley, *Cenci* (1819); George Byron, *Cain: a Mystery* (1821) and *Manfred* (1817).

earthly politics, as a way of underlining their determinist views. Implicit in their method is the depressing possibility that the fallen condition itself determines a repetition of the Fall: we might see this as a politicization of the idea of original sin, used to explain the cyclical patterns of tyranny and revolution observable through history.

More radically, through the revision or undermining of Milton's terms, it was possible to expose God Himself as the origin of evil. Writers using this second approach – and Blake is the outstanding example – are enabled by their critique of Milton's system to uncover the roots of societal oppression, and at the same time to suggest a different explanation for the cycles of history: moral categories, according to this view, should be read as the contingent products of warring ideologies, and not as entities in themselves. God is the origin of evil, since He is the creator of a repressive order which invites rebellion. The fall from grace is necessary, as an expression of the autonomy of the individual. Rebellion can be identified as good from a radical, bad from a conservative, angle. The emergence of evil as a separate category from good is therefore an expression of the status quo's will to power. By giving evil its bad name, the status quo attempts to isolate and contain what it is threatened by, and in so doing perpetuates the hierarchy which invites rebellion.

To some extent, these two modes of allusion cross over or coincide within individual Romantic texts or writers, and in so doing replicate the ambiguity which I have suggested is central to *Paradise Lost*.

From **Sandra M. Gilbert and Susan Gubar**, ***The Madwoman in the Attic: the Woman Writer and the Nineteenth-century Literary Imagination*** (New Haven, Conn.: Yale University Press, 1979), pp. 187–9

It is startling to discover just how many women have responded creatively to Milton's poetry. This extract comes from a much cited volume of feminist criticism, which explores the impediments placed upon the woman writer by a patriarchal tradition. It suggests that we see Milton as representative of a cultural misogyny against which the woman writer must consciously struggle to liberate herself. This necessary revolt against authority is, it is argued, a form of transgression which will link the woman writer not just to Eve in Milton's poem but to the Satanic role. The subversive creative energies harnessed by this thesis are empowering but it comes at too great a cost if we must accept a reductive placement of Milton as 'bogeyman' without question. The women writers cited here actually produce extremely shrewd and careful readings of Milton.

To resurrect "the dead poet who was Shakespeare's sister," Virginia Woolf declares in *A Room of One's Own*, literate women must "look past Milton's bogey, for no human being should shut out the view."[1] The perfunctory reference

1 [Gilbert's note.] Virginia Woolf, *A Room of One's Own*, p. 118.

to Milton is curiously enigmatic, for the allusion has had no significant development, and Woolf, in the midst of her peroration, does not stop to explain it. Yet the context in which she places this apparently mysterious bogey is highly suggestive. Shutting out the view, Milton's bogey cuts women off from the spaciousness of possibility, the predominantly male landscapes of fulfillment Woolf has been describing throughout *A Room*. Worse, locking women into "the common sitting room" that denies them individuality, it is a murderous phantom that, if it didn't actually kill "Judith Shakespeare," has helped to keep her dead for hundreds of years, over and over again separating her creative spirit from "the body which she has so often laid down."

Nevertheless, the mystery of Woolf's phrase persists. For who (or what) *is* Milton's bogey? Not only is the phrase enigmatic, it is ambiguous. It may refer to Milton himself, the real patriarchal specter or – to use Harold Bloom's critical terminology – "Covering Cherub" who blocks the view for women poets.[2] It may refer to Adam, who is Milton's (and God's) favored creature, and therefore also a Covering Cherub of sorts. Or it may refer to another fictitious specter, one more bogey created by Milton: his inferior and Satanically inspired Eve, who has also intimidated women and blocked their view of possibilities both real and literary. That Woolf does not definitively indicate which of these meanings she intended suggests that the ambiguity of her phrase may have been deliberate. Certainly other Woolfian allusions to Milton reinforce the idea that for her, as for most other women writers, both he and the creatures of his imagination constitute the misogynistic essence of what Gertrude Stein called "patriarchal poetry."

As our discussion of the metaphor of literary paternity suggested, literary women, readers and writers alike, have long been "confused" and intimidated by the patriarchal etiology that defines a solitary Father God as the only creator of all things, fearing that such a cosmic Author might be the sole legitimate model for all earthly authors. Milton's myth of origins, summarizing a long misogynistic tradition, clearly implied this notion to the many women writers who directly or indirectly recorded anxieties about his paradigmatic patriarchal poetry. A minimal list of such figures would include Margaret Cavendish, Anne Finch, Mary Shelley, Charlotte and Emily Brontë, Emily Dickinson, Elizabeth Barrett Browning, George Eliot, Christina Rossetti, H. D., and Sylvia Plath, as well as Stein, Nin, and Woolf herself. In addition, in an effort to come to terms with the institutionalized and often elaborately metaphorical misogyny Milton's epic expresses, many of these women devised their own revisionary myths and metaphors.

Mary Shelley's *Frankenstein*, for instance, is at least in part a despairingly acquiescent "misreading" of *Paradise Lost*, with Eve-Sin apparently exorcised from the story but really translated into the monster that Milton hints she is. Emily Brontë's *Wuthering Heights*, by contrast, is a radically corrective "misreading" of Milton, a kind of Blakeian Bible of Hell, with the fall from Heaven to Hell transformed into a fall from a realm that conventional theology would associate with "hell" (the Heights) to a place that parodies "heaven" (the Grange).

2 [Gilbert's note.] Harold Bloom, *The Anxiety of Influence*, p. 35. The *OED* gives three meanings for the word *bogey* or *bogy*, all relevant here: "1. As quasi-proper name: the evil one, the devil. 2. A bogle or goblin; a person much dreaded. 3. *fig*. An object of terror or dread; a bugbear."

Similarly, Elizabeth Barrett Browning's "A Drama of Exile," Charlotte Brontë's *Shirley*, and Christina Rossetti's "Goblin Market" all include or imply revisionary critiques of *Paradise Lost*, while George Eliot's *Middlemarch* uses Dorothea's worship of that "affable archangel" Casaubon specifically to comment upon the disastrous relationship between Milton and his daughters. And in her undaughterly rebellion against that "Papa above" whom she also called "a God of Flint" and "Burglar! Banker – Father," Emily Dickinson, as Albert Gelpi has noted, was "passionately Byronic," and therefore, as we shall see, subtly anti-Miltonic.[3] For all these women, in other words, the question of Milton's misogyny was not in any sense an academic one. On the contrary, since it was only through patriarchal poetry that they learned "their origin and their history" – learned, that is, to define themselves as misogynistic theology defined them – most of these writers read Milton with painful absorption.

3 [Gilbert's note.] Albert Gelpi, *Emily Dickinson: The Mind of the Poet* (Cambridge, Mass.: Harvard University Press, 1965), p. 40.

3

Key Passages

Introduction

Paradise Lost was published in 1667 as a ten-book epic poem. A second edition was published in 1674. This second edition included fifteen new lines of poetry but restructured the contents of the epic poem so that there were twelve books. This was done by splitting both Book 7 and Book 10 into two (i.e., Book 7 in 1667 contained the materials now to be found in Books VII and VIII while Book 10 held the materials now found in Books XI and XII). All textual references within the sourcebook are to the twelve-book epic, unless otherwise marked.[1] The text used for the key passages represents a partial modernisation. I have updated the spelling and reduced the capitalisation, italicisation and contractions a little but have not modernised the punctuation. What to do about punctuating *Paradise Lost* has always been something of a contested point among Milton editors (see **p. 29**). You may find that the punctuation here is lighter than you are used to. This should be seen as an advantage. It allows the verse paragraph to flow freely and sets off multiple suggestive connections within the reading process. If you read the lines out loud you will discover that the punctuation within a verse paragraph is there in the main to suggest breathing points rather than the division of one discrete thought from another.

These key passages, read alongside the headnotes, offer a coherent guide to both the narrative of *Paradise Lost* and its overall structure. My intention has been to choose passages that will shed light on the main action of the poem and also admit critical consideration of the strands of philosophical, metaphysical, theological, psychological, political, pedagogical and generic inquiry developed within it. Those already familiar with the poem are bound to have their own favourite passages, particularly from Books I, IV and IX where almost every line is eminently quotable. I hope they will not be disappointed by my selection but ask them to remember that the full text of the poem is well over 10,500 lines long. Some difficult decisions had to be made.

Today's practice of setting only certain books of *Paradise Lost* for study can seriously limit the student's appreciation of the development of Milton's argument and the nuances of his language, so extracts from each book have been

1 My references to the books of the 1667 edition use Arabic numerals [i.e. 1, 2, 3], and to the 1674 edition Roman numerals [i.e., I, II, III].

included here for analysis and detailed comment. I consider it important to foreground for the student the structural balances inherent to the epic as a whole and to encourage a fuller acquaintance with the poem's compositional strengths.[2] The reading experience famously begins in epic fashion, *in medias res* [in the midst of things]. Every reader must make a choice of which events, speeches, analogues and linguistic terms to recall, and possibly reinterpret, as the poem progresses. It is important to be aware that this is a crucial and unavoidable part of the reading experience and to widen one's knowledge of the poem accordingly. Here is just one example of what I mean. The generic structure of Book IX as a classical tragedy is refigured as a Christian drama when read in conjunction with Book X but Book X also deserves to be considered against the doctrine expounded in Book III. The Son's judgement of Adam and Eve in Book X activates his voluntary undertaking to be both mediator and redeemer for mankind made in Book III. His justice balances due punishment with hope, embedded in the protevangelium [*Genesis* 3.15]. Adam will need to be taught to understand its meaning and Michael's visit in Books XI and XII is intended to teach him how to identify the divine redemptive plan in future human history. Adam learns so well that he acknowledges the Son as his Redeemer, thereby becoming the first Christian, and indeed the first Protestant (see *PL* XII 572–3). In Book X, however, before he comprehends the Christian story of salvation, Adam despairs. His lengthy speech is an acknowledgement of his own guilt and an admission by our first father of the justice of God in sentencing man. This is an internal 'proof' of the epic undertaking to justify God's ways (*PL* I 26) and complements the harsh truth of Book III, 'Die he or justice must' (*PL* III 210). Adam at this stage cannot see beyond despair but his later emotional recovery becomes experiential proof of God's mercy and grace as embodied in the Son's voice in Book III. Adam's attitude to self-guilt is also a direct counter to Satan's conclusions made in similar circumstances in Book IV.

It is only by standing back to look at the epic in its entirety that the multivalency of its structural composition can be appreciated. Such an overview also makes one aware of the 'timing' issues within the poem and its complex weave of narration. I have therefore also provided a book-by-book summary of the epic and an alternative synopsis based on the internal chronology of events.

2 In the 1674 edition, the invocation to Book VII marks the halfway point of a twelve book narrative where Books I & II and XI & XII deal with the aftermath of a fall, Books III and X are books of judgement, Books IV and IX delineate the human estate before and after the Fall, and Books V, VI, VII and VIII retell the visit of Raphael. For more on the structures of the 1667 and 1674 editions, see Fowler (1998), pp. 25–9.

Book-by-book Breakdown of *Paradise Lost* (1674)

Book I

Invocation; Description of Hell; Satan, now fallen from Heaven with his army, after an unsuccessful rebellion against God's rule, remains defiant; his stirring rhetoric rouses his troops; a long litany of the devils' names; the construction of Pandaemonium as a place of assembly and the seat of government in Hell.

Book II

Satan's throne; Council in Hell ending with Satan's acceptance of the mission to ruin God's newest creation, mankind; Satan encounters Sin and Death at the Gates of Hell and then must traverse Chaos.

Book III

Invocation; A divine perspective upon the universe and Satan's vengeful activity; Theodicy – a long dialogue between the Father and the Son which affirms both divine justice and mercy and explicates the doctrines of free will and of election; Satan arrives at the bounds of the created universe and crosses the Paradise of Fools; Satan disguises himself in order to request directions from the angel in the sun, Uriel.

Book IV

Satan's speech on Mount Niphates; Satan invades Paradise; Lengthy description of the delights of the Edenic ecosystem; Satan sees Adam and Eve in the garden and overhears their conversation; Satan's jealousy; Night approaches – Eve's love lyric and her question about the stars; Adam and Eve retire to the nuptial bower; Satan, disguised as a toad, squats at the ear of the sleeping Eve and disturbs her dreams; Satan is discovered by the angels guarding Paradise, he reads his defeat in the stars and flees.

Book V

Eve recalls her dream to Adam and he comforts her; Morning prayers; The arrival of the archangel Raphael in Eden, sent by the Father as a kind of heavenly tutor – the human couple converse with their heavenly guest and share a meal with him; Raphael encourages them to remain obedient and begins his story of rebellion in Heaven; Raphael tells of Satan's envy at the exaltation of the Son, and of how the angel Abdiel kept faith and rebuked Satan for his apostasy.

Book VI

Raphael continues his narrative of the angelic War in Heaven – Satan is wounded in single combat by the archangel Michael, the rebels invent gunpowder, a stalemate is reached; On the third day of the war, the Son rides out in the chariot of paternal deity, at which sight the rebels turn, flee, and throw themselves down from Heaven; Raphael concludes his story (and the book) with a further warning, 'Remember and fear to transgress'.

Book VII

Invocation; Raphael recounts the six days of creation and the angelic hymns of thanksgiving on the sabbath.

Book VIII

Adam asks about astronomy but Raphael advises him to concentrate on matters closer to home; Eve leaves to tend the flowers; Adam recounts his first memories to Raphael, including his dialogue with God over a mate and the subsequent creation of Eve; A discussion of human passion and of angelic sex follows; Raphael departs at sunset.

Book IX

Invocation; Satan returns to Eden and incarnates himself into the serpent; Adam and Eve's morning debate regarding their workload and temptation; Eve leaves to garden alone; Description of the serpent as it approaches Eve; Satan's persuasive rhetoric; Eve's fall; Adam's reaction; Adam's fall; Their intoxication and lust; The couple wake to a realisation of their changed state and the book closes with their mutual recriminations.

Book X

The Son descends from Heaven to judge the human couple; Sin and Death build a bridge across Chaos in order to enter the fallen world and encounter Satan on his return journey to Hell; Satan's reception in Hell; A divine interpretation of the role of Sin and Death; The human couple struggle to understand their position – Adam contemplates suicide while Eve is distraught and offers self-sacrifice; Adam and Eve reunite and the book closes with their tearful prayers and humble penitence.

Book XI

God is pleased by the human couple's repentance; The archangel Michael arrives from Heaven to expel the human couple from Paradise but first he shows Adam visions of the future (Cain and Abel, the lazar-house, the sons of God and daughters of Cain, Enoch, Noah), and helps Adam to understand their meaning.

Book XII

Michael relates further Biblical events to Adam (Nimrod and the tower of Babel, Abraham, David's line to the new Joshua [i.e., Jesus], the persecution of the faithful in a corrupt world); Eve's final speech; The Expulsion.

Internal Chronology

An alternative way to consider the events of the poem is via the internal chronology.[1] [N.B. Milton follows Biblical practice and counts a day from one sunset to the next.]

Day 1: The anointing of the Son is the earliest event recorded within the poem.
Day 2–4: Satan's rebellion begins that evening and the War in Heaven lasts 3 days.
Day 4–13: The rebels throw themselves from Heaven and fall for 9 days.
Day 13–22: The rebel angels then lie chained to the fiery lake for a further 9 days. [At some point during this time the Creation takes place. It takes 7 days.]
Day 22: The events of Books I & II take a day in Hell.
Day 23: Satan traverses Chaos and the Paradise of Fools in a journey of uncertain duration but it takes a day from Satan's alighting at midnight on the universe in Book III to evening in Eden in Book IV.
Day 24: Eve's dream, Satan's expulsion from Eden, and Raphael's visit (Books IV–VIII).
Day 24–31: Satan spends this time encircling the earth.
Day 32: Satan returns at midnight, the Fall takes place at noon and the Judgement occurs in the early evening (Books IX–X).
Day 33: Michael arrives at sunrise. The expulsion is at noon, precisely 24 hours after the Fall.

1 See Fowler (1998), p. 31.

Key Passages

Book I 1–26: the first epic invocation

As one might expect, the opening invocation is a formal presentation of the main themes for the epic. The theme is 'man', by which is meant all mankind and all human history. The story is inclusive – it is 'our woe' in line three, an inclusive promise of restoration for 'us' in line five, and an undertaking to justify God's ways to 'men' in line 26. This is in strong contrast to all three of the main classical epics which immediately identify a single figure (i.e., Achilles in the *Iliad*, Odysseus in the *Odyssey*, Aeneas in the *Aeneid*) as the central protagonist of the poem. We can see just how radical a departure we are already making from classical epic if we consider the opening phrase of Virgil's *Aeneid*, *Arma virumque cano* [Arms and the man I sing]. There, three elements are introduced to us: battle, a hero and a bard to tell the tale. Milton's opening is significantly different. This is not to be the story of a single extraordinary military hero but a story for every man, nor is it an undertaking for the bard alone (*cf. cano* [I sing]). The narrator will not prove sufficient unless he has the support of a 'heavenly muse' and it is actually the muse who is required to sing *Paradise Lost* and not the poet. However, we should also note that the grand, instigating verbal command, 'sing', is delayed until line six. It is preceded by an initial run of sub-clauses that explain the complexity of this new epic subject – its theme is disobedience, loss *and* restoration – but also prove through their syntactic poise the technical control and authority of this narrator.

This is to be a story about beginnings, 'Of man's *first* disobedience', and its source of inspiration will be the same heavenly muse which previously inspired Moses to write down the first five books of the Old Testament [i.e. the Pentateuch: *Genesis* to *Deuteronomy*]. In effect, the narrator is claiming primacy over all previous classical authors and proposing a fuller revelation of the Word of God than that offered even to the great prophet, Moses. Moses gave us *Genesis*, 'In the beginning how the heavens and earth / Rose . . .', but this bard can also include a New Testament promise when he employs the phrase ['In the beginning was the Word and the Word was with God and the Word was God' is the opening of the *Gospel of St John*]. It is no wonder then that there is some anxiety over the legitimacy of this undertaking. The ambition is immense but so too is its confidence as an inspired Christian text. Look back now to lines four and five where a hero, 'one greater man', was promised but with no details given as to his identity or his role. This is a significant, though oblique, reference to Jesus Christ and it will be important for every reader to consider how the narrator introduces Christian witness into an epic that retells events from the very beginning of mankind's history. Such Christian witness also quickly turns out to have a political component. It is telling that in this primary reference to Jesus Christ, he should be said to 'restore' rather than redeem us. The term restoration has immediate political resonance in the 1660s. By the close of the epic when the very last human word is also 'restore' (see **p. 156**), we have a much fuller concept of what that term might connote for Milton. The radical nature of this epic is further emphasised in its conception of Creation. The source of inspiration invoked here is the same Spirit that played both a nurturing ('brooding') and an inseminating ('madest it pregnant') role at the time of the Creation of the universe. In a repeat of that primary moment of Creation, this narrator wants to be both guided ('instruct') and filled with divine inspiration ('illumine') as he begins his own creative endeavour. In that way he will be able to 'assert eternal Providence / And justify the ways of God to men'. We should pause momentarily on these famous lines. It is important to take the two lines together and to tease out their full meaning. To 'assert' is to proclaim or to state, while to 'justify' is to engage in persuasive debate. We need to remember that the poem makes this distinction. It does not necessarily intend to justify all of God's ways to men, only those aspects of the Almighty's 'ways' that concern mankind. Yet, in doing that, a fuller amount of evidence will be set in front of us as readers of this inspired poem than has ever been previously available.

At the close of this first invocation, we have a sense of just how privileged we are to be readers of this sacred text but equally how strenuous an undertaking it will be for us, and even more so for the narrator, and how important it is that he be authorised in his task. We know that this is a Christian epic *and* that it is an English epic. It may seem obvious to remark upon the language choice but, given that Milton was a superb Latinist, he really has made the choice to write the epic in English. It is a compliment to the vernacular language that he considers it to be a sufficient medium to maintain his undertaking. It is also a challenge to his fellow Englishmen that the epic should be addressed to them but take as its theme loss and woe rather than conquest and imperial supremacy. The invocation is also the first verse paragraph of the poem and we have now learnt how to read Milton's blank verse. It is iambic pentameter but it does not restrict the thought to a single line or to a couplet. Instead, it moves on through complex rhythmic patternings and the use of enjambment, and it plots the flow of its discourse through the particular emphasis it sets on certain words. Here, the key terms have been 'fruit', 'taste', 'woe', 'restore' and 'justify' and a number of verbs were also given prominence by their pronounced placement on the line, i.e., 'sing', 'instruct' and 'illumine'.

Of Man's First Disobedience, and the Fruit[1]
Of that Forbidden Tree, whose mortal taste
Brought Death into the World,[2] and all our woe,
With loss of *Eden*, till one greater Man
Restore us, and regain the blissful Seat,
Sing Heavenly Muse, that on the secret top
Of *Oreb*, or of *Sinai*,[3] didst inspire
That Shepherd, who first taught the chosen Seed,
In the Beginning how the Heavens and Earth
Rose out of *Chaos*: Or if *Sion* Hill[4]
Delight thee more, and *Siloa's* Brook[5] that flowed
Fast by the Oracle of God; I thence
Invoke thy aid to my adventurous Song,
That with no middle flight intends to soar
Above the *Aonian* Mount,[6] while it pursues
Things unattempted yet in Prose or Rhyme.
And chiefly Thou O Spirit,[7] that dost prefer
Before all Temples the upright heart and pure,[8]
Instruct[9] me, for Thou know'st; Thou from the first
Wast present, and with mighty wings outspread
Dove-like satst brooding on the vast Abyss
And madest it pregnant: What in me is dark
Illumine, what is low raise and support;
That to the highth[10] of this great Argument[11]
I may assert Eternal Providence,
And justify the ways of God to men.

Book I 59–69: the first description of Hell

Any seasoned reader of epic will know not to expect a linear narration. We begin *in medias res* [in the midst of things]. Nevertheless, our precipitous arrival in Hell is unexpected and disorientating. Our own discomfiture may help us

1 Outcome or result (as in fruit of your labour), as well as the literal reference to a food substance.
2 Eating the fruit was a mortal sin. More specifically it was a deadly action, in that human mortality is a consequence of the Fall.
3 Two Biblical names for the mountain where Moses received the Ten Commandments.
4 The site for a sanctuary. Mount Zion is the site of the Temple in Jerusalem.
5 A reference to a (sacred) spring flowing near Mount Zion. Possibly also a reference to the pool of Siloam (*John* 9.1–11) where Jesus sends a blind man to wash and have his eyesight restored.
6 Helicon, a mountain in Greece sacred to the muses.
7 A reference to the Holy Spirit as source of inspiration and instruction.
8 A strongly Protestant articulation of the primacy of inner virtue and faith. Paul teaches that each individual must make their body a temple to the Holy Spirit (*I Corinthians* 6.19).
9 Teach me, give me authorised directions. The Latin root *struere* means to pile up or build, which links back to the idea of the upright heart as a temple and forward to the epic composition.
10 Height. This poetic usage is common in the poem.
11 'Argument' here means subject matter, not a subject for debate.

relate to Satan's dire extremity. Certainly, our discovery of the place is closely linked to our encounter with the rebel leader, though the narratorial voice always acts as a counterweight to the rhetoric flourishes of the Father of Lies. This passage gives us the first description of Hell (as seen through Satan's eyes) and it makes the dire consequences of rebellion against the Almighty achingly concrete. Our senses are crippled. No light penetrates here and the fires of Hell give out no light but rather only further enforce the utter darkness of the place. The desolate thought is expertly contained in the puzzling phrase 'darkness visible' (on this phrase see Bentley's emendation and Swift's repost, **pp. 45–6**). This is a truly perverse situation. There is no light, no peace, no hope and the very mention of such terms has a draining quality. We reach for their supportive meaning, only to have it denied. One can feel the moral emptiness of Hell and it should be stressed that Milton is more interested in recording Hell as a place of psychological despair than in reiterating traditional descriptions of its physical torments.

At once as far as Angels' ken[1] he views
The dismal Situation waste and wild,
A Dungeon horrible, on all sides round
As one great Furnace flamed, yet from those flames
No light, but rather darkness visible
Served only to discover sights of woe,
Regions of sorrow, doleful shades, where peace
And rest can never dwell, hope never comes
That comes to all; but torture without end
Still urges, and a fiery Deluge, fed
With ever-burning Sulphur unconsumed:

Book I 84–126: Satan's first speech

This is the first direct speech within the poem. Satan shows prodigious resolve in the circumstances but the circumstances should not be overlooked. The contingent identification of the friend and the wider recognition of the ruinous present state are based upon an insurmountable contrast between past bliss and present circumstance. The gulf is encapsulated in Satan's syntactic flaws, most dramatically in the opening conditional phrase that is left to stand unsupported, 'If thou beest he'. Note that Satan is struck first by the diminution of heavenly light in his companion's appearance. The light that shines from the countenance of all rational creatures when they remain in union with the Godhead is a recurrent motif within the epic. The loss of this brightness then is

1 Range of knowledge or sight.

demonstrative evidence of the rebels' change of state. Given that Satan's name when he was a heavenly creature was Lucifer [the morning star], his lament for diminished light is hardly altruistic. Note also that no names are used by the fallen angels during any of their speeches in Hell. They lost their heavenly names by rebelling against the Creator (I 361–75) and will have to wait until the pagan era on earth before they can get new ones.

Satan sounds like a leader and a military hero. In point of fact, he sounds a lot like Aeneas at this point. In Virgil's *Aeneid* (II 268ff.), Aeneas recounts how the ghost of the great Trojan warrior, Hector, appeared to him in order to prophesy the restoration of Troy at its very moment of collapse and to authorise Aeneas's own flight from destruction as the chosen founder of the new Latin empire. However, Satan lacks any such legitimisation. He is a rebel and an apostate, not *pius* [dutiful, pious] Aeneas. This is made obvious by the fact that he must authorise his imperial ambitions himself and ordain his own epic quest.

Despite his shock and destabilisation, Satan keeps talking, promoting the 'unconquerable will' and revenge as the new constants of Hell. Many readers have been, and continue to be, moved by the energy and individualism surging through his speech. (See, for example, P. B. Shelley's remarks, **p. 51**.) Midway through the speech, Satan proposes a future for the rebels, 'What though the field be lost? /All is not lost; . . .'. It is little more than a trick of oratory but the conception and control of this dis-locution provides the space for Satan to build up an oppositional rhetoric (consider his use of such terms as Thunder, fate, tyranny and glory) and reconfigure Hell. Is it the case that as a reader you necessarily fall into error and submit to the Satanic rhetoric? Or is it possible for you to remain a more detached observer of his oratory, identifying its amalgam of indomitable courage and fallacious logic? Certainly, the narrator's interpretative interjection as Satan's speech closes is intended to keep us on the straight and narrow.

If thou beest he; But O how fallen! how changed[1]
From him, who in the happy Realms of Light
Clothed with transcendent brightness didst out-shine
Myriads[2] though bright: If he whom mutual league,
United thoughts and counsels, equal hope
And hazard in the Glorious Enterprise,
Joined with me once, now misery hath joined
In equal ruin: into what Pit thou seest
From what highth fallen, so much the stronger proved
He with his Thunder: and till then who knew
The force of those dire Arms? yet not for those
Nor what the Potent Victor in his rage

1 Aeneas is shocked by the vision of Hector's shade, not least because his ghost bears the marks of the abuse meted out on it by Achilles. Aeneas laments Hector's demise, 'Ah me! what aspect was his! how changed . . .' (*Aeneid* II 274–5).

2 The vast numbers (of other angels).

Can else inflict do I repent or change,
Though changed in outward lustre; that fixed mind
And high disdain, from sense of injured merit,
That with the mightiest raised me to contend,
And to the fierce contention brought along
Innumerable force of Spirits armed
That durst dislike his reign, and me preferring,
His utmost power with adverse power opposed
In dubious Battle on the Plains of Heaven,
And shook his throne. What though the field be lost?
All is not lost;[3] the unconquerable Will,
And study of revenge, immortal hate,
And courage never to submit or yield:
And what is else not to be overcome?
That Glory never shall his wrath or might
Extort from me[4]. To bow and sue for grace
With suppliant knee, and deify[5] his power,
Who from the terror of this Arm so late
Doubted his Empire,[6] that were low indeed,
That were an ignominy[7] and shame beneath
This downfall; since by Fate the strength of Gods
And this empyreal[8] substance cannot fail,
Since through experience of this great event
In Arms not worse, in foresight much advanced,
We may with more successful hope resolve
To wage by force or guile eternal War
Irreconcilable, to our grand Foe,
Who now triumphs, and in the excess of joy
Sole reigning holds the Tyranny of Heaven.
  So spake the Apostate[9] Angel, though in pain,
Vaunting[10] aloud, but racked with deep despair: . . .

3 The term 'All' has deep theological importance within the poem and often relates to union in God, (see *PL* VI 732 and cf. Marvell's usage of the term). Despite Satan's rhetorical stance here, the irony of this moment will become clear as we read on, by rejecting their place within God's plan the rebels quite definitely lost 'All'.

4 Satan is claiming that God unjustly employs unlawful force to get His way. However, Satan is twisting the meaning of words to make this claim.

5 The verb 'deify' means to make a God of. Satan would accuse God of forcing the angels to worship His power but from what we will discover from Satan's own speeches and from Raphael's narrative of the War in Heaven, it is Satan who idolises power for its own sake.

6 i.e., [I will never humble myself before God] when so recently my military strength made Him fear for His empire.

7 Dishonour or infamy. The term comes from the Latin *nomen* [name]. There is a telling irony in this worry over a shameful name or reputation given that the rebels have lost their names completely.

8 Belonging to the sky or heavens. There is now an irony in its alternative meaning – belonging to the sphere of fire.

9 An apostate is an extremely strong term. It means someone who has denied their beliefs or abandoned their religion.

10 Boasting.

Book I 192–208: the epic simile of the whale

The focus shifts from Satan's rhetorical prowess to his prostrate body chained on the burning lake. He is monstrously large and resembles a sea-serpent. The classical references link him both to the Titan, Briareos, and to the Giant, Typhon. Both races and both named individuals fought against Jupiter. The references made here are intentionally imprecise: the main thrust of the analogy being a sense of a vast, ill-controlled bulk with rebellious tendencies. What follows in this extract is the first of the epic similes within the poem. Such epic similes are literary pieces, extended comparisons where the flow of the narrative action has been suspended so that the comparison may be developed in its own right. They are particularly prominent in Books I, II and IX. This first simile can tell us a lot about our own role as readers of the epic. We would expect the simile to help us understand the extraordinary experience of Hell by comparing it to something with which we were familiar. However, Milton's syntactical versatility seems here to have been employed to set us a puzzle and it is likely that you will want to go back over the lines a number of times. This then is a textual meander that reproduces in the reading experience an experience of confusion. If we were to paraphrase the simile it would work like this:

> Maybe [haply] there is a boat in difficulties, lost because of the darkness and possibly in danger of sinking as a result [night-foundered]. Its pilot believes that he has found by chance [haply] an island and sheltered anchorage but in fact he has encountered the sleeping Leviathan. Unwittingly, the pilot drops anchor on the body of the whale. Daylight is eagerly awaited. This tale is told by the sailors as being a common occurrence.

There is a lot going on in a very compact space and we are given no indication of how to employ the information. Are we perhaps to speculate that when day returns the pilot would see just how perilous his situation was and weigh anchor quickly? Now that would be a story to tell to other sailors later! Or, as seems more likely, are we to presume that anchoring on whales is a sure way never to see the light of day again? When the whale dives, the boat will sink and everyone on board will be lost, not realising their predicament until it is too late. There is a certain thrill in the way that the simile leaves the boat to its fate [hap]. With chance as the presiding ideology of Hell, the reader's predicament here should also be considered. What are we to do with the whale simile now that we have stumbled across it? What choices can we make? If a lesson is to be learnt, it is that one should not 'anchor in whales' (i.e., one should not place one's trust in anything no matter how secure it seems without testing it first). Surely that means that we should not trust anything that is going on here. But is it really possible to avoid one's fate? A critic such as Stanley Fish (see **pp. 59–60**) would take an episode such as this as evidence of the reader's deficiency. We have 'anchored' not just in Satan but in rhetoric and have fallen into the depths of error. Other critics would argue that the reader is not on that boat but has been offered the simile as a warning and an active exercise in avoiding such error because in order to read the complex syntax, we have necessarily employed our reasoning powers.

Thus Satan talking to his nearest Mate
With Head up-lift above the wave, and Eyes
That sparkling blazed, his other Parts besides
Prone on the Flood, extended long and large
Lay floating many a rood, in bulk as huge
As whom the Fables name of monstrous size,
Titanian, or *Earth-Born*, that warred on *Jove*,
Briareos or *Typhon*, who the Den
By ancient *Tarsus*[1] held, or that Sea-beast
Leviathan,[2] which God of all his works
Created hugest that swim the Ocean stream:
Him haply[3] slumbering on the *Norway* foam
The Pilot of some small night-founder'd Skiff,[4]
Deeming some Island, oft, as Sea-men tell,
With fixed Anchor in his scaly rind
Moors by his side under the Lee,[5] while Night
Invests the Sea, and wished Morn delays:

Book I 242–63: Satan claims dominion in Hell

Satan's speech on raising himself from the burning lake glories in his own strength, though we should note that the narrator has just told us that Satan's movements are occurring only because of divine providence. Satan's tone is now imperious and his key terms here are 'freedom' and 'choice', though he perverts both ideals. The speech presumes a myth of resistance to tyranny on the part of the rebel angels and proposes a heroic constancy of purpose which will bring with it imperial rewards, 'Better to reign in Hell, than serve in Heaven'. This final axiom stands proud and it is the founding ideology for Satan's regrouping of his troops and the construction of Pandaemonium. However, when Satan's argument is dissected, the weakness of his position is revealed. He is in effect teaching himself to be blind both to his circumstances and to the weakness of his logic. So, for example, he finds it acceptable to consider his own strength as not far short of omnipotence and suggests that God can feel envy. As part of the resistance argument, he advocates a mind constant enough not to be swayed by changes in circumstance. His intention is to suggest that it will

1 Capital of Cilicia in Turkey where Typhon was supposed to live but the place name also has Biblical connotations.
2 First a reference to the sea-monster in *Job* 41 but, in the subsequent phrases, a whale.
3 'Hap' means fate and it is a common term in Hell; 'haply' could mean 1. by fate 2. by chance or 3. perhaps. Despite the bulk of Leviathan, it is actually this little term that governs the simile.
4 A skiff is a ship's working boat.
5 Out of the predominant wind.

be possible for the rebel angels to turn the new location, Hell, into a Heaven of sorts. However his phrasing actually admits that, for those who think as he does, the mind is an inescapable prison which would make a torment of any location, even Heaven. Satan will later admit the full truth of this in his speech addressed to the sun in Book IV, (32–113, see **pp. 105–7**).

Is this the Region, this the Soil, the Clime,
Said then the lost Arch Angel, this the seat
That we must change for Heaven, this mournful gloom
For that celestial light? Be it so, since he
Who now is Sovereign can dispose and bid
What shall be right: furthest from him is best
Whom reason hath equalled, force hath made supreme
Above his equals.[1] Farewell happy Fields[2]
Where Joy for ever dwells: Hail horrors, hail
Infernal world, and thou profoundest Hell
Receive thy new Possessor: One who brings
A mind not to be changed by Place or Time.
The mind is its own place, and in it self
Can make a Heaven of Hell, a Hell of Heaven.
What matter where, if I be still the same,
And what I should be, all but less than he
Whom Thunder hath made greater?[3] Here at least
We shall be free; the Almighty hath not built
Here for his envy, will not drive us hence:
Here we may reign secure, and in my choice
To reign is worth ambition though in Hell:
Better to reign in Hell, then serve in Heaven.

Book I 587–612: archangel ruined

After a lengthy digression for the litany of devils' names and catalogue of idolatrous practices, we return to Satan. His heart swells with pride as he surveys his troops. This description of Satan is rightly famous and Edmund Burke (see **p. 47**) chose it for a core example of poetic sublimity. Satan's obscured glory, his ruined state, somehow seizes the imagination more strongly than any

1 Satan never mentions the Son by name in Books I and II and until Raphael's narrative we have no way of filling in the blanks here. Satan's jealousy with regard to the Son would seem to motivate this argument.
2 A paraphrase of the classical term, Elysium.
3 Satan is claiming that the only difference between himself and God is that God had the advantage of controlling the 'Thunder' [i.e., amoral strength]. Satan's repeated identification of the Godhead with Thunder suggests the classical analogy of Jupiter.

description of heavenly perfection. It seems possible to empathise with his blighted hopes and conscious loss and simultaneously to be in awe of his grandeur in defeat. Why this should be the case and what it says about the human psyche is something for each individual reader to consider. Meanwhile, we should also note that this passage is the only part of the poem known to have attracted the eye of the Restoration licenser [censor].

Thus far these beyond
Compare of mortal prowess, yet observed
Their dread commander: he above the rest
In shape and gesture proudly eminent
Stood like a Tower; his form had yet not lost
All her Original brightness, nor appeared
Less then Arch Angel ruined, and the excess
Of Glory obscured: As when the Sun new risen
Looks through the Horizontal misty Air
Shorn of his Beams, or from behind the Moon
In dim Eclipse disastrous twilight sheds
On half the Nations, and with fear of change
Perplexes Monarchs.[1] Darkened so, yet shone
Above them all the Arch Angel: but his face
Deep scars of Thunder had intrenched,[2] and care
Sat on his faded cheek, but under Brows
Of dauntless courage, and considerate[3] Pride
Waiting revenge: cruel his eye, but cast
Signs of remorse and passion to behold
The fellows of his crime, the followers rather
(Far other once beheld in bliss) condemned
For ever now to have their lot in pain,
Millions of Spirits for his fault amerced[4]
Of Heaven, and from Eternal Splendours flung
For his revolt, yet faithful how they stood,
Their Glory withered.

1 i.e., the sun enfeebled by morning mists or eclipsed by the moon presages general calamity but a specific shadow is cast over monarchs, because of their common acceptance of the sun as a symbol of their power. John Toland (in Darbishire, pp. 40–1) noted that these lines had been thought politically subversive by the Licenser for the Press. That anxiety is partly explained by the fact that there had actually been a solar eclipse in June of 1666. For more on the commonplace association of monarchy with the sun, see **pp. 23–4**.

2 His face was riven with deep scars of Thunder. This might suggest that Satan's own ire has marked his face, though we know that Satan refers to God as the Thunderer. We discover a more specific reference when Raphael (VI 858) relates how the Son in the chariot drives the rebels 'Thunderstruck' before him until they cast themselves from Heaven.

3 Premeditated.

4 Deprived of.

Book I 710–51: the building of Pandaemonium

The seat of government in Hell rises as if to music but also as if pumped up with air. It is grandiose but ill-proportioned, a monument to falsehood and idolatry. This is Pandaemonium (I 756) [seat or assembly of devils], a term that is familiar to us but was in fact Milton's coinage here. Because the description of Pandaemonium follows on from a long section naming the pagan gods and indicating the barbarous practices involved in their worship, it is easy to identify this construction as a type for all such earthly idolatry. Its architectural construction is described in some detail. Above the pillars is the architrave, above that the frieze, above that the cornice with relief carvings and above that the roof is covered over with ornate golden decoration. We are encouraged to look up and up but however much one cranes one's neck, this remains affectation and aspirationalism devoid of true worth. It should be contrasted with the inherent vigour of Creation and its upward impulse towards the real sky as related in Book VII, see **pp. 125–7**.

It is worth noting that the mining of the minerals and precious metals required in order to construct this edifice is described as a violation of their mother earth (I 684–90). Pandaemonium is founded on exploitation, greed and destructive ambition – an attitude summed up in the passage's final phrase 'to build in Hell'. The architect for Pandaemonium is known to the Romans as the god Vulcan or Mulciber. We are not given the equivalent Greek name (Hephaistos), though the myth of his fall used here comes from Homer (*Iliad* I 591–5). We do, however, have an English rendition of the Greek name for Italy, 'Ausonian land'. The narrator's polyglot knowledge initially strikes us as impressive, if a little over-complicated, and this description of Mulciber's fall has become one of the most-quoted passages from the epic. The rhythmic control and elegant phrasing is turning Mulciber's vertiginous fall into decorous myth, until the unexpected admission that such fables are not just untrue but morally suspect. This bombshell explodes in the skilful placement of a single word, 'Erring', at the start of a new line. The new information is equivalent to the (unmentioned) crash that we can speculate must have occurred when Mulciber hit the ground. It throws our understanding of the previous lines off-balance and forces us to reconsider our perspective on cosmic events. Standing and falling within the epic take place not just on a vertical axis but also on a moral axis.

Anon out of the earth a Fabric huge
Rose like an Exhalation, with the sound
Of Dulcet Symphonies and voices sweet,
Built like a Temple, where *Pilasters* round[1]
Were set, and Doric pillars overlaid
With Golden Architrave; nor did there want

1 Pilasters are square columns, so there is a momentary ironic contradiction in suggesting that they are round. As one continues to read, 'round' becomes an adverb, i.e., set around.

Cornice or Freeze, with bossy Sculptures graven,
The Roof was fretted[2] Gold. Not *Babilon*,
Nor great *Alcairo*[3] such magnificence
Equalled in all their glories, to enshrine
Belus or *Serapis*[4] their Gods, or seat
Their Kings, when *Egypt* with *Assyria* strove
In wealth and luxury. The ascending pile
Stood fixed her stately highth, and straight the doors
Opening their brazen folds discover wide
Within, her ample spaces, o'er the smooth
And level pavement: from the arched roof
Pendant by subtle Magic many a row
Of Starry Lamps and blazing Cressets fed
With naphtha and asphaltus[5] yielded light
As from a sky. The hasty multitude
Admiring entered, and the work some praise
And some the Architect: his hand was known
In Heaven by many a Towered structure high,
Where Sceptred Angels held their residence,
And sat as Princes, whom the supreme King
Exalted to such power, and gave to rule,
Each in his Hierarchy, the Orders bright.
Nor was his name unheard or unadored
In ancient *Greece*; and in *Ausonian*[6] land
Men called him *Mulciber*; and how he fell
From Heaven, they fabled, thrown by angry *Jove*
Sheer o'er the Crystal Battlements: from Morn
To Noon he fell, from Noon to dewy Eve,
A Summer's day; and with the setting Sun
Dropped from the Zenith like a falling Star,
On *Lemnos* the *Aegaean* Isle: thus they relate,
Erring[7]; for he with this rebellious rout
Fell long before; nor aught availed him now
To have built in Heaven high Towers; nor did he scape
By all his Engines,[8] but was headlong sent
With his industrious crew to build in hell.

2 Carved with decoration that is raised from the surface in order to give an appearance of solidity.
3 Cairo.
4 'Belus' is the Babylonian Baal; 'Serapis' is an Egyptian god. These names reinforce the references to idol-worship made throughout the long litany of devils' names. The implication is that Pandaemonium is akin to a pagan temple or a spectacular barbaric palace.
5 Asphalt or pitch would be burnt in the cressets (iron baskets), while naphtha (an oil from asphalt) would go in the lamps.
6 Italy.
7 i.e., the myth is told in a meandering or wandering fashion but it is also factually wrong and (as a pagan fable) morally questionable.
8 Devices, ingenious productions.

Book II 1–10: Satan enthroned in Pandaemonium

The opening of Book II sees Satan enthroned in state in his newly completed capital, Pandaemonium. The opulence of this spectacle does little to mask the fact that the grandeur is based on cruelty and exploitation, wonderfully expressed in the phrase 'barbaric pearl and gold'. The display of imperial power is made so very obvious that the religious reference might easily be missed. Every phrase here is damning but specifically the lines recall Paul's *Letter to the Romans* I 18–22.

> For the wrath of God is revealed from Heaven against all ungodliness and unrighteousness of men, who hold the truth in unrighteousness; . . . Because that, when they knew God, they glorified him not as God, neither were thankful; but became vain in their imaginations, and their foolish heart was darkened. Professing themselves to be wise, they became fools.

Following on from the description of Pandaemonium, it is now the enthroned Satan who would rise higher. His rebellious aspirations contradict divine inspiration and also run counter to his own previous experience of defeat. But then, if we follow the Pauline allusion, Satan is a fool.

High on a Throne of Royal State, which far
Outshone the wealth of *Ormus* and of *Ind*,[1]
Or where the gorgeous East with richest hand
Showers on her Kings *Barbaric* Pearl and Gold,
Satan exalted sat, by merit raised
To that bad eminence; and from despair
Thus high uplifted beyond hope, aspires
Beyond thus high, insatiate[2] to pursue
Vain[3] War with Heaven, and by success untaught
His proud imaginations thus displayed.

Book II 648–73: Satan encounters Sin and Death at the Gates of Hell

Much of Book II is taken up with the Council in Hell. As we may well guess, that turns out to be something of a sham as Satan manipulates the outcome to his

1 Hormuz lies in the Persian gulf and was famous as a market for jewels. India was also famous for its wealth and opulence. These geographical references refer us to the early modern world of European expansionist travel, trade wars and mercantile exploitation.
2 Never to be satisfied.
3 Useless, foolish. The Latin *vanus* means empty or devoid of substance. The modern connotations of personal vanity are also pertinent to Satan's desire for the admiration of others.

own ends. It is his own audacious self-assertion that leads him to propose an epic quest to discover and pervert God's new Creation. His journey is by flight, a common metaphor for ambition and human presumption ever since Icarus. Undertaking the flight leads Satan not just to the boundaries of Hell but into a new dimension, that of allegory. It is introduced as an overtly fictive formula, and something of a joke at Satan's expense. Satan's whole 'epic' journey will be allegorical – a flight across Hell to its gates and from there through Chaos, and on past the Paradise of Fools before he comes to the newly created universe.

At the gates of Hell, Satan encounters two monstrous forms. He is preparing to fight with Death until Sin intervenes and announces that Satan is the Father of both herself and Death. This lands Satan in an incestuous family romance and produces an infernal Trinity (one of a number of orthodox doctrinal positions which Milton has relegated to Hell). The allegorical contortions of Sin and Death at the gates of Hell are singularly emblematic of the dislocation that defines Hell and also, as his offspring, ironic evidence of Satan's 'proud imaginings' (II 10, see **p. 96**). The tripartite form of Sin in this description is emblematic of the act of sin: pleasant at first, then all-encompassing and with a sting in the tail. She is also 'voluminous' [large and made up of volumes], a figure replete with possible sources and analogues from literary and Biblical texts, e.g., Spenser's figure of Errour from *The Faerie Queene* (I.i.14–20), or the genealogy of death in the *Epistle of James* 1.14–15. Recent feminist criticism has been extremely interested in the imagery of sexual deviancy, monstrous births and gaping orifices in the description of Sin. Earlier readers such as Burke and Coleridge (see **pp. 50–1**) were more taken by the self-cancelling, and somewhat melodramatic, description of Death. It is presumably intentional that the description of Death starts at line 666, the number of the Antichrist.

    Before the Gates there sat
On either side a formidable shape;
The one seemed Woman to the waist, and fair,
But ended foul in many a scaly fold
Voluminous and vast, a Serpent armed
With mortal sting: about her middle round
A cry of Hell Hounds never ceasing barked
With wide *Cerberean*[1] mouths full loud, and rung
A hideous Peal: yet, when they list, would creep,
If aught disturbed their noise, into her womb,
And kennel there, yet there still barked and howled,
Within unseen. Farr less abhorred than these
Vexed *Scylla* bathing in the Sea that parts

1 Cerberus was the three-headed dog that guarded the entrance to Hades.

Calabria from the hoarse *Trinacrian* shore:[2]
Nor uglier follow the Night-Hag, when called
In secret, riding through the Air she comes
Lured with the smell of infant blood, to dance
With *Lapland* Witches, while the labouring Moon
Eclipses at their charms. The other shape,
If shape it might be called that shape had none
Distinguishable in member, joint, or limb,
Or substance might be called that shadow seemed,
For each seemed either; black it stood as Night,
Fierce as ten Furies, terrible as Hell,
And shook a dreadful Dart; what seemed his head
The likeness of a Kingly Crown had on.

Book III 1–6, 21–55: the second invocation

The second invocation stands as a hymn to celestial light and a prayer for divine illumination. It begins with an address to light as both a divine entity and as a metaphoric way of conceptualising divinity. The narrator's journey through Hell and Chaos is over and he is greatly relieved to have been returned safe to the regions of light. Soon, he will address the sun directly but his first and primary celebration is of God as light. The first six lines of this book are the most esoteric formulation in the epic. It is impossible to comprehend the Godhead fully, and this is part of the admission being made in this inwoven celebration of light as an expression of divine transcendence and omnipresence. The flow of the argument is based in the movement of 'light' and 'bright' through the lines but if I were to hazard a paraphrase it would be this:

> The addressee is holy Light. This light is either God's first Creation (*Genesis* 1.2 'Let there be light') or it is a way of thinking about the Son as a 'coeternal' expression of the Father. Certainly it is a struggle to produce an adequate linguistic description and the narrator is anxious about his own limitations and those of his medium. His subject is the divine itself, since God is light (*I John* 1.5) and dwells eternally in light ('Dark with excessive bright' III 380). This means that God dwells in the holy Light which the narrator has hailed as his own source of inspiration and for which he will now produce the inclusive nomination, 'Bright effluence of bright essence increate' – the bright emanation [light] that flows from the noncreated spiritual substance [God].

It is fitting that the divine should be celebrated at the start of Book III as

2 Three-cornered, a reference to the shape of Sicily. The terrible obstacles of Scylla and Charybdis are faced by those sailing between Sicily and the Italian mainland. The choice is either to sail close to the rocks of Scylla, described as yelping dogs that will snatch and devour random crew members, or close to Charybdis, a whirlpool that will destroy the entire ship. Ovid tells Scylla's own story (*Metamorphoses* XIV 1–74), presenting her as a nymph punished unjustly by the gods and transformed while she was bathing into this monstrous form.

an awesome and transcendent power, far beyond the limits of human understanding. Book III will be committed to justifying the ways of God, offering a divine colloquy between God the Father and the Son, where the divine reasoning which made possible both man's Fall and his Redemption is revealed to us. Before we grow too accustomed to thinking about God as a speaking figure within the poem, we should remember that the deity is equally to be appreciated through intense formulations such as this. We might think also at this point of the description of the Son riding forth on the Chariot of Paternal Deity (VI 749–66, see **pp. 122–3**).

In the second section here, the narrator has turned his attention to the benevolent power of the sun. Its light and heat are 'vital' [life-giving] to all on earth but the narrator laments that his blindness means that he is no longer able personally to see the light of the sun. Despite this disability, he will continue with his epic undertaking, safe in the knowledge that blindness can be a mark of divine favour, as it was for the precursors whom he names here. The inspired individual, be he poet or prophet or both, is vulnerable and has a great responsibility placed upon him. Yet, he also has a great gift, and it is the personal gift held by the poet that we now turn to consider, 'Then feed on thoughts, that voluntary move / Harmonious numbers'. To say that his thoughts 'move' voluntarily would seem to be a way for the narrator to suggest not only that the poetry is spontaneous but that he has made a free choice in accepting divine inspiration. Moreover, this use of 'move' is also transitive: the thoughts move themselves but are also acting upon [moving] the 'numbers'. 'Harmonious numbers' suggests the rhythms and metrics of versification, and they too are quite willing to be so moved in this intensely collaborative expression of the creative moment.

The narrator's best way of clarifying his meaning is to turn to the example of the nightingale, which remains awake, producing the most exquisite music almost as a spiritual gift in the physical darkness of the night. The phrase 'sings darkling' is admirably subtle. It refers to the nightingale's solitude but also its modesty – the way it sends its music forth but is not seen itself. It also suggests the tantalising fragility of the song from a source that can be deduced but remains unseen and, as a metaphor, it may also hint at a secret or a mystery caught up in the beauties of the nightingale's song. The thought of the nightingale's song, which brings solace and beauty from out of the dark, functions as an important parallel to the narrator's prayer for inspiration as a spiritual light that will 'irradiate' [fill with light] the darkness of his physical blindness.

Yet, despite his commitment, there remains a real poignancy in the blind man's lament. He grieves that his loss of sight means that he can no longer enjoy God's works set out all around him in what we still often term the book of nature. In particular, he misses the subtle changes in the daylight that occur at dawn and dusk, the beauties of spring and summer and above all other things he laments the fact that he can no longer see the faces of other human beings. The phrasing here is both accurate and sensitive, he calls it the 'human face divine'. It is often said that the eyes are the mirrors to the soul but within the epic we will find an even stronger insistence that the true glories of the Creator reside in the intelligence and openness of the human face. This is the hardest loss that the narrator bears. Yet, he has the courage to continue and the climax to this invocation is a prayer for a cleansing inner light that will burn off the narrator's personal impurities and make him adequate to the task ahead. In Book III he undertakes a divine theodicy but with Book IV we will enter Eden. There, the majestic descriptions of Paradise's eternal spring and of the human face divine (e.g., IV 264–8, 291–301, see **pp. 107–9**) are proof, should we require it, that the blind bard has been compensated for his loss of sight with an inspired revelation beyond that previously given to any poet or prophet.

Hail holy Light, offspring of Heaven first-born,
Or of the Eternal Coeternal beam
May I express thee unblamed? since God is light,
And never but in unapproached light
Dwelt from Eternity, dwelt then in thee,
Bright effluence of bright essence increate.[1]
. . . thee I revisit safe,
And feel thy sovereign vital Lamp; but thou
Revisitst not these eyes, that roll in vain
To find thy piercing ray, and find no dawn;
So thick a drop serene hath quenched their Orbs,
Or dim suffusion[2] veiled. Yet not the more
Cease I to wander where the Muses haunt
Clear Spring, or shady Grove, or sunny Hill,
Smit with the love of sacred song; but chief
Thee *Sion* and the flowery Brooks beneath
That wash thy hallowed feet, and warbling flow,
Nightly I visit: nor sometimes forget
Those other two equalled with me in Fate,
So were I equalled with them in renown,
Blind *Thamyris* and blind *Maeonides*
And *Tiresias* and *Phineus* Prophets old.[3]
Then feed on thoughts, that voluntary move
Harmonious numbers; as the wakeful Bird
Sings darkling, and in shadiest Covert hid
Tunes her nocturnal Note. Thus with the Year
Seasons return, but not to me returns
Day, or the sweet approach of Even or Morn,

1 Not created.
2 Milton probably suffered from what we would call glaucoma. Here, he includes two literal translations of seventeenth-century medical terms relating to his condition, *gutta serena* becomes 'drop serene' and *suffusion nigra*, 'dim suffusion'.
3 Two blind poets of renown and two blind prophets – Thamyris was from Thrace, blinded for boasting that he could outdo the muses; Maeonides is a reference to Homer; Tiresias was blinded by Juno in punishment but received the gift of prophecy from Jupiter in recompense; Phineus was a mythical king of Thrace, blinded but a prophet.

Or sight of vernal bloom, or Summer's Rose,
Or flocks, or herds, or human face divine;
But cloud in stead, and ever-during dark
Surrounds me,[4] from the cheerful ways of men
Cut off, and for the Book of knowledge fair
Presented with a Universal blank
Of Nature's works to me expunged and razed,
And wisdom at one entrance quite shut out.
So much the rather thou Celestial light
Shine inward, and the mind through all her powers
Irradiate,[5] there plant eyes, all mist from thence
Purge and disperse, that I may see and tell
Of things invisible to mortal sight.

Book III 93–134, 183–202, 236–41: theodicy

The epic has undertaken to 'justify the ways of God to men'. The greater part of Book III is concerned with this theodicy. It involves a long conversation between the Father and the Son in Heaven. They look down from Heaven at the glories of Creation and at Satan scrambling around, before they discuss the forthcoming Fall of man. The Father's voice represents justice and it is answered and complemented by the Son's mercy. The core statements are: the Father's assertion of the doctrine of free will; his explanation of why divine omniscience does not hinder creaturely free will; the question of election and the role of individual conscience; the Son's acceptance of his role as man's Redeemer. It is also helpful to remember that the divine colloquy has been framed by the narrator's invocation to light and the angelic hymns of thanksgiving, which give creaturely support to the divine theodicy.

The first extract reads much like the argument in favour of freedom of choice in Milton's prose text, *Areopagitica* (1644), see **pp. 18–20**. The difference of course is that here the argument has been put into the mouth of God. The introduction of God as a character within the epic has been seen as the greatest flaw within the poem. As soon as 'God' is restricted to a role within the narration, His position is reduced. 'God' has become a limited and definable part of the aesthetic creation of *Paradise Lost* in a way that runs counter to the basic theological argument that the Creator is *not* a creation. It is a short step from viewing 'God' as an anthropomorphic failure to terming 'Milton's God' [i.e., his defence of Christianity] tyrannical and advocating instead a humanist reading of the text (see Empson, **pp. 60–1**). A short step but, within the providential plan at least, a false one. It is not God who is limited but our human reason and our human language. This is why this presentation in Book III

4 Cf., VII 26–8, **p. 125**.
5 Cf., the positioning of the verb 'Illumine' in the first invocation (I 23, **pp. 85–6**).

suggests voices in conversation as an appropriate way for man to approach the omnifaceted reality of God.

According to the Father in this first extract, both mankind and the angels have the freedom either to obey or disobey divine commands. God chose to give them this freedom at their creation. It means He cannot thereafter manipulate their actions. However, that does not amount to a limiting of His omnipotence, because it lay in His power as the Almighty to grant that freedom to His rational creatures in the first place. By means of his free will, man is defined as a self-determining agent, capable of making morally significant choices. However, in consequence, he also becomes directly responsible for his actions. As much as the doctrinal detail in this passage, we hear the strength of the term, 'Ingrate' (line 97). Its grating tone stops the creative cycle of communication between God and his rational creation. This is not God's fault. His term is accurate. Disobedient man is the 'ingrate', no longer grateful and no longer in a state of grace. The narrator's description of the first couple (IV 288–324, see **pp. 109–10**), Raphael's narration of the creation of man on day six of the creation (VII 505–34, see **pp. 127–8**), and Adam and Eve's spontaneous prayers of thanksgiving to the Creator (IV 720–35, V 144–209) all occur after Book III but help to justify this speech. Man's role as the masterwork in creation is to complete the cycle, voluntarily returning thanks from the creation to the Creator.

For man will hearken to his glozing[1] lies,
And easily transgress the sole Command,
Sole pledge of his obedience: So will fall,
He and his faithless Progeny: whose fault?
Whose but his own? ingrate, he had of me
All he could have; I made him just and right,
Sufficient to have stood, though free to fall.
Such I created all the Ethereal Powers
And Spirits, both them who stood and them who failed;
Freely they stood who stood, and fell who fell.
Not free, what proof could they have given sincere
Of true allegiance, constant Faith or Love,
Where only what they needs must do, appeared,
Not what they would? what praise could they receive?
What pleasure I from such obedience paid,
When Will and Reason (Reason also is choice)
Useless and vain, of freedom both despoiled,
Made passive both, had served necessity,
Not me. They therefore as to right belonged,
So were created, nor can justly accuse
Their maker, or their making, or their Fate;

1 Cf., IX 549, see **p. 137** and footnotes.

As if Predestination over-ruled
Their will, disposed by absolute Decree
Or high foreknowledge; they themselves decreed
Their own revolt, not I: if I foreknew,
Foreknowledge had no influence on their fault,
Which had no less proved certain unforeknown.
So without least impulse or shadow of Fate,
Or aught by me immutably foreseen,
They trespass, Authors to themselves in all
Both what they judge and what they choose; for so
I formed them free, and free they must remain,
Till they enthrall[2] themselves: I else must change
Their nature, and revoke the high Decree
Unchangeable, Eternal, which ordained
Their freedom, they themselves ordained their fall.
The first sort by their own suggestion fell,
Self-tempted, self-depraved: Man falls deceived
By the other first:[3] Man therefore shall find grace,
The other none: in Mercy and Justice both,
Through Heaven and Earth, so shall my glory excel,
But Mercy first and last shall brightest shine.

This second extract feels bleaker and the problem of God's language comes to the fore. God is saying that He will give man every opportunity to repent and that only those who refuse to hear His call will be excluded. Particular importance is placed by God on His 'umpire conscience', as reason is to be man's best guide through all persecution and religious disputation. However, the tone of the last sentence is harsh. The rhetorical techniques jar, particularly the rhyme on grace/taste and the way that repetition seals men's fate. What we take from the final line is a divine decree that God will exclude some men from His grace, although what God is saying is that some men will be excluded from grace because they exclude themselves.

Some I have chosen of peculiar grace
Elect above the rest;[4] so is my will:
The rest shall hear me call, and oft be warned
Their sinful state, and to appease betimes

2 A reflexive verb meaning to enslave oneself. This exonerates the Creator by positioning the initial transgression as a reflexive action on the part of a creature endowed with free will. (Cf., Abdiel to Satan during the War in Heaven, 'Thy self not free, but to thyself enthralled' (VI 181).)

3 i.e., by the fallen angel, Satan.

4 Milton's use of the term 'elect' normally suggested a general opportunity available to all 'believers' rather than a preselected [predestined] minority. Milton's God, though, would seem to be differentiating between an elect group of dissenting saints, and a general call for reformation that will be heard by some but not by others.

The incensed Deity,[5] while offered grace
Invites; for I will clear their senses dark,
What may suffice, and soften stony hearts
To pray, repent, and bring obedience due.[6]
To Prayer, repentance, and obedience due,
Though but endeavoured with sincere intent,
Mine ear shall not be slow, mine eye not shut.
And I will place within them as a guide
My Umpire *Conscience*, whom if they will hear,
Light after light well used they shall attain,
And to the end persisting, safe arrive.[7]
This my long sufferance and my day of grace
They who neglect and scorn, shall never taste;
But hard be hardened, blind be blinded more,
That they may stumble on, and deeper fall;
And none but such from mercy I exclude.

Finally, here is the Son's volitional acceptance of his role as Redeemer. The conversation between God the Father and the Son is intended to allow for a fuller expression of how God's justice is mitigated by His mercy. The Son is responding to the justice required by the Father, 'Die he or justice must; unless, for him / Some other able, and as willing, pay / The rigid satisfaction, death for death' (210–12). There is a legal requirement, a debt to be paid. The Son is agreeing to fulfil the law by taking man's sins upon himself, and dying in atonement. The phrase 'Account me man' therefore brings into the poem the mystery of the Incarnation, when God became man and dwelt amongst us.

Behold me then, me for him, life for life
I offer, on me let thine anger fall;
Account me man; I for his sake will leave
Thy bosom, and this glory next to thee
Freely put off, and for him lastly die
Well pleased, on me let Death wreck[8] all his rage;

5 i.e., they will be warned to pacify God's anger in good time by satisfying His requirement of repentance.
6 Compare the final lines of Book X (1097–1104). Note the grammar here, as one sentence closes with the verbal construction and the next sentence shifts the specific action into general nouns.
7 Cf., XII 537–51.
8 Wreak or vent; but also suggesting that Death will not overcome the Son.

Book IV 32–92, 114–19: Satan addresses the sun

At the close of Book III, Satan disguised himself as a 'stripling cherub' (III 636) and fooled the angel in the sun, Uriel (Light of God), into giving him directions to Eden. The difficulty faced even by an archangel when encountering hypocrisy should be remembered when Eve is initially confronted by the speaking snake. Satan has now landed on the top of Mount Niphates, the mountain from which the river Tigris, one of the rivers in Paradise, was reputed to originate. His long, somewhat melodramatic, speech is a quite remarkable invention by Milton (see **pp. 27–9** for more on its date of composition). The speech should be contrasted with the invocation to Book III (see **pp. 98–101**) where the narrator prays for light and internalises inspiration and insight and it also works as a comparison to Adam's articulation of guilt and despair in Book X (see **pp. 144–7**).

Satan's speech starts in bluster with a rejection of the sun's benevolent presence but soon shifts into an examination of conscience. He admits his guilt but rejects repentance. He feels pain more than he does remorse, and he fears to humiliate himself in front of his followers more than he fears to deny God. While conceding his own responsibility for his actions and the totally unjustifiable nature of his actions, he will not recant and would rather curse God and reject His love. The speech has Satan damn himself out of his own mouth, and the fact that he is irredeemable by his own volition is important for the theodicy of the poem. Intriguingly, however, we still lack an adequate explanation of why it is that an original rebellion took place, although Satan wants to believe that an act of disobedience was bound to occur because it was possible for it to occur.

O thou that with surpassing Glory crowned,
Lookst from thy sole[1] Dominion like the God
Of this new World; at whose sight all the Stars
Hide their diminished heads; to thee I call,
But with no friendly voice, and add thy name
O Sun, to tell thee how I hate thy beams
That bring to my remembrance from what state
I fell, how glorious once above thy Sphere;[2]
Till Pride and worse Ambition threw me down
Warring in Heaven against Heaven's matchless King:
Ah wherefore! he deserved no such return
From me, whom he created what I was
In that bright eminence, and with his good
Upbraided none; nor was his service hard.
What could be less then to afford him praise,
The easiest recompense, and pay him thanks,

1 Pun on *sol*, the Latin term for the sun.
2 We might remember that in Heaven Satan's name was Lucifer (morning star).

How due! yet all his good proved ill in me,
And wrought but malice; lifted up so high
I sdeigned[3] subjection, and thought one step higher
Would set me highest, and in a moment quit
The debt immense of endless gratitude,
So burthensome, still paying, still to owe;
Forgetful what from him I still received,
And understood not that a grateful mind
By owing owes not, but still pays, at once
Indebted and discharged;[4] what burden then?
O had his powerful Destiny ordained
Me some inferior Angel, I had stood
Then happy; no unbounded hope had raised
Ambition. Yet why not? some other Power
As great might have aspired, and me though mean
Drawn to his part; but other Powers as great
Fell not, but stand unshaken, from within
Or from without, to all temptations armed.
Hadst thou the same free Will and Power to stand?
Thou hadst: whom hast thou then or what to accuse,
But Heaven's free Love dealt equally to all?
Be then his Love accurst, since love or hate,
To me alike, it deals eternal woe.
Nay cursed be thou; since against his thy will
Chose freely what it now so justly rues.
Me miserable![5] which way shall I fly
Infinite wrath, and infinite despair?
Which way I fly is Hell; my self am Hell;[6]
And in the lowest deep a lower deep
Still threatening to devour me opens wide,
To which the Hell I suffer seems a Heaven.
O then at last relent: is there no place
Left for Repentance, none for Pardon left?
None left but by submission; and that word
Disdain forbids me, and my dread of shame
Among the spirits beneath, whom I seduced
With other promises and other vaunts

3 Scorned.

4 i.e., forgetful of the constant gifts of God and not understanding that a rational creature's sense of gratitude is sufficient to pay the 'debt' owed to God and to renew constantly the bond between creature and Creator. This is an important admission from Satan, particularly in its use of the term 'grateful' (cf. III 97, see **p. 102**) and also the argument in Milton's early Latin poem to his father, *Ad Patrem*.

5 A Latinism.

6 The devil, Mephistophilis, in *Dr Faustus*, says something similar, 'Why, this is hell, nor am I out of it./ Thinkst thou that I, who saw the face of God, / And tasted the eternal joys of Heaven, / Am not tormented with ten thousand hells, / In being deprived of everlasting bliss?' (A text. I iii 78–82). *Christopher Marlowe, Doctor Faustus. A- and B- texts (1604, 1616)*, ed. David Bevington and Eric Rasmussen (Manchester: Manchester University Press, 1993), p.130.

Then to submit, boasting I could subdue
The Omnipotent. Ay me, they little know
How dearly I abide that boast so vain,[7]
Under what torments inwardly I groan;
While they adore me on the Throne of Hell,
With Diadem and Sceptre high advanced
The lower still I fall, only Supreme
In misery; such joy Ambition finds. [. . .]
  Thus while he spake, each passion dimmed his face
Thrice changed with pale, ire, envy and despair,
Which marred his borrowed visage, and betrayed
Him counterfeit, if any eye beheld.
For heavenly minds from such distempers foul
Are ever clear.

Book IV 264–324: description of Paradise and the human couple

Satan has reached Eden and the garden of Paradise. This passage opens with musical wordplay. The birds delighting in their setting are singing. Their music is 'vernal airs', songs of spring composed of and in the pastoral atmosphere of Paradise. This music is carried on the springtime breezes and, when it reaches the plants and trees, their leaves become a tuned instrument taking part in these delightful harmonies. The movement of the verse here is intricate but graceful and it is enjoyable to tease out the verbal interplay. The next part of the passage develops an Ovidian perspective upon this vibrant pastoral scene. In Ovid's texts, innocence and virginal existence are always on the verge of change or destruction and the emphasis in the story of Proserpina on mortality and grief is a case in point. However, we should notice how the Ovidian perspective is introduced in a negative manner. Paradise is *not* that fair field of Enna; yet, now that the connection has been made, we may find it difficult to forget the threat of violent disruption completely. The fragility of our conception of Eden, which needs to be a place that is not just beautiful but perfect, is consciously brought to our attention just as we first encounter its delights.

It is quite likely that a good number of modern readers will skip over the next few lines, replete as they are with classical and geographical references. Those who intend to do so might invoke the simile of the whale in their defence (I 192–208, see **pp. 90–1**). It is a characteristic technique within this epic to produce a list of possible analogues which require our fixed attention but which are ultimately to be rejected as insufficient or completely fallacious. The negatives here train the reader both to acknowledge and to dismiss his fallen preconceptions, to reject the fictions of classical myth and to ignore those who

7 i.e., how much pain I now suffer continuously because of that vain boast.

would 'map' Paradise in terms of our current landmasses. Only after that process will the narrator allow us to see the masterwork of creation and to admire the decorous simplicity and uncomplicated joys of human existence in Paradise. You will find that the syntax and lexical choice for the description of Adam and Eve are not difficult to understand in comparison to the narrator's prolegomena [learned introduction]. What is important in this first encounter is that we have a loving couple; that they stand tall; that they exist in 'filial freedom' and 'naked majesty'. Only once you have grasped these points fully should you move on to the infamously problematic line, 'he for God only, she for God in him'. We might argue that the woman is there to bring out, and respond to, only the best in man but ultimately this phrasing would seem to condone the subordination of the female sex and the authority of the male even before the Fall.

The Birds their choir apply; airs, vernal airs,
Breathing the smell of field and grove, attune
The trembling leaves, while Universal *Pan*
Knit with the *Graces* and the *Hours* in dance
Led on the Eternal Spring. Not that fair field
Of *Enna*, where *Proserpine* gathering flowers
Her self a fairer Flower by gloomy *Dis*
Was gathered, which cost *Ceres* all that pain
To seek her through the world;[1] nor that sweet Grove
Of *Daphne* by *Orontes*, and the inspired
Castalian Spring might with this Paradise
Of *Eden* strive;[2] nor that *Nyseian* Isle
Girt with the River *Triton*, where old *Cham*,
Whom Gentiles *Ammon* call and *Libyan Jove*,
Hid *Amalthea* and her Florid Son
Young *Bacchus* from his Stepdame *Rhea's* eye;[3]
Nor where *Abassin* Kings their issue Guard,
Mount *Amara*, though this by some supposed
True Paradise under the *Ethiop* Line
By *Nilus* head, enclosed with shining Rock,

1 Proserpina was snatched by Dis [better known as Pluto, god of the underworld], while she was gathering flowers in the field of Enna. Her mother Ceres [goddess of the harvest] abandoned everything to search the world for her daughter. The world became barren as a result. Ceres discovers her daughter in the underworld but, as Proserpina has eaten pomegranate seeds there, she cannot be restored unconditionally. She will be allowed to spend six months of every year with her mother but then must return to her husband, Dis. Ceres grieves during her daughter's absences in Hell, bringing winter to the earth. (See Ovid *Fasti* iv 420ff.) Stories such as this which explain the cause of a natural occurrence (e.g. winter) are termed aetiological myths.

2 Orontes is the name of a river near Antioch. Daphne was pursued there by a lascivious god and was saved by being turned into a laurel. The grove where these events were said to have occurred was named after her. It also contained a water source named after Parnassus ['the inspired/ Castalian spring'].

3 The island of Nysa is near modern Tunis. The Lybian king Ammon hid his lover [Amalthea] and her child, Dionysus [Bacchus], there away from his wife's [Rhea] sight. King Ammon was identified with Jupiter (see *PL* IX 508 'Ammonian Jove') and also with Noah's son, Ham [Vulgate *Cham*].

A whole day's journey high,[4] but wide remote
From this *Assyrian* Garden,[5] where the Fiend
Saw undelighted all delight,[6] all kind
Of living Creatures new to sight and strange:
Two of far nobler shape erect and tall,
Godlike erect, with native Honour clad
In naked Majesty seemed Lords of all,
And worthy seemed, for in their looks Divine
The image of their glorious Maker shone,
Truth, wisdom, Sanctitude severe and pure,
Severe, but in true filial freedom[7] placed;
Whence true authority in men; though both
Not equal, as their sex not equal seemed;[8]
For contemplation he and valour formed,
For softness she and sweet attractive Grace,
He for God only, she for God in him:[9]
His fair large Front and Eye sublime declared
Absolute rule; and Hyacinthine Locks[10]
Round from his parted forelock manly hung
Clustering, but not beneath his shoulders broad:
She as a veil down to the slender waist
Her unadorned golden tresses wore
Dishevelled, but in wanton[11] ringlets waved
As the Vine curls her tendrils, which implied
Subjection, but required with gentle sway,
And by her yielded, by him best received,
Yielded with coy submission, modest pride,

4 The Kings of Abyssinia held their male offspring in a fortress on Mount Amara in order to prevent sedition. The location was so pleasant that it was thought a Paradise. Milton notes that it lies by the equator ['Ethiop line'] and near the head-waters of the Nile. This mountain was so high that it would take a day to ascend and was said to have been enclosed with shining rock.

5 The extended list of negative comparisons draws to a close and we return to Eden, which is not to be found near Mount Amara but far remote from that Assyrian garden.

6 The word Eden is associated in Hebrew with the word for delight. Satan may be in a delightful location but he refuses to respond to it openly (cf. IV 75, see **p. 106**) and footnote 6. The narration has followed Satan the interloper into the garden and now records his, as well as our, first sight of the human couple. It is therefore possible to blame any problematic aspects of this first description on Satan's partiality.

7 Filial means 'pertaining to a son or daughter'. It refers to the duty owed by mankind to the Creator as Father, and to the liberty given by the Father to mankind as to his sons. It also develops a political sense by XII 64–71 (see **p. 153**), where all sons are born free and none should usurp power over another.

8 The term 'equal' can suggest identicality as well as a comparative, hierarchical, ranking. That man and woman are not physically identical should perhaps be seen as an enrichment of the human state rather than a divisive issue.

9 Cf. Paul, *I Corinthians* xi.3. 'The head of every man is Christ; and the head of the woman is the man; and the head of Christ is God'.

10 i.e., close curls.

11 A much discussed term but if Eve is not to be thought morally suspect her hair is promiscuous only in the sense that it is profuse.

And sweet reluctant amorous delay.[12]
Nor those mysterious parts were then concealed,[13]
Then was not guilty shame, dishonest shame
Of nature's works, honour dishonourable,
Sin-bred, how have ye troubled all mankind
With shows instead, mere shows of seeming pure,
And banished from man's life his happiest life,
Simplicity and spotless innocence.
So passed they naked on, nor shunned the sight
Of God or Angel, for they thought no ill:
So hand in hand they passed, the loveliest pair
That ever since in love's embraces met,
Adam the goodliest man of men since born
His Sons, the fairest of her Daughters *Eve*.

Book IV 460–527: Eve's memories and Satan's envy of the human couple

The first human words heard in the epic are Adam's to Eve, 'Sole partner and sole part of all these joys/ Dearer thy self than all . . .' (IV 411–12). As that conversation continues, Eve retells the story of her first memories. Most critics (starting with Patrick Hume in 1695) have identified the literary echo of the Ovidian myth of Narcissus within Eve's narrative (see *Metamorphoses* III 341–510). Narcissus refused a heterosexual union with Echo, became enamoured of his own reflection, pined away and died by the water's edge. It should be obvious that Eve's situation runs contrary to that of Narcissus, though many critics have rightly indicated the potential for self-love in Eve's first experiences. The introduction of this particular Ovidian myth allows the poet to play a game with textual reflection. Is it the same thing or isn't it? Of course it is not, and the Edenic version turns out to have more dimensions to it than the pagan myth. It even quotes the Latin text against itself by reintroducing the words in which Ovid's narrator comments on Narcissus's doom (words which Narcissus cannot hear) as a voice which directly speaks to Eve within her narrative, warning her of her danger and taking her out of the reflexive situation. It is often said that this 'voice' within Eve's narrative is that of God (Adam says as much at VIII 485 but he has no real grounds for making that identification) but really it is just as likely to be her own voice of conscience or a citation game between poets.

It is essential to Milton that our first parents understand the nature of their marital bond. The difference between a reflection and a man is the potential for physical union in the heterosexual union. Adam's touch is an important element

12 A wonderfully well-balanced expression of the erotic interaction between our first parents. The lines are teased out for our aesthetic delectation but simultaneously give a sense of satisfaction and completion through the rhyme on sway/delay.
13 i.e., genitals.

in winning Eve over. He does not look as attractive as her reflection does and, even though he has identified her as his 'other half', she is still drawn back to beauty until he 'seizes' her hand. A masculine erotic strength is implied here – 'seized' is a powerful, almost a violent, term yet that is modified by the fact that this hand is 'gentle' [noble and courteous]. Almost immediately thereafter, we look on as the couple embrace. It is a highly charged tactile moment, intensified by the fact that Eve's long golden hair continues to separate her naked body from that of her husband. Partnership is the theme of this first conversation. We are discovering how Adam and Eve as two separate individuals became partners and what that means to them. The concluding embrace should be seen as a significant element of this first conversation [a term that can mean both verbal and physical union at this time, cf., our current usage of the word 'intercourse'], championing the erotic potential of sexual difference.

It is startling to be reminded that Satan is in fact watching this embrace. His predatory gaze threatens the couple's future happiness just as the memory of a reflected gaze was an obstacle on the path to present union. Satan's aching desire, his frustration, and the intense loneliness that underpins his destructive jealousy are positioned in a highly dramatic fashion right next to the united bodies of our first parents. The privacy of the couple has already been violated by this voyeur but his jealousy cannot yet taint their innocent pleasures. Situated so close to happiness, Satan's own unhappiness and dissatisfaction become abundantly clear. He can rightly term the human couple's union an 'imparadising' but he cannot join with the couple and instead must speak to himself – or to us. It is an unpleasant thought that we may pair off with Satan at this point. We certainly understand his fallen emotions very well and the techniques that he intends to apply in order to destroy the innocence in front of him. He has been listening in only to exploit the situation and to gain information. Now he tells us his plan – to 'excite their minds/ With more desire to know'. Knowledge, put to the wrong ends, will be the downfall of humanity.

As I bent down to look, just opposite,
A Shape within the watery gleam appeared
Bending to look on me, I started back,
It started back, but pleased I soon returned,
Pleased it returned as soon with answering looks
Of sympathy and love; there I had fixed
Mine eyes till now, and pined with vain desire,
Had not a voice thus warned me, What thou seest,
What there thou seest fair Creature is thy self,
With thee it came and goes:[1] but follow me,
And I will bring thee where no shadow stays

1 Cf. Ovid *Metamorphoses* III 432–6. 'O fondly foolish boy, why vainly seek to clasp a fleeting image? What you seek is nowhere; but turn away, and the object of your love will be no more. That which you behold is but the shadow of a reflected form and has no substance of its own. With you it comes, with you it stays, and it will go with you – if you can go.'

Thy coming, and thy soft embraces, he
Whose image thou art, him thou shall enjoy
Inseparably thine, to him shalt bear
Multitudes like thy self, and thence be called
Mother of human Race: what could I do,
But follow straight, invisibly thus led?
Till I espied thee, fair indeed and tall,
Under a Platan,[2] yet methought less fair,
Less winning soft, less amiably mild,
Than that smooth watery image; back I turned,
Thou following cried'st aloud, Return fair *Eve*,
Whom fly'st thou? whom thou fly'st, of him thou art,
His flesh, his bone; to give thee being I lent
Out of my side to thee, nearest my heart
Substantial Life, to have thee by my side
Henceforth an individual solace dear;
Part of my Soul I seek thee, and thee claim
My other half: with that thy gentle hand
Seized mine, I yielded, and from that time see
How beauty is excelled by manly grace
And wisdom, which alone is truly fair.
  So spake our general Mother, and with eyes
Of conjugal attraction unreproved,
And meek surrender, half embracing leaned
On our first Father, half her swelling Breast
Naked met his under the flowing Gold
Of her loose tresses hid: he in delight
Both of her Beauty and submissive Charms[3]
Smiled with superior Love, as *Jupiter*
On *Juno* smiles, when he impregns[4] the Clouds
That shed *May* Flowers; and pressed her Matron lip
With kisses pure: aside the Devil turned
For envy, yet with jealous leer malign
Eyed them askance, and to himself thus plained.[5]
  Sight hateful, sight tormenting! thus these two
Imparadised in one another's arms
The happier *Eden*, shall enjoy their fill
Of bliss on bliss, while I to Hell am thrust,
Where neither joy nor love, but fierce desire,

2 A plane tree.
3 Eve yields (line 489) and now is described as having 'submissive' charms, i.e., she places herself willingly under the authority of another [Adam]. This fuels his love and 'delight' (a common Edenic term). Consideration of this exchange as the basic experience of a heterosexual erotic will tell us a lot about our cultural norms but we should remember that 'superior Love' need do little more than suggest that Adam is the taller of the two.
4 Impregnates.
5 Complained. The verb, to 'plain', is often associated with the pleas made by a lover. Satan is jealous of the innocent love enjoyed by Adam and Eve but he is also envious of the beauty of Eve and will speak to her like a suitor or seducer in both her dream and the temptation proper.

Among our other torments not the least,
Still unfulfilled with pain of longing pines;
Yet let me not forget what I have gained
From their own mouths; all is not theirs it seems:
One fatal Tree there stands of Knowledge called,
Forbidden them to taste: Knowledge forbidden?
Suspicious, reasonless. Why should their Lord
Envy them that? can it be sin to know,
Can it be death? and do they only stand
By Ignorance, is that their happy state,
The proof of their obedience and their faith?
O fair foundation laid whereon to build
Their ruin! Hence I will excite their minds
With more desire to know, and to reject
Envious commands, invented with design
To keep them low whom knowledge might exalt
Equal with Gods; aspiring to be such,
They taste and die: what likelier can ensue?

Book V 15–25, 48–93: Eve's dream

Book V begins in Paradise early in the morning following Eve's diabolically induced dream. Adam wakes first and admires Eve's beauty as she sleeps, though the narration notes that her face is flushed (V.10). In his aubade [early morning song] Adam delights in his partnership with Eve and celebrates the fecundity of nature. Adam's love song contains strong echoes of the Bridegroom's song from the *Song of Solomon*. This highly erotic Old Testament text was taken by Paul to express the mystery of Christ's union with His church but in Eden its terms can be associated with frank erotic enjoyment, or what Adam terms 'rational delight' (VIII 391). Eden pulses with vitality and growth on this new day and Adam looks forward to reviewing the difference that the human couple's work is making in helping the plants to 'spring'. The verb is intentionally dynamic, expressing the energy in the garden as the plants burst forth and bloom in Paradise's perpetual springtime. It is significant that Adam is interested in the human input to this natural process. Man's husbandry [care of the garden and self-governance] and the application of his reasoning powers come into focus in Book V, beginning with the issues raised by Eve's dream.

Eve wakes startled and tells Adam of her disturbing dream. She dreamt that she heard a voice which she took to be Adam's. It called her forth to be seen by the 'eyes' (line 44) of the stars which are attracted 'by thy beauty still to gaze' (line 47). She 'rose as at thy call' and walked to the Tree of Knowledge where she met a figure winged like an angel. He ate the fruit in front of her and then encouraged her to eat. Eve relates that she felt compelled to taste and then that the consequence of tasting was flight. There is therefore a gap in the narrative where the act itself must be presumed to take place. Finally, Eve says she sank down and 'fell' asleep. The dream has of course attracted much critical attention and it does seem a quite remarkable addition for Milton to have made to Adam and Eve's innocent experience. The conventional critical debate is over Eve's inherent weakness and the possibility that she inclines towards a fallen state even during the prelapsarian narrative. It would however be unfair to judge Eve's moral standing on what happens in a diabolically induced dream. This episode is more subtle than that. It is about experiencing the potential for error at a time when reason is not in control. Adam's view is that there is nothing to worry about so long as the 'misjoining shapes' (line 111) of the dream remain 'unapproved' (line 118) by the conscious mind. Eve, silent and passive in a dream, will not be held to account for what unfolds but, awake and rationally alert, she should now be on her guard against such disobedient action. The ways in which this dream passage reworks previous textual information (especially Eve's love lyric and question about the stars IV 639–58), and the way in which it is itself refashioned during the temptation in Book IX, (e.g., see **p. 140**) are fascinating areas to explore. A psychoanalytical approach to the idea of flight or a feminist approach to the importance of the (male?) extended gaze upon Eve throughout her dream, and again during her temptation in Book IX, would also prove rewarding.

. . . ; then with voice
Mild, as when *Zephyrus* on *Flora* breaths,[1]
Her hand soft touching, whispered thus. Awake
My fairest, my espoused, my latest found,
Heaven's last best gift, my ever new delight,
Awake,[2] the morning shines, and the fresh field
Calls us, we lose the prime,[3] to mark how spring
Our tended Plants, how blows the Citron Grove,
What drops the Myrrh, and what the balmy Reed,
How Nature paints her colours, how the Bee
Sits on the Bloom extracting liquid sweet.[4]
[. . .]
I rose as at thy call, but found thee not;
To find thee I directed then my walk;

1 Zephyrus is the west wind, Flora the goddess of flowers. (See Ovid *Fasti* v.195ff.). These lines might be compared to IV 264–8, see **p. 108** or to IX 394–6.

2 Cf., *Song of Solomon* 2.10ff. 'My beloved spake, and said unto me, Rise up, my love, my fair one, and come away . . . The flowers appear on the earth; the time of the singing of birds is come, and the voice of the turtle [dove] is heard in our land; The fig tree putteth forth her green figs, and the vines with the tender grape give a good smell. Arise, my love, my fair one, and come away.'

3 The first hour of the day (sunrise in Paradise is at 6 am). An additional suggestion that this is the best time of day.

4 The repeated application of the term 'sweet' as this passage progresses is worth noting. It moves from being a reference to nectar as a product of nature, through a reference to the cadence of the nightingale's song, to the perverse suggestion that it is a property of the forbidden fruit itself. Misappropriation of this term is particularly noticeable because of its repeated usage in descriptions of Eden and Eve. It was a prominent term in Eve's own love lyric addressed to Adam on the evening before her dream (IV 639–58).

And on, methought, alone I passed through ways
That brought me on a sudden to the Tree
Of interdicted[5] Knowledge: fair it seemed,
Much fairer to my Fancy then by day:
And as I wondering looked, beside it stood
One shaped and winged like one of those from Heaven
By us oft seen; his dewy locks distilled
Ambrosia; on that Tree he also gazed;
And O fair Plant, said he, with fruit surcharged,
Deigns none to ease thy load and taste thy sweet,
Nor God, nor Man; is Knowledge so despised?
Or envy, or what reserve forbids to taste?
Forbid who will, none shall from me withhold
Longer thy offered good, why else set here?
This said he paused not, but with venturous Arm
He plucked, he tasted;[6] me damp horror chilled
At such bold words vouched with a deed so bold:
But he thus overjoyed, O Fruit Divine,
Sweet of thy self, but much more sweet thus cropt,
Forbidden here, it seems, as only fit
For Gods, yet able to make Gods of Men:
And why not Gods of Men, since good, the more
Communicated, more abundant grows,
The Author not impaired, but honoured more?[7]
Here, happy Creature, fair Angelic *Eve*,
Partake thou also; happy though thou art,
Happier thou mayst be, worthier canst not be:
Taste this, and be henceforth among the Gods
Thy self a Goddess, not to Earth confined,
But sometimes in the Air, as we, sometimes
Ascend to Heav'n, by merit thine, and see
What life the Gods live there, and such live thou.
So saying, he drew nigh, and to me held,
Even to my mouth of that same fruit held part
Which he had plucked; the pleasant savoury smell
So quickened[8] appetite, that I, methought,
Could not but taste. Forthwith up to the Clouds
With him I flew, and underneath beheld
The Earth outstretched immense, a prospect wide
And various: wondering at my flight and change

5 Forbidden, prohibited by decree.

6 Note how the rhythm slows here and how dramatic the line becomes through the employment of two sequential verbs (Cf. IX 781, see **p. 140** and the note on the importance of the word 'taste', see **p. 132**, footnote 1 and **p. 144**, footnote 6. See also Turner **p. 72**).

7 A subtle perversion of logic. Communicating the 'good' that is God is best done through a grateful heart not through breaking a commandment and it would be idolatrous to believe that the fruit itself has the power to transfer 'goodness' to the consumer. In any case, all rational creatures should be keenly aware that there can only be one God, the Creator of all things.

8 Stimulated, sharpened.

To this high exaltation; suddenly
My Guide was gone, and I, me thought, sunk down,
And fell asleep; but O how glad I waked
To find this but a dream!

Book V 468–543: Raphael's explanation of the universal scale

The archangel Raphael is sent by God to assist Adam and Eve after the disturbance of Eve's dream and to warn them of the need for vigilance. The conversation between the angel and the human couple is an immensely important episode set at the very heart of the epic (Books V–VIII). From Raphael's courteous discourse we gain information on numerous subjects – the universal scale, nutrition, angels, obedience, sin, rebellion, faith, war, God's Creation, astronomy, passion – and a repeated message that all knowledge must be employed for the greater glory of the Creator and not for selfish motives. It is a great privilege for man to be able to discourse on equal terms with the angels and a proof within the epic both of man's prelapsarian capabilities and of the Creator's benevolence.

Raphael is willing not only to converse but to eat with the human couple. This double communion between man and angel is an active example of Raphael's theoretical explanation of the elemental unity underpinning creational diversity and the essential indivisibility of spirit and matter. Within this key passage, Raphael chooses to explain this theory of monist materialism through the metaphor of the plant. This organic organism can be considered as the whole of its composite parts (root, stalk, leaves, flower). It grows higher, becoming more 'airy' until its flowers both breathe in the air and send out perfume into the air. A similar scale of positive aspiration, to grow closer to spirit though rooted in matter, defines all created forms in their perfect state. It governs nature on earth and it also defines the angelic substance. Raphael has chosen the plant as his example in part because it will be familiar to prelapsarian man and partly because he is currently engaged in eating a fructarian meal. He specifically states that, like man, he too will receive nourishment from this source, though he will convert and digest the food in a slightly different manner than man does. Raphael's extended discourse on the scale of nature becomes more speculative as he continues the argument by suggesting that man, living in innocence, may in time ascend 'by steps' to a more spiritual form. This offers a remarkable sense within the epic of Edenic existence as progressive rather than static. It also acts to dissuade man from the misconception of Eve's recent dream that it might be possible to attain a higher status by one single action (i.e., eating one piece of fruit in an act of disobedience won't do it but eating lots of fruit while remaining obedient will). The opportunity for such refinement of the body relies on humanity's volitional obedience and Raphael will soon be encouraging Adam to be aware of his responsibility in this respect. It is not surprising to find that the heavenly messenger reiterates the doctrine of free will. As readers, we know of the doctrine from the divine colloquy in Book III but Raphael will now instruct the human couple, speaking as one rational creature to another not imposing a doctrine from on high.

To whom the winged Hierarch replied.
O *Adam*, one Almighty is, from whom
All things proceed, and up to him return,
If not depraved from good, created all
Such to perfection, one first matter all,
Indued with various forms, various degrees
Of substance, and in things that live, of life;
But more refined, more spirituous, and pure,
As nearer to him placed or nearer tending
Each in their several active Spheres assigned,
Till body up to spirit work, in bounds
Proportioned to each kind. So from the root
Springs lighter the green stalk, from thence the leaves
More airy, last the bright consummate[1] flower
Spirits odorous breathes: flowers and their fruit
Man's nourishment, by gradual scale sublimed
To vital Spirits aspire, to animal,
To intellectual, give both life and sense,
Fancy and understanding, whence the Soul
Reason receives, and reason is her being,
Discursive, or Intuitive; discourse
Is oftest yours, the latter most is ours,[2]
Differing but in degree, of kind the same.
Wonder not then, what God for you saw good
If I refuse not, but convert, as you,
To proper substance; time may come when men
With Angels may participate, and find
No inconvenient Diet, nor too light Fare:
And from these corporal nutriments[3] perhaps
Your bodies may at last turn all to Spirit
Improved by tract of time, and winged ascend
Ethereal, as we, or may at choice
Here or in Heavenly Paradises dwell;
If ye be found obedient, and retain
Unalterably firm his love entire
Whose progeny you are.[4] Mean while enjoy

1 Perfect. The description of the plant is brought to completion in its flower.
2 Man employs his reason through argument (and language); angels have an immediate comprehension based on vision not words. The common ground between both is that, rightly employed, reason will further the creature's knowledge of God.
3 Food for the body.
4 i.e., and remain true to His love. 'Progeny' means offspring.

Your fill what happiness this happy state
Can comprehend, incapable of more.
  To whom the Patriarch of mankind replied.
O favourable spirit, propitious guest,[5]
Well hast thou taught the way that might direct
Our knowledge, and the scale of Nature set
From centre to circumference, whereon
In contemplation of created things
By steps we may ascend to God. But say,
What meant that caution joined, *if ye be found*
Obedient? can we want[6] obedience then
To him, or possibly his love desert
Who formed us from the dust, and placed us here
Full to the utmost measure of what bliss
Human desires can seek or apprehend?
  To whom the Angel. Son of Heaven and Earth,
Attend[7]: That thou art happy, owe to God;
That thou continuest such, owe to thy self,
That is, to thy obedience; therein stand.
This was that caution given thee; be advised.
God made thee perfect, not immutable;
And good he made thee, but to persevere
He left it in thy power, ordained thy will
By nature free, not over-ruled by Fate
Inextricable, or strict necessity;
Our voluntary service he requires,
Not our necessitated, such with him
Finds no acceptance, nor can find, for how
Can hearts, not free, be tried whether they serve
Willing or no, who will but what they must
By Destiny, and can no other choose?
My self and all the Angelic Host that stand
In sight of God enthroned, our happy state
Hold, as you yours, while our obedience holds;
On other surety none; freely we serve
Because we freely love, as in our will
To love or not; in this we stand or fall:
And some are fallen, to disobedience fallen,
And so from Heaven to deepest Hell; O fall
From what high state of bliss into what woe!

5 Gracious.
6 Lack. i.e., Adam is saying that the idea of *not* being obedient to the Creator is new to him.
7 Listen, take note.

Book V 600–17: Raphael recounts God's exaltation of the Son

This is as far back as it is possible to go within the internal chronology of the poem. Our knowledge of events and our reckoning of time begin here with the voice of God, though we know of the proclamation only through the recollection of Raphael. The Son is anointed [marked out] and appointed as head of all the ranks of angels. In honouring the Son, the angels will honour God and manifest divine union. However, it is just this addition of a point of mediation between the created entity and the Godhead that causes envy (line 662) and pride (line 665) in Lucifer/Satan, who we are soon to be told 'thought himself impaired' (line 665). The declaration of the Son is based on Psalm 2, often called the coronation psalm. Milton translated this psalm in the 1650s, emphasising its apocalyptic message and the humbling of all secular monarchs that takes place with the appearance of the Son.

Hear all ye Angels, Progeny of Light,
Thrones, Dominations, Princedoms, Virtues, Powers,
Hear my Decree, which unrevoked shall stand.
This day I have begot whom I declare
My only Son, and on this holy Hill
Him have anointed, whom ye now behold
At my right hand; your Head I him appoint;
And by my Self have sworn to him shall bow
All knees in Heaven, and shall confess him Lord:
Under his great Vice-regent[1] Reign abide
United as one individual Soul
For ever happy: him who disobeys
Me disobeys, breaks union, and that day
Cast out from God and blessed vision, falls
Into utter darkness, deep engulfed, his place
Ordained without redemption, without end.
  So spake the Omnipotent, and with his words
All seemed well pleased, all seemed, but were not all.

Book V 853–907: Raphael recounts Satan's apostasy and Abdiel's fidelity

Raphael's story of the War in Heaven begins with the exaltation of the Son (V 600–15) and Satan's 'envy' (V 662). Satan then removes his cohorts to the

1 Vice regent, one ruling by deputed power, one appointed by a monarch to rule in his place.

North and plans rebellion. Only one angel will speak against him. This is Abdiel, whose name means Servant of God. The fierce disagreement between Satan and Abdiel is the climax of Book V, an important structural position particularly in the first (ten-book) edition of *Paradise Lost* (1667). The courage of a lone individual, who confirms his faith despite general contempt, is an important type for dissenters after the Restoration, and Abdiel's witness will be renewed through the motif of the 'one just man' in the Biblical episodes related in Books XI and XII. Both of these models are available to Adam but for the reader there will be one more brave witness to admire and imitate, the narrator, who in the invocation to Book VII describes himself as 'with dangers compassed round' (VII 27, see **p. 125**).

This extract opens mid-speech as Satan denies that he was created at all. His logic is puerile – 'I don't remember that happening, therefore it did not happen.' In fact, as the epic repeatedly shows, one of the defining characteristics of being a created entity is that you do not know the moment of your own birth but have it narrated to you by another being. (The only entity for whom this is not the case is Sin, who narrates the story of her own birth at II 752–61, but then again Sin may not be a reliable source of information!) As readers, we are already familiar with the Satanic mode of argument but within the internal chronology of events this is an early example of his sneering, punning, bullying manner. He is already vying with God, and attempting to control the rhetorical moment by his quip on 'beseeching' or 'besieging'. However, the episode has been framed to expose his fallacy and deny him rhetorical supremacy. It is important that the first rejection of Satan and the epic's central proclamation of his doom should come from the mouth of a faithful angel, rather than God. It is part of the wider justification of God's ways that rational creatures can vindicate His truth in this fashion and ultimately it is Abdiel who gains our respect in this episode. He does so by standing firm and being brave enough to tell Satan to his face that his claims are false and perverse.

That we were formed then sayst thou? and the work
Of secondary hands, by task transferred
From Father to his Son? strange point and new!
Doctrine which we would know whence learnt: who saw
When this Creation was? remember'st thou
Thy making, while the Maker gave thee being?
We know no time when we were not as now;
Know none before us, self-begot, self-raised
By our own quickening[1] power, when fatal course
Had circled his full Orb, the birth mature
Of this our native Heav'n, Ethereal Sons.
Our puissance[2] is our own, our own right hand

1 Life-giving. In the following lines Satan claims that they are the product of their environment, sons of the air.
2 Strength, power.

Shall teach us highest deeds, by proof to try
Who is our equal: then thou shalt behold
Whether by supplication we intend
Address, and to begirt the Almighty Throne
Beseeching or besieging. This report,
These tidings carry to the anointed King;[3]
And fly, ere evil intercept thy flight.
He said, and as the sound of waters deep[4]
Hoarse murmur echoed to his words applause
Through the infinite Host, nor less for that
The flaming Seraph fearless, though alone
Encompassed round with foes, thus answered bold.
O alienate from God, O spirit accurst,
Forsaken of all good; I see thy fall
Determined, and thy hapless crew involved
In this perfidious fraud, contagion spread
Both of thy crime and punishment: henceforth
No more be troubled how to quit the yoke
Of God's *Messiah*; those indulgent Laws
Will not be now vouchsafed, other Decrees
Against thee are gone forth without recall;
That Golden Sceptre which thou didst reject
Is now an Iron Rod to bruise and break
Thy disobedience. Well thou didst advise,
Yet not for thy advice or threats I fly
These wicked Tents devoted, least the wrath
Impendent,[5] raging into sudden flame
Distinguish not:[6] for soon expect to feel
His Thunder on thy head, devouring fire.
Then who created thee lamenting learn,
When who can uncreate thee thou shalt know.
So spake the Seraph *Abdiel* faithful found,
Among the faithless, faithful only he;
Among innumerable false, unmoved,
Unshaken, unseduced, unterrified
His Loyalty he kept, his Love, his Zeal;[7]
Nor number, nor example with him wrought
To swerve from truth, or change his constant mind

3 Messiah [the anointed one] – a sneering reference to God's decree (V 600–15, see **p. 119**).
4 In *Revelation* 19.6 such a sound implies worship.
5 Imminent; hanging over you.
6 i.e., Abdiel says that he is leaving not because of any threat made by Satan but because God's wrath will soon break on the heads of the rebels and he does not want to be in the wrong place at the wrong time. His departure echoes *Numbers* 16.26–33 where Moses warns the Israelites not to support a rebellion but to depart from the 'tents of these wicked men' (cf. 'wicked tents' in line 890). In the Old Testament story, the ground opens to swallow the rebels up and take them down to Sheol [Hell] alive.
7 Ardent faith and righteous indignation.

Though single.[8] From amidst them forth he passed,
Long way through hostile scorn, which he sustained
Superior, nor of violence feared aught;
And with retorted scorn[9] his back he turned
On those proud Towers to swift destruction doomed.

Book VI 749–66: Raphael recounts how the Son rode forth in the Chariot of Paternal Deity

The revelation of the Son throned in the chariot of paternal deity is a spectacle of power. He rides forth on the third day of the War in Heaven, not to engage in combat but rather to expose the insignificance of the rebels in the face of God's power. They turn tail at the sight of the Son and prefer to throw themselves from Heaven than face him. This is a theophany but at the same time the Son in the 'chariot of parental deity' is also the ultimate symbol of free obedience and total commitment to God. The chariot symbolises overwhelming triumph, judgement and power. This victorious sight is crucial to the argument of the epic and, as Fowler (1998, p. 26) notes, on a count on the number of lines in the first edition of the epic (1667), it has been placed at the very centre of the entire poem. The description of the chariot is based on Ezekiel's vision in *Ezekiel* 1 and it reinforces the presentation of the Son within the epic as a transcendent being, a revelation of power and glory and light. The chariot moves by its own spirit. It is kinetically overpowering. Indeed, the very sound of the passage insists on its movement. The onomatopoeia of the terms used to describe its action, (whirl, rush, flash) suggest light and movement caught in sound and the 'whirlwind sound' dominates the passage, twisting grammar and definition, confusing the boundaries of sense perception. The Son here outshines all imitation, and out-tropes any royalist analogy of monarch to sun. He both emits light and is an emanation of light.

. . . forth rushed with whirlwind sound
The Chariot of Paternal Deity,
Flashing thick flames, Wheel within Wheel undrawn,
It self instinct with Spirit, but convoyed
By four Cherubic shapes, four Faces each
Had wondrous, as with Stars their bodies all
And Wings were set with Eyes, with Eyes the wheels
Of Beryl, and careering Fires between;
Over their heads a crystal Firmament,
Whereon a Sapphire Throne, inlaid with pure

8 i.e., even though he was alone, neither their numbers nor their behaviour inclined him to alter his opinion.

9 i.e., Abdiel returns scorn with scorn. The previous lines suggest that he has had to endure much goading and abuse before he is clear of the rebel forces.

Amber, and colours of the showery Arch.[1]
He in Celestial Panoply[2] all armed
Of radiant *Urim*,[3] work divinely wrought,
Ascended,[4] at his right hand Victory
Sat Eagle-winged, beside him hung his Bow
And Quiver with three-bolted Thunder stored,
And from about him fierce Effusion[5] rolled
Of smoke and bickering[6] flame, and sparkles dire;

Book VII 1–39: the third invocation

The third of the four invocations in the epic occurs here at the start of Book VII. As line 21 indicates, we have reached an important structural divide: we are halfway through the epic (particularly so in the twelve-book format of the second edition) and are returning now to earthly matters and away from supra-human occurrences; halfway also through Raphael's narration; and at line 21 halfway through this invocation. It seems an appropriate point to pause. We might expect the narrator to congratulate himself on how much he has achieved but instead the invocation is filled with a sense of personal anxiety. The vulnerability of the narrator is acute. He has gone far beyond his natural element in telling of the War in Heaven and he fears a 'fall'. For the only time in the poem the muse is given a name, Urania. In classical terms this would indicate the muse of astronomy, a fitting choice given that this book will consider God's creation of the universe. However, the narrator is hesitant as to whether this is the correct name for his Christian muse, whom he knows to be truly heavenly and not just a pagan myth. He needs the security of a Christian muse, both as guide in his epic endeavour and as protector because of the darkness that surrounds him. His phrasing 'In darkness and with dangers compassed round' initially recollects the invocation to Book III, where the darkness of blindness was so poignantly described (III 40–55, see **pp. 100–1**). However there has been a definite shift in emphasis. Now the 'days' are evil and the darkness is malevolent. We are not discussing blindness here but politics. The allusion to Bacchus [God of wine] and his revellers seems a blunt reference to the court of Charles II and its Cavalier *mores*, while the narrator's stance is akin to that of the faithful angel Abdiel, who stood 'Encompassed round with foes' (V 876). The public euphoria surrounding the Restoration itself made it an extremely

1 Colours of the rainbow.
2 i.e., clad in complete heavenly armour. The term is often used figuratively to refer to 'the whole armour of God' (*Ephesians* 6.11, 13).
3 Urim is a now unknown stone which was worn by the Jewish priesthood when entering the Holy of Holies, see *Exodus* 28.30.
4 The mid-lines of *Paradise Lost* (1667) are 'work divinely wrought/Ascended'. The work may be the chariot or the Son or both. It may also hint at a reference to the epic poem itself. See Fowler (1998), p. 26.
5 A pouring forth.
6 Flashing or quickly moving.

threatening time for Milton. Although he was not personally named as one of those to be excluded from the General Pardon in 1660, he would have been an easy target for any drunken group and he feared reprisals long after his release from prison in December 1660. When we recall that a number of the surviving regicides were less lucky than Milton and were publicly hung, drawn and quartered, even the Orpheus reference does not seem too far-fetched.

This is going to be the epic's hexameron: Book VII is taken up in its entirety by Raphael's account to Adam of the six days of God's Creation and of the Sabbath. Adam is granted knowledge of the Creation because his intention is to praise the Creator, 'the more/To magnify his works, the more we know' (VII 96–7). This chimes with the angelic hosanna at the close of Book VII. And yet we begin not with joy and profusion but with the narrator in postlapsarian misery and physical vulnerability, struggling heroically to keep faith. It is a subtle foil to the poem's celebration of creational perfection that we have been reminded of what man's inhumanity to man has made of God's gifts.

Descend from Heaven *Urania*, by that name
If rightly thou art called, whose Voice divine
Following, above the *Olympian* Hill I soar,
Above the flight of *Pegasean* wing.[1]
The meaning, not the Name I call: for thou
Nor of the Muses nine, nor on the top
Of old *Olympus* dwell'st, but Heavenly born,
Before the hills appeared, or fountain flowed,
Thou with Eternal wisdom didst converse,
Wisdom thy sister, and with her didst play
In presence of the Almighty Father,[2] pleased
With thy Celestial Song. Up led by thee
Into the Heaven of Heavens I have presumed,
An earthly guest, and drawn empyreal air,
Thy tempering;[3] with like safety guided down
Return me to my native element:
Least from this flying steed unreined, (as once
Bellerophon, though from a lower clime)
Dismounted, on the *Aleian* field I fall

1 Mount Olympus was the home of the classical gods but here it dwindles to a hill as the poet soars above it, higher even than the winged horse Pegasus (a common emblem for poetic inspiration) could have taken him.
2 This is a reference to *Proverbs* 8, where Wisdom is brought forth before there were fountains or hills. She is said to be beside God, 'I was daily his delight, rejoicing [Vulgate *ludens* could be translated as playing] always before him' (*Proverbs* 8.30). The intense sexuality of this mystery transfers into Milton's wording. His muse is not Wisdom but is to be conceived of in related terms.
3 i.e., he has been able to breathe heavenly air because (a) it was modified by the muse and (b) his capacities were increased by the muse.

Erroneous,[4] there to wander and forlorn.
Half yet remains unsung, but narrower bound
Within the visible diurnal sphere;[5]
Standing on earth, not rapt above the pole,
More safe I sing with mortal voice, unchanged
To hoarse or mute, though fallen on evil days,
On evil days though fallen, and evil tongues;
In darkness, and with dangers compassed round,
And solitude;[6] yet not alone, while thou
Visit'st my slumbers nightly, or when morn
Purples the East:[7] still govern thou my Song,
Urania, and fit audience find, though few.
But drive far off the barbarous dissonance
Of *Bacchus* and his revellers, the race
Of that wild rout that tore the *Thracian* bard
In *Rhodope*,[8] where woods and rocks had ears
To rapture,[9] till the savage clamour drowned
Both harp and voice; nor could the muse defend
Her son.[10] So fail not thou, who thee implores:
For thou art Heavenly, she an empty dream.

Book VII 453–74, 505–50: Raphael recounts events on the sixth day of Creation

These extracts relate events from the sixth day of Creation. The imaginative expansion made from the account of the creative process in *Genesis* I 24–31 is quite remarkable. Milton births his animals fully formed and mature from the womb of mother earth. The vigour of the life force in each creature dominates the passage as each strives to rise up out of the ground. The basic idea is that they are as natural a product of the earth as plants (472–3). There is a delightful

4 Bellerophon tried to fly to Heaven on Pegasus but Jupiter sent an insect to sting the horse and the rider was thrown. He fell to earth on the Aelian plain in Lycia. Falling into error (with an aetiological pun on wandering) is a fear that the bard must face both physically and in terms of his literary ambition. Cf., the tale of Mulciber (and its enjambment) 'thus they relate/ Erring;' (I 746–7, see **p. 95**).
5 The second half of the epic will relate to events taking place in the created universe, where time can be measured in days.
6 Cf., V 875–6, see **p. 121**.
7 A reference to Milton's compositional method (see **pp. 27–9**) but you may also wish to compare Milton's Sonnet XIX, 'Methought I saw my late espoused saint'.
8 A mountain in Thrace, sacred to Dionysus. The Thracian bard is Orpheus.
9 Ovid *Metamorphoses* 11. Orpheus was able to excite a response from nature and inanimate objects through his music.
10 The Muse Calliope was the mother of Orpheus. Milton's preoccupation with Orpheus's fate is long-standing (see *Lycidas* 58–63). He was ripped apart by a mob of female Bacchanates [followers of Bacchus]. Their barbarism is indicated here by the cacophony that drowns out the voice of the poet.

game of identification to be played as the animals come forth – the lion gets halfway and must push to free himself, the stag has to negotiate its exit with a full set of antlers on its head – but there is also an important political lesson and a metaphysical message to be expounded (see Edwards, **pp. 67–8** and Fallon, **pp. 64–6**). The extreme energy in evidence here could even be thought subversive. The celebration of the life force is tellingly heterodox with a surprising emphasis placed upon the fertility of a mother earth. Moreover, the naming game enjoyed by the poet, via Raphael, has actually taken the place in the epic of any detailed celebration of Adam's first naming of the animals (though that event is referred to on a number of occasions, e.g., VIII 349–54).

The creation of man as the climax of God's creation of the entire universe is given a lengthy preamble by Raphael. We are forced to stop and consider what man's creation means before we are admitted to the great event. The defining difference between man and the beasts is identified as God's holy gift of reason, termed here 'sanctity of reason'. That gift lifts man above the animals – he stands erect and, conscious of his place in Creation, can govern on earth while gratefully acknowledging the ultimate sovereignty of the Creator. The creation of Adam is another perfect opportunity for Raphael to enforce a message not just of God's goodness and benevolence but of monist materialism. Adam, the first man was dust [*ha'adama*, the dust of the ground] but is now a living corporeal thing, and moreover the image of God, through the power and goodness of the Creator. This information, like the extended metaphor of the plant (V 469–505, see **pp. 116–17**), should reinforce his awareness of the single substance underpinning all divine creation but Raphael will also reiterate man's freedom of choice within the garden as part of his rendering of the divine prohibition upon eating the fruit of the Tree of Knowledge.

The Earth obeyed, and straight
Opening her fertile Womb teemed at a Birth
Innumerous living Creatures, perfect forms,
Limbed and full grown: out of the ground up rose
As from his lair the wild beast where he wons[1]
In Forest wild, in Thicket, Brake, or Den;
Among the Trees in Pairs they rose, they walked:
The Cattle in the Fields and Meadows green:
Those rare and solitary, these in flocks
Pasturing at once, and in broad Herds upsprung:
The grassy Clods now Calved, now half appeared
The Tawny Lion, pawing to get free
His hinder parts, then springs as broke from Bonds,
And rampant shakes his brinded main;[2] the Ounce,

1 Lives.
2 The sovereign of beasts is named first. The heraldic term 'rampant' is appropriate to the newly created lion as it rears its forepaws in the air, stretching and shaking itself as it enjoys its new freedom. 'Brinded' means brownish or marked with different colours. Other big cats follow the lion – the lynx (ounce), the leopard (libbard) and the tiger.

The Libbard, and the Tiger, as the Mole
Rising, the crumbled Earth above them threw
In Hillocks; the swift Stag from under ground
Bore up his branching head: scarce from his mould
Behemoth biggest born of Earth upheaved
His vastness:[3] Fleeced the Flocks and bleating rose,
As Plants:[4] ambiguous between Sea and Land
The River Horse and scaly Crocodile.
[. . .]
There wanted yet the Master work, the end
Of all yet done; a Creature who not prone
And Brute as other Creatures, but endued
With Sanctity of Reason, might erect
His Stature, and upright with Front serene[5]
Govern the rest, self-knowing, and from thence
Magnanimous to correspond with Heaven,
But grateful to acknowledge whence his good
Descends, thither with heart and voice and eyes
Directed in devotion, to adore
And worship God Supreme, who made him chief
Of all his works: therefore the Omnipotent
Eternal Father (For where is not he
Present) thus to his Son audibly spake.
 Let us make now Man in our image, Man
In our similitude, and let them rule
Over the Fish and Fowl of Sea and Air,
Beast of the Field, and over all the Earth,
And every creeping thing that creeps the ground.
This said, he formed thee, *Adam*, thee O Man
Dust of the ground, and in thy nostrils breathed
The breath of Life; in his own Image he
Created thee, in the Image of God
Express, and thou becamest a living Soul.
Male he created thee, but thy consort
Female for Race;[6] then blessed Mankind, and said,
Be fruitful, multiply, and fill the Earth,
Subdue it, and throughout Dominion hold
Over Fish of the Sea, and Fowl of the Air,
And every living thing that moves on the Earth.

3 The elephant is the biggest creature on earth and when it is first rises up, it looks like a vast piece of the earth is moving.

4 This is Milton enjoying himself. The sheep come up in flocks with their fleece already in place, so they even look like plants but they are bleating like sheep because that is what they are. The phrase is amusing in the creational context but later poets over-indulged in such poetic diction [extravagant phrasing] as 'Fleecy flocks' rather than call a sheep a sheep.

5 Literally this means something like unwrinkled forehead but a wider sense of calm demeanour is more appropriate. Cf. IV 291–4, 300–01, **p. 109**.

6 Raphael gives only half a line to the creational division of humanity into two sexes.

Wherever thus created, for no place
Is yet distinct by name, thence, as thou know'st
He brought thee into this delicious[7] Grove,
This Garden, planted with the Trees of God,
Delectable both to behold and taste;
And freely all their pleasant fruit for food
Gave thee, all sorts are here that all the Earth yields,
Variety without end but of the Tree
Which tasted works[8] knowledge of Good and Evil,
Thou mayst not; in the day thou eat'st, thou diest;
Death is the penalty imposed, beware,
And govern well thy appetite, least sin
Surprise thee, and her black attendant Death.
Here finished he, and all that he had made
Viewed, and behold all was entirely good;
So Even and Morn accomplished the Sixth day:

Book VIII 379–92: Adam recounts how he asked God for a helpmate

Raphael has finished his narration and in Book VIII Adam now offers to relate his own memories to Raphael. His narration functions as an expansion and exposition of *Genesis* 2, just as Raphael's account in Book VII was a gloss on *Genesis* 1. Within Adam's narrative of his first experience of life, man initially rejoices both in the Creation around him and his own physical being. The intense joy in physical movement is part of his learning process. From a survey of his own body, Adam can move to a consideration of his surroundings and this immediately prompts a desire for contact with the creating force (VIII 267–82). The conference between God and Adam is a Miltonic addition to the *Genesis* story. It stands as a remarkable proof of man's reasoning powers and an educative process in its own right. In the Argument for Book VIII, the debate is termed 'his talk with God concerning solitude and fit society'. In other words, the communication over a mate for Adam is identified by Milton as the theme that brings God and man closest together within the text of *Paradise Lost*. The wording of Adam's request is significant. The first man sees his need as being for a companion capable of 'fellowship' and what he terms 'rational delight', a phrase which would seem to combine intellectual and erotic interaction. This is a highly sophisticated definition of marriage which takes the bond far beyond mere physical procreation.

7 Highly pleasing, especially to the senses of taste and smell. Both this term and 'delectable' are etymologically related to 'delight'.
8 Brings about.

Let not my words offend thee, Heavenly Power,
My Maker, be propitious[1] while I speak.
Hast thou not made me here thy substitute,
And these inferior far beneath me set?
Among unequals what society
Can sort,[2] what harmony or true delight?
Which must be mutual, in proportion due
Given and received; but in disparity
The one intense, the other still remiss
Cannot well suite with either, but soon prove
Tedious alike: Of fellowship I speak
Such as I seek, fit to participate
All rational delight, wherein the brute
Cannot be human consort; . . .

Book VIII 462–99: Adam recounts the creation of Eve

Adam now relates his memory of the birth of Eve. Although Milton retains the fact that woman is created from Adam's rib, his account is markedly different from that in *Genesis* 2. Moreover, when Adam wakes, Eve is not there. He has to seek her out and win her over. Her version of events, which is not quite identical with what Adam says here, has already been retold (IV 440–91, **pp. 110–12**). The fact that Adam and Eve both enter into the marriage agreement as willing individuals accords with the view expressed by Milton in his divorce tracts that marriage is primarily a human contract. In the prose tracts, this proposition was necessary to explain why some marriages might not be successful. A marriage could legally be annulled only on the grounds of physical incompatibility or consanguinity but Milton advocated divorce for those couples who proved either morally or intellectually incompatible. Within *Paradise Lost*, we see the flip-side of this argument, where a perfect human marriage is shown to be a complete and inclusive union. Adam inaugurates the marriage bond in words very similar to *Genesis* 2 23–4 but markedly extends this definition of marriage beyond physical union. Adam will unite with Eve not only as one flesh but as one heart and one soul.

Abstract as in a trance methought I saw,
Though sleeping, where I lay, and saw the shape
Still glorious before whom awake I stood;

1 Be gracious, look favourably upon me.
2 Adam argues that without equality there can be no true union. He extends his point through musical analogies. He wants a marriage based on fellow feeling with both intellectual and physical pleasures. 'Sort' here means to be suited or to accord. If such a bond can be achieved, then Adam's question of what 'can sort' will be answered in his 'consort'.

Who stooping opened my left side, and took
From thence a Rib, with cordial[1] spirits warm,
And life-blood streaming fresh; wide was the wound,
But suddenly with flesh filled up and healed:
The rib he formed and fashioned with his hands;
Under his forming hands a Creature grew,
Manlike, but different sex, so lovely fair,
That what seemed fair in all the World, seemed now
Mean, or in her summed up, in her contained
And in her looks, which from that time infused
Sweetness into my heart, unfelt before,
And into all things from her air inspired
The spirit of love and amorous delight.
She disappeared, and left me dark, I waked
To find her, or for ever to deplore
Her loss, and other pleasures all abjure:
When out of hope, behold her, not far off,
Such as I saw her in my dream, adorned
With what all Earth or Heaven could bestow
To make her amiable: On she came,
Led by her Heavenly Maker, though unseen,
And guided by his voice, nor uninformed
Of nuptial sanctity and marriage rites:
Grace was in all her steps, Heaven in her eye,
In every gesture dignity and love.
I overjoyed could not forbear aloud.
  This turn hath made amends; thou hast fulfilled
Thy words, Creator bounteous and benign,
Giver of all things fair, but fairest this
Of all thy gifts, nor enviest.[2] I now see
Bone of my bone, flesh of my flesh, my self
Before me; Woman is her Name, of Man
Extracted; for this cause he shall forgo
Father and Mother, and to his Wife adhere;[3]
And they shall be one flesh, one heart, one soul.

Book VIII 614–29: Raphael explains angelic sex

Raphael is warning Adam against erotic passion, as it amounts to a submission of reason to lesser pleasures. Adam asks how the angels express their love, and

1 Belonging to the heart.
2 An odd inclusion. Adam is praising the Creator for this final act of Creation and also grateful that the Creator has given so lavishly and without reluctance. The phrasing however 'nor enviest' is noteworthy as it actively contrasts with Satanic allegations regarding God.
3 Cleave; unite.

this is the remarkable insight into heavenly intercourse offered by Raphael in reply. Raphael tells Adam that, because angels are spirit rather than body, they fuse completely. The theory expounded here is once again monist and should be considered alongside Raphael's discussion of the heavenly scale of being in Book V (468–543, see **pp. 116–18**) and also against his explanation of how angelic 'bodies' heal (VI 344–53).

Bear with me then, if lawful what I ask;
Love not the heavenly Spirits, and how their Love
Express they, by looks only, or do they mix
Irradiance,[1] virtual or immediate[2] touch?
   To whom the Angel with a smile that glowed
Celestial rosy red, Love's proper hue,[3]
Answered. Let it suffice thee that thou knowest
Us happy, and without Love no happiness.
Whatever pure thou in the body enjoyest
(And pure thou wert created) we enjoy
In eminence,[4] and obstacle find none
Of membrane, joint, or limb, exclusive bars:
Easier then Air with Air, if Spirits embrace,
Total they mix, Union of Pure with Pure
Desiring; nor restrained conveyance need
As Flesh to mix with Flesh, or Soul with Soul.

Book IX 1–33: the fourth invocation

The last of the four epic invocations stands at the beginning of Book IX (lines 1–47). It opens with a negative formation, setting a tone of lament that will invest the narration from now on. It is time to introduce the 'tragic' note, as the story of man's Fall must be retold (see **p. 16** for more on the dramatic implications here). This is a 'sad task' but the narrator claims it as a more heroic [i.e., epic] undertaking than anything to be found in the classics. This bard would teach us to rethink our cultural value systems and move beyond a celebration of heroism that glorifies only physical strength and acts of aggression. We should note how wonderfully dismissive the references to the three great classical epics are, dealing in turn with Homer's *Iliad*; Virgil's later Roman epic *The Aeneid*; and then back to Homer and the *Odyssey*. Each is caught in amber in just

1 Light (and heat?).
2 Without any mediation.
3 Raphael is blushing but he is not therefore to be thought abashed or ashamed. This is an appropriate response in discussing matters of love.
4 (a) To a higher degree; (b) on high in Heaven.

two or three lines, and the choice of summary term in each case (wrath, rage, ire) makes it seem as if the three greatest stories ever told are in fact very similar indeed. The Christian bard on the other hand is not interested in military splendour or courtly grandeur. He identifies true heroism as being found elsewhere: in the individual's spiritual struggle. This he claims as the appropriate topic for solemn and substantial consideration.

Suddenly the story from *Genesis* of two individuals in a garden can come to have epic significance. In their individual trials is held an exploration of the human condition, in their fate lies the future of the whole human race. And, because of that, this is not just the story of a man and a woman, it is all our stories. Taking on this challenge is in itself a heroic undertaking. The narrator's struggle to impart his inspired tale adequately is itself a part of the new concept of human epic. He is also the narrator of a Christian epic and we cannot fail but hear a Christian reference in the phrasing 'patience and heroic martyrdom', although that meaning will be elaborated in Books X–XII rather than in Book IX. This then is the new domestic epic, a story of the individual and of our personal relations, rather than of battlefields and imperial aspirations. It will be an investigation of what goes on inside one's head rather than an itemisation of the blows that can be inflicted upon a warrior's physical body. Most previous literary epics were produced as celebrations of a particular ruler, or a particular nation's military and imperial supremacy. Virgil, for example, looked back from the times of the Roman Emperor, Augustus Caesar, to tell the history of Rome's foundation, and most of the Renaissance epics sought to flatter a specific secular patron. The narrator here sets the relationship between himself and his muse in place of such secular patronage and its compromises. This poem is inspired. It came directly to the poet from his 'celestial patroness'. His role is to speak its truth as best he can under her guidance. This is truly a new kind of epic.

No more of talk where God or Angel Guest
With Man, as with his Friend, familiar used
To sit indulgent, and with him partake
Rural repast, permitting him the while
Venial discourse unblamed: I now must change
These Notes to Tragic; foul distrust, and breach
Disloyal on the part of Man, revolt,
And disobedience: On the part of Heaven
Now alienated, distance and distaste,[1]
Anger and just rebuke, and judgement given
That brought into this World a world of woe,[2]

1 The preface 'dis' has occurred five times in the last four lines. Perhaps we are supposed to hear a pun on the classical term for Hell, Dis. The general theme here is traumatic severance and the last usage 'distaste' is particularly telling. It is as if the fact that man has eaten the apple leaves a bad taste in the mouth. Taste is a resonant term in Book IX (taste-tasting-tasted occurs 26 times within Book IX) and is part of a key network of words within the epic which link intellectual and experiential knowledge.

2 Cf. I, 3.

Sin and her shadow Death, and Misery
Death's Harbinger: Sad task, yet argument[3]
Not less but more Heroic then the wrath[4]
Of stern *Achilles* on his Foe pursued
Thrice Fugitive about *Troy* Wall; or rage
Of *Turnus* for *Lavinia* disespoused,
Or *Neptune's* ire or *Juno's*, that so long
Perplexed the *Greek* and *Cytherea's* Son;[5]
If answerable style I can obtain
Of my Celestial Patroness, who deigns
Her nightly visitation unimplored,
And dictates to me slumbering, or inspires
Easy my unpremeditated[6] Verse:
Since first this subject for Heroic Song
Pleased me long choosing, and beginning late;
Not sedulous by Nature to indite
Wars,[7] hitherto the only Argument
Heroic deemed, chief mastery to dissect
With long and tedious havoc fabled Knights
In Battels feigned; the better fortitude
Of Patience and Heroic Martyrdom
Unsung; . . .

Book IX 335–75: the separation scene

Adam and Eve are in disagreement over whether they should spend the day working separately in the garden or whether, as previously, they should work side by side. Their debate stems from a worry expressed by Eve that their labour may not be productive enough and that the garden's vigorous growth requires more diligent attention. Adam however is more willing to combine gardening with social interaction and conversation (IX 235–41). It is remarkable that Milton's depiction of an unfallen state allows this level of debate and autonomy. The scene is an audacious addition to the *Genesis* story and is unprecedented. If he can persuade us of the concept of mature human beings remaining in innocence it must be through our response to episodes such as this. There has been much critical anxiety over whether or not Adam and Eve demonstrate fallen traits during this conversation. It is a provoking and

3 As at I 24, this means subject matter, as opposed to an issue to be debated.
4 The opening lines of the *Iliad* translate thus, 'The wrath, sing, goddess, of Peleus' son Achilles, the accursed wrath which brought countless sorrows upon the Achaeans, . . .' *Iliad* I 1–2.
5 Odysseus. Cytherea is another name for Venus.
6 Spontaneous. The information given here regarding the composition of the epic accords with that offered by Cyriack Skinner, see **p. 28**.
7 i.e., it would not be my personal choice to write about war. 'Sedulous' means eager; 'indict' means to put into words, to write about.

fascinating admission that prelapsarian man could be fractious. Yet, neither individual has actually sinned here. There has been no deliberate act of disobedience or choice of evil. Eve will go off on her own at the end of this passage and the narrator will lament her imminent Fall. However, we should pause to consider what would have happened if she had not met Satan. Say that no temptation had occurred on this day, what then? What would the outcome of this experiment have been? Is it possible to conceptualise the possibility of the couple remaining unfallen and going on to make decisions based on what they had learnt from this experience?

Adam is trying to dissuade Eve from separating from him. Unfortunately, Eve's final argument is the trump card, based on the argument presented against censorship in *Areopagitica* (1644) (see **pp. 18–20**). Even so, Eve's application of the term 'imperfect' is ill-advised. She seems to have forgotten that human perfection rests on their freedom to choose. She should know that there is always a possibility of making the wrong choice and that there could be no real freedom of choice without that option being available. The 'happy state' of voluntary obedience is sufficient to repel evil but its perfection lies in its exposure to trial, and hence to imperfection. After her dream in Book V, when her 'happy state' was so readily disturbed, she should be more acutely aware of this. Adam seems to have grasped the argument more fully. He agrees that they must both be constantly on their guard but would rather not go seeking trials only in order to prove his constancy. To some extent, Adam would seem to be advocating a 'cloistered virtue' (see **p. 19**). Such an option is not valid in postlapsarian surroundings but is Adam wrong here? He knows enough of the arguments of individual liberty to know that he cannot force his wife to stay with him. He concludes by saying that Eve must make her own mind up. So must the reader.

And what is Faith, Love, Virtue unassayed[1]
Alone, without exterior help sustained?
Let us not then suspect our happy state
Left so imperfect by the Maker wise,
As not secure to single or combined.
Frail is our happiness, if this be so,
And *Eden* were no *Eden* thus exposed.
  To whom thus *Adam* fervently replied.
O Woman, best are all things as the will
Of God ordained them, his creating hand
Nothing imperfect or deficient left
Of all that he created, much less Man,
Or aught that might his happy State secure,
Secure from outward force; within himself
The danger lies, yet lies within his power:

1 Unproven, untested.

Against his will he can receive no harm.
But God left free the will, for what obeys
Reason, is free, and Reason he made right,
But bid her well beware, and still erect,
Least by some fair appearing good surprised
She dictate false,[2] and misinform the Will
To do what God expressly hath forbid.
Not then mistrust, but tender love enjoins,
That I should mind thee oft, and mind thou me.[3]
Firm we subsist, yet possible to swerve,
Since Reason not impossibly may meet
Some specious object by the Foe suborned,[4]
And fall into deception unaware,
Not keeping strictest watch, as she was warned.
Seek not temptation then, which to avoid
Were better, and most likely if from me
Thou sever not:[5] Trial will come unsought.
Wouldst thou approve[6] thy constancy, approve
First thy obedience; the other who can know,
Not seeing thee attempted, who attest?[7]
But if thou think, trial unsought may find
Us both securer than thus warned thou seem'st,
Go; for thy stay, not free, absents thee more;[8]
Go in thy native innocence, rely
On what thou hast of virtue, summon all,
For God towards thee hath done his part, do thine.

Book IX 494–518, 532–51: Satan begins his seduction of Eve

Satan has already incarnated himself in the snake. He spies Eve alone and her beauty stops him in his tracks. For a moment he is 'stupidly good' (IX 465), i.e.,

2 i.e., unless the will takes the wrong decision, surprised and taken unawares by something that looks attractive and seems good.
3 To 'mind' can mean to warn; to give heed to; to care for.
4 i.e., it is feasible that we might be tricked (unless we keep strict watch) by the foe's underhanded procurement of some attractive but ultimately fallacious object.
5 i.e., it would be better to avoid temptation if possible rather than to go out looking for it and you are more likely to avoid temptation by staying with me. This is a highly problematic argument and would not hold in the postlapsarian world but each reader needs to consider whether or not it is valid before the Fall.
6 Prove, demonstrate.
7 i.e.,if there is no witness to your temptation then it brings no commendation. This is a weak argument.
8 '[W]hat is at stake in this scene, as in the whole epic, is the meaning of human liberty' says Joan Bennett, *Reviving Liberty: Radical Christian Humanism in Milton's Great Poems* (Cambridge, Mass.: Harvard University Press, 1989), p. 95.

detached from his malicious plans he takes unthinking delight in the beauty in front of him. However, he soon recollects his purpose and reminds himself that his only pleasure now is in destruction, and so he applies himself to gaining Eve's attention. He wants to attract her eye and then to gain her ear. His motion and his rhetoric are equally oblique and seductive (cf., IX 634–45 where Satan is compared to a will-o'-the-wisp and IX 664–76 where he is compared to a classical orator). The initial stages of the temptation rely heavily on sight: firstly, the sight of this extremely phallic snake and then the insidious suggestion that Eve deserves to have more refined admirers of her beauty than are available to her in the garden. His initial address puns on 'wonder' and aims to make Eve consider herself as an object of beauty – i.e., 'do not marvel at me, a speaking snake, when you are the object most worthy of admiration'. The half rhyme linking 'gaze' and 'gloze' should not be overlooked by the reader, nor should the embedded acrostic S-A-T-A-N [enemy] at lines 510–14.

So spake the Enemy of Mankind, enclosed
In Serpent, Inmate bad, and toward *Eve*
Addressed his way, not with indented wave,
Prone on the ground, as since, but on his rear,
Circular base of rising folds, that towered
Fold above fold a surging Maze, his Head
Crested aloft, and Carbuncle[1] his Eyes;
With burnished Neck of verdant Gold, erect
Amidst his circling Spires, that on the grass
Floated redundant:[2] pleasing was his shape,
And lovely, never since of Serpent kind
Lovelier, not those that in *Illyria* changed
Hermione and *Cadmus*, or the god
In *Epidaurus*; nor to which transformed
Ammonian Jove, or *Capitoline* was seen,
He with *Olympias*, this with her who bore
Scipio the height of *Rome*.[3] With tract oblique
At first, as one who sought access, but feared
To interrupt, side-long he works his way.
As when a Ship by skilful steersman wrought
Nigh river's mouth or foreland, where the Wind

1 Red or fiery. As a name for a precious stone, carbuncle suggests ruby or garnet but the term also connotes inflammation as in medical usage the term refers to a malignant tumour.

2 Like waves, i.e., the head and neck of the snake are raised erect above its many rippling coils. The Edenic serpent moves in this upright fashion in part to explain why in *Genesis* the Judgement on the snake for its part in the deception of Eve was to go on its belly in the dust.

3 A veritable nest of classical tales about serpents. Ovid *Metamorphoses* IV 572 ff. relates how Cadmus having been changed into a snake embraced his wife, Hermione, and she too metamorphosed into a serpent. Aesculapius is the god of healing and father of medicine. He lived in Epidaurus and had the power to transform himself into a snake. Jove could transform himself into a snake to further his amours, and did so to sleep with Alexander the Great's mother, Olympias, and also with the mother of the great Roman, Scipio Africanus.

Veers oft, as oft so steers, and shifts her Sail;
So varied he, and of his tortuous Train
Curled many a wanton wreath in sight of *Eve*,
To lure her Eye;
[. . .]
Wonder not, sovereign Mistress, if perhaps
Thou canst, who art sole Wonder,[4] much less arm
Thy looks, the Heaven of mildness, with disdain,
Displeased that I approach thee thus, and gaze
Insatiate, I thus single; nor have feared
Thy awful brow, more awful thus retired.
Fairest resemblance of thy Maker fair,
Thee all living things gaze on, all things thine
By gift, and thy Celestial Beauty adore
With ravishment beheld, there best beheld
Where universally admired; but here
In this enclosure wild, these Beasts among,
Beholders rude, and shallow to discern
Half what in thee is fair, one man except,
Who sees thee? (and what is one?) who shouldst be seen
A Goddess among Gods, adored and served
By Angels numberless, thy daily Train.
  So glozed the Tempter, and his Proem tuned;[5]
Into the Heart of *Eve* his words made way,
Though at the voice much marvelling;

Book IX 684–717, 762–92, 816–33: the temptation and fall of Eve

Satan has brought Eve to the Tree of Knowledge. She initially refuses to eat but does continue to listen to the spurious argument of the tempter. Echoes of Eve's dream (V 28–93, see **pp. 113–16**) have littered Satan's seduction. The speaking snake has called Eve a goddess and has spoken idolatrously of the inherent (almost magical) qualities of this specific fruit. Eve does not challenge this strongly enough, and does not stand firm when the justice of God is questioned. At this point we should contrast her position with that of Abdiel, who refuses to hear more Satanic falsehoods and instead speaks out, witnessing to the fundamental goodness and justness of God as the Creator (V 822–31).

4 The scene is reminiscent of Ferdinand's first speech to Miranda in William Shakespeare's *The Tempest* (I ii.422–8), another literary moment where a courteous and sophisticated male addresses himself to a completely innocent woman.

5 A memorable line. To 'gloze' is to gloss – to explain in a plausible but insincere manner, to flatter, to give a deceptively fair surface. Remember that God the Father in Book III foretold that man would 'harken to his glozing lies' (III 93). 'Proem' is the prefatory introduction in the formal rhetorical construction of a speech.

This extract shows Satan's speech circling around the meaning of 'death', inserting dubieties wherever possible: the fruit brings life not death; God is a 'Threatener' not a benevolent Creator; maybe death will prove no bad thing but just a transition to a higher state of being. It is an outrageous perversion of logic to propose that it is good to 'know' evil in order to be better prepared to shun it in the future. The argument may be superficially similar to that in *Areopagitica* where abstract knowledge from books might be of assistance to a fallen individual but the difference is that Satan is endorsing a literal or carnal knowledge not an abstract comprehension of options in order that they might be avoided. Nor does he stop there. He asks how God can be just if he keeps his creatures from information that would assist them in rejecting evil and suggests that God is in reality restricting liberty and keeping mankind in ignorance (cf., IV, 521–7, see **p. 113**). The snake slips between the terms 'good' and 'God' with incredible audacity. He proposes that 'If it is good to know evil, then it would not be just to be reprimanded for taking the necessary steps to achieve that goal' and that 'If God were to reprimand you, then He would not be just, and if God would punish His creatures unjustly then He is not [good]/God'.

'Not just, not God.' Milton always gives the tempters in his poems good debating skills but this is the crowning achievement for the Father of Lies. The goodness and justice of God are the pulse of the entire poem. The justification of God's ways to men is our theme. Yet, here is Satan turning that endeavour on its head in one gloriously spurious half line. It is an exceptional addition to the epic undertaking that this argument has been included for our detached consideration. Beyond the theological debate, it offers us insight into our reasoning powers and the power of rhetoric to sway our decisions. Within God's universe, it is a second great moment of apostasy. Satan publicly denied that God was his creator in Book V (V 853–69, see **pp. 120–21**). Here he would deny that God exists at all. Note, however, that having (rhetorically at least) demolished the existence of the Almighty in this way, all Satan can offer in His place is pagan idolatry and the ambition to be like the gods. (See Bennett, **pp. 69–71**, for an extended discussion of the arguments presented in the temptation scene.)

Queen of this Universe, do not believe
Those rigid threats of Death; ye shall not Die:
How should ye? by the Fruit? it gives you Life
To Knowledge. By the Threatener? look on me,
Me who have touched and tasted, yet both live,
And life more perfect have attained than Fate
Meant me, by venturing higher than my Lot.
Shall that be shut to Man, which to the Beast
Is open? or will God incense his ire
For such a petty Trespass, and not praise
Rather your dauntless virtue, whom the pain
Of Death denounced, whatever thing Death be,
Deterred not from achieving what might lead
To happier life, knowledge of Good and Evil;

Of good, how just? of evil, if what is evil
Be real, why not known, since easier shunned?
God therefore cannot hurt ye, and be just;
Not just, not God; not feared then, nor obeyed:
Your fear it self of death removes the fear.
Why then was this forbid? Why but to awe,
Why but to keep ye low and ignorant,
His worshippers; He knows that in that day
Ye eat thereof, your Eyes that seem so clear,
Yet are but dim, shall perfectly be then
Opened and cleared, and ye shall be as Gods,
Knowing both Good and Evil as they know.
That ye should be as Gods, since I as Man,
Internal Man, is but proportion meet,
I of brute human, ye of human Gods.
So ye shall die perhaps, but putting off
Human, to put on Gods, death to be wished,
Though threatened, which no worse than this can bring.
And what are Gods that Man may not become
As they, participating God-like food?

Eve now repeats her own version of the snake's logic to herself but it is becoming ever more garbled. Despite Adam's warning at the moment of their separation (IX 360–3, see **p. 135**), Eve does not doubt the veracity of the speaker. However, even though hypocrisy is a behavioural pattern which all innocent creatures have difficulty in identifying, Eve's logic is also at fault. It is extremely bad logic to presume that because the fruit has given speech to the snake the equivalent transition in man will be to gain the status of a god. That simply does not follow, but her decision is made and she eats of the Tree of Knowledge of Good and Evil. It seems a small, almost an insignificant action from one perspective but on a cosmic level there are immediate signs of the significance of this event. The earth itself responds, lamenting that 'all was lost' (see footnote 3, **p. 89**). With enormous irony, the narration tells us that Eve now finds 'delight' [a synonym for Eden] in the forbidden fruit. Having lost her innocence, and with it her temperance, she gorges herself, sensual pleasures taking precedence over all other concerns.

. . . In the day we eat
Of this fair Fruit, our doom is, we shall die.
How dies the Serpent? he hath eaten and lives,
And knows, and speaks, and reasons, and discerns,
Irrational till then. For us alone
Was death invented? or to us denied
This intellectual food, for beasts reserved?
For Beasts it seems: yet that one Beast which first
Hath tasted, envies not, but brings with joy

The good befallen him, Author unsuspect,[1]
Friendly to man, far from deceit or guile.
What fear I then, rather what know to fear
Under this ignorance of good and Evil,
Of God or Death, of Law or Penalty?
Here grows the Cure of all, this Fruit Divine,
Fair to the Eye, inviting to the Taste,
Of virtue to make wise: what hinders then
To reach, and feed at once both Body and Mind?
So saying, her rash hand in evil hour
Forth reaching to the Fruit, she plucked, she ate:[2]
Earth felt the wound, and Nature from her seat
Sighing through all her Works gave signs of woe,
That all was lost. Back to the Thicket slunk
The guilty Serpent, and well might, for *Eve*
Intent now wholly on her taste, naught else
Regarded, such delight till then, as seemed,
In Fruit she never tasted, whether true
Or fancied so, through expectation high
Of knowledge, nor was God-head from her thought.
Greedily she engorged without restraint,
And knew not eating Death: [. . .]

Eve first worships the tree before turning her attention to whether her trespass will have been noted by God. She hopes He will not have noticed what just happened but her attention moves almost immediately to consider what to do about Adam. Should she share her new knowledge or use it to gain superiority? In convincing herself that love is her motive in sharing the fruit with Adam, she fails to hide the fact that she will be bringing death to Adam. See **pp. 24–5**, for a wide-ranging list of sins that can be seen as inherent to the original sin of Adam and Eve.

[. . .] But to Adam in what sort
Shall I appear? Shall I to him make known
As yet my change, and give him to partake
Full happiness with me, or rather not,
But keep the odds of Knowledge in my power
Without Copartner? So to add what wants
In female sex, the more to draw his love,
And render me more equal, and perhaps,
A thing not undesirable, sometime

1 i.e., the fact that the snake is ready to share this information with man, proves that it is not subject to suspicion.
2 Cf. V 65, see **p. 115** and footnote 6.

Superior; for inferior who is free?
This may be well: but what if God have seen,
And Death ensue? then I shall be no more,
And *Adam* wedded to another *Eve*,
Shall live with her enjoying, I extinct;
A death to think. Confirmed then I resolve,
Adam shall share with me in bliss or woe:
So dear I love him, that with him all deaths
I could endure, without him live no life.

Book IX 886–916: Adam's recognition that Eve is lost

Adam is coming to find his wife, as she leaves the tree to find him. He brings with him a garland of roses with which he intends to crown Eve, presumably in honour of her work and in recompense for the tension between them earlier in the day. However, Eve's foolish admittance of Satanic flattery has dethroned her from innocence and she is no longer an Edenic Queen of the May. Adam recognises the change in Eve immediately and his astonishment is complete. At this most poignant moment in the love story, our attention is placed on a minor movement of his hand and the garland as it falls to the ground. The coronet that was to have marked Eve's efforts is instead a proof of the changes taking place in the Edenic ecosystem – the roses fade as mortality has now entered the world. Eve has repeatedly been associated with the flowers of Eden. When she left Adam's side earlier in the day and was first seen by Satan it was through a veil of floral perfume, while the narrator described her as 'fairest unsupported flower' (line 432). Now, the grace and glory of her innocence are lost and her 'fall' finds its objective correlative in the faded roses. The technical skill with which this is achieved is almost cinematographic but, metrically, it relies on two stresses in the first foot of line 893.

The moment is also important for Milton's construction of a *domestic* epic. Half mankind is lost and the world is irrevocably changed. Yet, instead of some great military action, we have had only a woman eating fruit. However, the image of the garland takes the Homeric epic's lament for a hero fallen in battle and dextrously repositions it for a pastoral setting with no loss of pathos. Consider by way of comparison the much-lamented death of Patroklos in the *Iliad* XVI.786ff. Patroklos has overestimated his own strength in going to battle dressed in the armour of his friend, Achilles. As his fate catches up with him, the bard focuses on the ornate helmet (borrowed by Patroklos from Achilles) that crashes to the ground and rolls in the dust. That shining helmet has never previously been besmirched by dust but now it lies on the ground as an omen that its wearer is marked for death.

The period of time when one half of the couple is fallen but the other is not is extended in Book IX in order to have Adam reason through his situation. This should provide us with a perfect man's response to human disobedience but

Adam is less concerned with keeping faith with God than we might have expected. It is noteworthy that he speaks to himself. In Adam's first memories of life, retold in Book VIII, his solitariness did not result in soliloquy. He was monotheistic from the very first and sought a fuller understanding of his relationship with the divinity. Now he does not seek such a relationship but relies on his own emotions. It is a quite remarkable moment in human history, as Adam decides to surrender to death rather than lose his wife. His Fall is presented by Milton in a significantly different manner from that of Eve and there is no *Genesis* authorisation for this decision to value the human relation above the relationship with God. This version of the story of Adam and Eve may be the greatest love story ever told. Even so, it is also a tale of cowardice and fallibility because Adam's love is not altruistic. A fear of loneliness is a significant factor in the sacrifice Adam makes for love. He is simply terrified of continuing without Eve. You should ask yourself whether you think that an insightful addition to this epic exploration of the human condition. Note also how we find Adam committed to 'woe' through the rhyming pattern embedded in the latter part of his argument (forgo-[forlorn] – [afford]-no, no – woe)

Thus *Eve* with Countenance blithe her story told;
But in her cheek distemper flushing glowed.
On the other side, *Adam*, soon as he heard
The fatal Trespass done by *Eve*, amazed,
Astonied[1] stood and Blank, while horror chill
Ran through his veins, and all his joints relaxed;
From his slack hand the Garland wreathed for *Eve*
Down dropped, and all the faded Roses shed:[2]
Speechless he stood and pale, till thus at length
First to himself he inward silence broke.
O fairest of Creation, last and best
Of all God's Works, Creature in whom excelled
Whatever can to sight or thought be formed,
Holy, divine, good, amiable, or sweet!
How art thou lost, how on a sudden lost,
Defaced, deflowered, and now to Death devote?[3]
Rather how hast thou yielded to transgress
The strict forbiddance, how to violate
The sacred Fruit forbidden! some cursed fraud
Of Enemy hath beguiled thee, yet unknown,
And me with thee hath ruined, for with thee
Certain my resolution is to Die;

1 Turned to stone.
2 Cf. *Iliad* XVI.793–6 'And from his head Phoebus Apollo struck the helmet, and it rang as it rolled beneath the feet of the horses – the crested helmet; and its plumes were befouled with blood and dust'.
3 A wonderfully alliterative line, summing up Eve's loss of virtue and virginal innocence.

How can I live without thee, how forgo
Thy sweet Converse[4] and Love so dearly joined,
To live again in these wild Woods forlorn?
Should God create another *Eve*, and I
Another Rib afford, yet loss of thee
Would never from my heart; no no, I feel
The Link of Nature draw me: Flesh of Flesh,
Bone of my Bone thou art, and from thy State
Mine never shall be parted, bliss or woe.

Book IX 997–1033: Adam's fall and the couple's lustful desire

Adam eats and the act of original sin is complete. The effects are felt immediately. There is a thunderstorm in Eden while the couple enter a heightened state of inebriation. Drunk, they think themselves growing wings (cf. V 86–93, see **pp. 115–16**) but the aspiration to leave the earth behind is soon forgotten in favour of earthly desires. Adam's first fallen discourse is full of sexual innuendo and puns. The perversion of Edenic thought is captured in that first compliment on Eve's discriminating 'taste'. The wit game suggests over-subtle refinement and a shift from the frank delights of innocence to an intellectual epicurism [refined sensuous enjoyment]. See Turner, **pp. 71–2** for more on this change in the language describing human sexuality.

. . . : he scrupled not to eat
Against his better knowledge, not deceived,
But fondly[1] overcome with Female charm.
Earth trembled from her entrails, as again
In pangs, and Nature gave a second groan,
Sky loured and muttering Thunder, some sad drops
Wept at completing of the mortal Sin
Original;[2] while *Adam* took no thought,
Eating his fill, nor *Eve* to iterate[3]
Her former trespass feared, the more to soothe
Him with her loved society, that now
As with new Wine intoxicated both
They swim in mirth, and fancy that they feel
Divinity within them breeding wings

4 Conversation is an inclusive term for the Edenic relationship, combining physical intercourse with rational discourse and emotional support.

1 Foolishly; through emotion rather than reason.
2 The only use of the phrase 'original sin' in the poem.
3 Repeat.

Wherewith to scorn the Earth: but that false Fruit
Far other operation first displayed,
Carnal desire enflaming, he on *Eve*
Began to cast lascivious[4] Eyes, she him
As wantonly repaid; in Lust they burn:
Till *Adam* thus, 'gan *Eve* to dalliance move.[5]
Eve, now I see thou art exact of taste,
And elegant, of Sapience[6] no small part,
Since to each meaning savour we apply,
And Palate call judicious; I the praise
Yield thee, so well this day thou hast purveyed.[7]
Much pleasure we have lost, while we abstained
From this delightful Fruit, nor known till now
True relish, tasting; if such pleasure be
In things to us forbidden, it might be wished,
For this one Tree had been forbidden ten.
But come, so well refreshed, now let us play,
As meet is, after such delicious Fare;
For never did thy Beauty since the day
I saw thee first and wedded thee, adorned
With all perfections, so enflame my sense
With ardour to enjoy thee, fairer now
Than ever, bounty of this virtuous Tree.

Book X 720–32, 741–93: Adam's despair

After their Judgement by the Son, Milton invents a lengthy episode in order to detail the couple's evolving understanding [*anagnorisis*] of what death will mean to them. This speech by Adam runs for over 120 lines (X 720ff.). It is a moving and psychologically plausible journey into the depths of one man's despair and a masterly exploration of the all-too-human experience of guilt. The essential bitterness of Adam's situation is summed up in his initial outburst, 'O miserable of happy'. 'Happy' has been one of the most commonly used synonyms for the Edenic experience and state of mind. Now comes a cruel reversal as the memory of innocent pleasure intensifies the pain felt in the current situation. This phrase might be compared to Satan's dismissal of joy in Hell (I 249–51, see **p. 92**) but Adam's entire complaint should be contrasted with Satan's address to the sun (IV 32–113, see **pp. 105–7**). Both rational created beings are

4 Inclined to lust.
5 Adam began to encourage Eve in amorous play.
6 Wisdom. The etymological root of sapience is the Latin *sapere*, meaning to have a taste. An interplay between abstract and experiential knowledge has been ongoing since the word play on 'fruit' and 'mortal taste' in the opening lines of the poem (see **p. 86**).
7 Provided. 'Purvey' includes the specific sense of supplying provisions or food – as such there is a reminder here of Eve's role and knowledge in Book V when she provided lunch for the angel Raphael.

conscious of their own fault but only Adam will admit the justice of God's punishment. Where Satan chooses to curse God's goodness, Adam in contrast accepts that the curses must fall on his own head for abusing God's goodness. He expects those curses to be heaped on his head by all mankind because his disobedience will have ramifications beyond the moment and beyond the self. He has in effect condemned all future generations to misery by his selfish action. The fact that the blessing of the Creator and the delights of the creative process, including the procreation of children, should by his actions have now become a sentence of death shocks him to the core of his being. (Eve will soon propose sexual abstinence as a way of restricting the effects of the Fall to one generation or, if abstinence is too difficult, she suggests suicide. Adam is not taken by either idea.)

The poetry expresses the individual's dejection admirably but Adam's reasoning here has further ramifications. It is Adam who admits the doctrine of original sin [the belief in an innate depravity inherited by each and every generation following the disobedience of our forefather] in his understanding that he will 'propagate' his own fault. The doctrine of original sin will be unpalatable to many modern secular readers but it was rarely questioned by Christian theologians. It is telling that Milton thought it appropriate to have Adam, as the father of mankind, reason it out for himself. One of the strengths of the speech is the circularity of its argument and the fact that it ends without consolation or contrition. Its bleak last lines are, 'O Conscience! into what Abyss of fears/And horrors hast thou driven me; out of which / I find no way, from deep to deeper plunged' (lines 842–4). Again, there is a doctrinal reason behind this. Adam has articulated his conviction of sin in this speech but, without the intervention of God's grace, he can proceed no further. It will take the rest of Book X for him to move towards repentance and, in a highly Miltonic addition, he will first have to show concern for another human being and be reconciled with his wife.

These additions to the *Genesis* account allow Milton to probe the human psyche. It also provides an opportunity for him to introduce one of his own heretical beliefs. Milton adheres to the heresy of mortalism, the belief that the soul of man dies with the body. His views on creation and monist materialism make the orthodox belief that the body and soul somehow split from each other at death, so that only the body is buried in the ground, an impossibility. The Miltonic reasoning is written into Adam's speech in what amounts to free thinking on the part of the first man. Adam's logic stems from a macabre speculation of what it might otherwise be like to be dead but is also deeply rooted in the account of his creation provided by Raphael in Book VII (VII 524–8, see **p. 127**).

O miserable of happy![1] is this the end
Of this new glorious World, and me so late
The Glory of that Glory, who now become
Accurst of blessed, hide me from the face

1 The term 'happy' has been used numerous times as an epithet for the Edenic state of being.

Of God, whom to behold was then my hight
Of happiness: yet well, if here would end
The misery, I deserved it, and would bear
My own deservings; but this will not serve;
All that I eat or drink, or shall beget,
Is propagated curse. O voice once heard
Delightfully, *Increase and multiply*,
Now death to hear![2] for what can I increase
Or multiply, but curses on my head?
[. . .]
. . . O fleeting joys
Of Paradise, dear bought with lasting woes!
Did I request thee, Maker, from my Clay[3]
To mould me Man, did I solicit thee
From darkness to promote me, or here place
In this delicious Garden? as my Will
Concurred not to my being, it were but right
And equal to reduce me to my dust,
Desirous to resign, and render back
All I received, unable to perform
Thy terms too hard, by which I was to hold
The good I sought not. To the loss of that
Sufficient penalty, why hast thou added
The sense of endless woes? inexplicable[4]
Thy Justice seems; yet to say truth, too late,
I thus contest; then should have been refused
Those terms whatever, when they were proposed:
Thou didst accept them; wilt thou enjoy the good,
Then cavil the conditions?[5] and though God
Made thee without thy leave, what if thy Son
Prove disobedient, and reproved, retort,
Wherefore didst thou beget me? I sought it not:
Wouldst thou admit for his contempt of thee
That proud excuse? yet him not thy election,
But Natural necessity begot.[6]
God made thee of choice his own, and of his own
To serve him, thy reward was of his grace,
Thy punishment then justly is at his Will.
Be it so, for I submit, his doom is fair,

2 Cf. VII 531, see **p. 127**.

3 An allusion to Adam's creation from the dust of the earth (*Genesis* 2.7). Remember that in Hebrew, Adam's name recalls this source material. The term 'clay' here suggests something with great plastic potential but compare Adam's later use of the term 'clod'.

4 Although Adam initially claims that God's justice is not comprehensible to man, his own reasoning in the next few lines will make him reverse that view.

5 i.e., will you first enjoy the benefits of life in Eden and only later raise spurious objections to the stipulated terms of the agreement (after you have failed to meet them)?

6 i.e., would you consider your own son justified if he were to upbraid his father for having begotten him? Yet offspring are the natural products of procreative existence not of particular selection.

That dust I am, and shall to dust return:
O welcome hour whenever! why delays
His hand to execute what his Decree
Fixed on this day? why do I overlive,
Why am I mocked with death, and lengthened out
To deathless pain?[7] how gladly would I meet
Mortality my sentence, and be Earth
Insensible, how glad would lay me down
As in my Mothers lap? there I should rest
And sleep secure; his dreadful voice no more
Would Thunder in my ears, no fear of worse
To me and to my offspring would torment me
With cruel expectation. Yet one doubt
Pursues me still, lest all I cannot die,
Lest that pure breath of Life, the Spirit of Man
Which God inspired, cannot together perish
With this corporeal Clod;[8] then in the Grave,
Or in some other dismal place, who knows
But I shall die a living Death? O thought
Horrid, if true! yet why? it was but breath
Of Life that sinned; what dies but what had life
And sin? the Body properly hath neither.
All of me then shall die: let this appease
The doubt, since human reach no further knows.[9]

Book X 867–73, 884–95, 909–36: Adam's abusive behaviour towards Eve

The action in Book X is extremely disrupted and for good reason as it is a reaction to the immense cosmic upheaval caused by man's Fall. We start in Heaven and move to Paradise for the sentencing of man, then we follow Satan back to Hell, before returning to Paradise to focus on Adam and Eve's long process of recovery from despair. With Adam and Eve at loggerheads, Milton can indulge in a little invective, a rhetorical skill which he put to such good use in his prose. We should note however that it is only after the Fall that man begins to think in an antagonistic, spiteful or misogynistic manner. When Adam starts to call Eve names, we should feel this to be perverse, a view confirmed when Adam later reconfirms the true meaning of Eve's name (XI 158–61). At this moment, however, Adam's Edenic perception of Eve as the last and best gift of

7 i.e., why am I threatened with death and left in this interim of endless pain anticipating death?
8 Raphael's account of man as invigorated only by the Creator's breath of life is essential to Adam's reasoning here.
9 i.e., it is enough for me to be certain that 'all of me' shall die, since I do not have the capacity to delve deeper into these mysteries.

the Creator (and indeed the whole monist materialism argument embedded in her creation) has been forgotten and replaced by the first anti-feminist rant. The wish that woman had never been created and that man had existed in some exclusively male society is especially peevish when we remember the audacious addition to the *Genesis* account made by Milton in Book VIII of his poem, in order that Adam might speak directly to God and request a mate (see **pp. 128–9**).

Out of my sight, thou Serpent, that name best
Befits thee with him leagued, thy self as false
And hateful; nothing wants, but that thy shape,
Like his, and colour Serpentine may show
Thy inward fraud, to warn all Creatures from thee
Henceforth; lest that too heavenly form, pretended
To hellish falsehood, snare them.
[. . .] a Rib
Crooked by nature, bent, as now appears,
More to the part sinister[1] from me drawn,
Well if thrown out, as supernumerary[2]
To my just number found. O why did God,
Creator wise, that peopled highest Heaven
With Spirits Masculine, create at last
This novelty on Earth, this fair defect
Of Nature, and not fill the World at once
With Men as Angels without Feminine,
Or find some other way to generate
Mankind? . . .

Eve's supplication is the turning point for the human couple. She humbly admits her fault and is willing to take the entire blame for events upon herself. The wording here echoes the Son's acceptance of his redemptive role in Book III (236–8, see **p. 104**). Some critics have therefore suggested a redemptive Christ-like role for Eve. That seems a little too strong. The Son's agreement to suffer for man's sins is a completely selfless act: Eve expresses some self-interest in her wish to be reunited with Adam. However, it is this commitment to the human relationship that will allow the couple to regain some composure and begin the process of repentance and reconciliation.

1 In *Genesis* 2, woman is created from a rib taken from Adam's left side. *Sinister* is the Latin for left but the term also connotes misfortune, or corrupt and deceptive practices. This was a common anti-feminist slur.

2 Extra, added after the due number. Adam declares that he considers himself well rid of this extra rib which he never needed, and which (through Eve's actions) has now proven itself to have been not just physically curved but morally crooked from the start.

He added not, and from her turned, but *Eve*
Not so repulsed, with Tears that ceased not flowing,
And tresses all disordered, at his feet
Fell humble, and embracing them, besought
His peace, and thus proceeded in her plaint[3].
Forsake me not thus, *Adam*, witness Heaven
What love sincere, and reverence in my heart
I bear thee, and unweeting[4] have offended,
Unhappily deceived; thy suppliant
I beg, and clasp thy knees; bereave me not,
Whereon I live, thy gentle looks, thy aid,
Thy counsel in this uttermost distress,
My only strength and stay: forlorn of thee,
Whither shall I betake me, where subsist?
While yet we live, scarce one short hour perhaps,
Between us two let there be peace, both joining,
As joined in injuries, one enmity
Against a Foe by doom express assigned us,
That cruel Serpent: On me exercise not
Thy hatred for this misery befallen,
On me already lost, me than thyself
More miserable; both have sinned, but thou
Against God only, I against God and thee,[5]
And to the place of judgement will return,
There with my cries importune Heaven, that all
The sentence from thy head removed may light
On me, sole cause to thee of all this woe,
Me me only just object of his ire.

Book XI 806–38: Michael extrapolates on the vision of Noah and the Flood

The archangel Michael's visit to Eden takes up most of Book XI and all of Book XII. His mission is to expel Adam and Eve from Paradise but first he prepares mankind for the struggles that lie ahead. Michael teaches Adam that God's covenant is with the individual. The majority of humanity will fail to keep God's commands but there will always be a remnant to witness to God's truth. This is spelt out here, 'Of them derided but of God observed / The one just man alive', and the model of the 'one just man' runs throughout Michael's narrative. The future (Biblical) history of mankind from the death of Abel through to the

3 Lament.
4 Unknowingly.
5 Cf., IV 299, see p. 109.

destruction of the earth by fire (XII 547–9) and the Last Judgement is revealed to Adam.

Within this inclusive sweep of postlapsarian human history, the story of the Flood and of Noah's survival in the Ark (*Genesis* 6–9), should occupy an important position. It marks the first destruction of the corrupt world by God through flood, an event transformed by divine providence into a new beginning for Noah and his descendants. In the restructured second edition of *Paradise Lost* (1674), these events gain just that pivotal placement. The explanation and vision of the Flood close Book XI and a hiatus between the old world and the postdiluvian world is structurally embedded in the new lines added to the start of Book XII. The important lesson sung by the angelic choir at the end of Book VII, that 'but to create / Is greater than created to destroy' (VII 606–7) is also renewed but with a difference. The postlapsarian world will often stand in need of purgation as a reformative process. The Flood is exemplar of the force of iconoclastic reform. It erases all in its path, cleansing the world of corruption and the process is comprehensive. Impious and morally depraved individuals will perish but so too will the 'mount of Paradise' that we have grown so accustomed to as our setting.

It is a shock to the system to find that the delights of Eden, built up at length in the central books of the poem, are to be erased so abruptly. The garden itself, we are told, will move from its current location at the time of the Flood and become stranded in the Gulf as a barren, unwelcoming island. It is a wrench to the reader (and to the author?) to give up Eden like this but its time is past. We are moving towards the paradise within (XII 587, see **pp. 154–5**) and must not remain nostalgic for a return to a Paradise lost.

So all shall turn degenerate,[1] all depraved,
Justice and Temperance, Truth and Faith forgot;
One Man except, the only Son of light
In a dark Age, against example good,
Against allurement, custom, and a World
Offended; fearless of reproach and scorn,
Or violence, he of their wicked ways
Shall them admonish,[2] and before them set
The paths of righteousness, how much more safe,
And full of peace, denouncing wrath to come
On their impenitence; and shall return
Of them derided, but of God observed
The one just Man alive; by his command
Shall build a wondrous Ark, as thou beheld'st,
To save himself and household from amidst
A World devote to universal rack.

1 Debased, having lost its original quality.
2 To counsel or warn. To remind someone of their duty.

No sooner he with them of Man and Beast
Select for life shall in the Ark be lodged,
And sheltered round, but all the Cataracts[3]
Of Heaven set open on the Earth shall pour
Rain day and night, all fountains of the Deep
Broke up, shall heave the Ocean to usurp
Beyond all bounds, till inundation rise
Above the highest hills: then shall this Mount
Of Paradise by might of waves be moved
Out of his place, pushed by the horned flood,[4]
With all his verdure spoiled, and trees adrift
Down the great River to the opening Gulf,
And there take root an Island salt and bare,
The haunt of Seals and Orcs, and Sea-mews clang.[5]
To teach thee that God attributes to place
No sanctity, if none be thither brought
By Men who there frequent, or therein dwell.

Book XII 24–74: Michael tells of Nimrod and the building of the Tower of Babel

Milton identifies Nimrod as the first king, thereby associating monarchical government with both secular tyranny and rebellion against God's sovereignty. Monarchical government is defined as a debasement of the equal status previously enjoyed by all men. The political message is very clear but Milton goes even further by having the father of all men exclaim against Nimrod's behaviour in the strongest terms. Adam, who was initially seen in 'naked majesty' (IV 290, see **p. 109**), is totally opposed to kingship on this model and curses the son who oppresses his brothers in this manner. It is little wonder that Beale made the comment that he did (see **p. 41**) and great wonder that this got past the licenser.

The name Nimrod means Rebellion and Rebellion means discord and division. The parallels with Satan (enemy of God) grow stronger as the narrative progresses. The Tower of Babel was actually referenced when the construction of Pandaemonium was described (I 694) and many of the key terms here are reminiscent of those commonly employed in Books I and II (pride, empire, ambition, rebellion, crew, tyranny, aspire). Nimrod and his crew are looking to gain fame and to 'get themselves a name'. The line recalls I 365, and its context

3 Literally, waterfalls but here floodgates.
4 A Virgilian phrase, a reference to the curved shape of the flood waters as they push against a landmass.
5 Eden is reduced to a barren island, uninhabited except for seals and monsters and the echoing cries of seabirds. One feels a deep sense of bereavement for the 'Wilderness of sweets' (V 294) that was Eden and the dissonance of 'clang' is almost heart-breaking.

of impiety, imprecision and pagan idolatry. This is not accidental. Creaturely ambition, infidelity and the imprecision of fallen language are once again central themes here. From Babel comes babble, when God in his righteousness topples the structure and punishes man for his pride by replacing the single Adamic language with our modern multiplicity of tongues. Since that day, humanity has been condemned to flawed communication, scrambling to convey meaning through an imperfect medium – as witnessed in the variant stories told of the fall of Mulciber, or should that be Hephaistos? (I 738 ff., see **pp. 94–5**).

. . .; till one shall rise
Of proud ambitious heart, who not content
With fair equality, fraternal state,
Will arrogate[1] Dominion undeserved
Over his brethren, and quite dispossess
Concord and law of Nature from the Earth;
Hunting (and Men not Beasts shall be his game)
With War and hostile snare such as refuse
Subjection to his Empire tyrannous:
A mighty Hunter thence he shall be styled
Before the Lord, as in despite of Heaven,
Or from Heaven claming second Sovereignty;
And from Rebellion shall derive his name,
Though of Rebellion others he accuse.
He with a crew, whom like Ambition joins
With him or under him to tyrannize,
Marching from *Eden* towards the West, shall find
The Plain, wherein a black bituminous gurge[2]
Boils out from under ground, the mouth of Hell;
Of Brick, and of that stuff they cast to build
A City and Tower, whose top may reach to Heaven;
And get themselves a name, lest far dispersed
In foreign Lands their memory be lost
Regardless whether good or evil fame.
But God who oft descends to visit men
Unseen, and through their habitations walks
To mark their doings, them beholding soon,
Comes down to see their City, ere the Tower
Obstruct Heaven Towers, and in derision sets
Upon their Tongues a various Spirit to raze
Quite out their Native Language, and instead
To sow a jangling noise of words unknown:
Forthwith a hideous gabble rises loud
Among the Builders; each to other calls

1 To claim for oneself something to which one is not entitled.
2 Latin term for whirlpool or abyss.

Not understood, till hoarse, and all in rage,
As mocked they storm; great laughter was in Heaven
And looking down, to see the hubbub[3] strange
And hear the din; thus was the building left
Ridiculous, and the work Confusion named.
  Whereto thus *Adam* fatherly displeased.
O execrable[4] Son so to aspire
Above his Brethren, to himself affirming
Authority usurped, from God not given:
He gave us only over Beast, Fish, Fowl
Dominion absolute; that right we hold
By his donation;[5] but Man over men
He made not Lord; such title to himself
Reserving, human left from human free.
But this Usurper his encroachment proud
Stays not on[6] Man; to God his Tower intends
Siege and defiance: Wretched man! . . .

Book XII 469–78: Adam's expression of joy at hearing of God's redemptive plan

Michael has completed his succinct relation of the life of Jesus and of the Son's apocalyptic Second Coming. This is the climax to God's redemptive plan and it produces the following exclamation of joy from Adam. His initial phrasing praises the extreme goodness of God. It recalls the paradox of a *felix culpa* [fortunate fall], so called because out of man's sin a greater good has proceeded. It is unlikely that we are actually supposed to agree fully with Adam here. The Fall cannot in itself be condoned. It would have been much preferable had mankind remained in a state of innocence. Then, they might have followed the path sketched out by Raphael (V 491–500, see **p. 117**) and the sufferings of the faithful which Michael has been relating would not have become necessary. However, God's redemptive plan remains a great blessing and it gives an opportunity for God's infinite mercy to be shown and for God to be glorified. The Christian reader will therefore find it difficult to disagree with Adam completely and for all readers the phrase 'Light out of darkness' will remain highly emotive, recalling as it does both the first act of Creation (VII 243) and the invocation to Book III (see **pp. 98–101**). Note also the prevailing lexical patterning (good – God – glory – grace).

3 A confused noise. The term is part of a cluster of onomatopoeic words suggestive of cacophony, cf., jangle, gabble, din. 'Hubbub' is a term derived from Irish.

4 Accursed, detestable. An extremely strong term suggesting that Adam is pronouncing a curse upon this particular son.

5 Gift.

6 Does not stop with.

O goodness infinite, goodness immense![1]
That all this good of evil shall produce,
And evil turn to good; more wonderful
Than that which by creation first brought forth
Light out of darkness! full of doubt I stand,
Whether I should repent me now of sin
By me done and occasioned, or rejoice
Much more, that much more good thereof shall spring,
To God more glory, more good will to Men
From God, and over wrath grace shall abound.

Book XII 575–87: Michael sums up his message

Having completed his narrative, Michael exhorts Adam to live in accordance with the lessons taught. From his newly acquired insight into the future history of mankind, Adam should commit himself to act henceforth in an obedient and virtuous manner. In that way, Adam will take an active part in bringing to fruition God's providential plan. If he behaves virtuously, then Adam will retain or rather regain an inner 'Paradise'. The cosmic geography of the epic is turning ever more clearly in these last books into a metaphor for moral states of being. The descriptions of the postlapsarian world have made it resemble a Hell on earth, but for the few committed to live in obedience to God's redemptive plan there can be a 'Paradise within'. We should note that Milton cannot resist having the archangel Michael endorse this new doctrine of a paradise within as 'happier far'. Just a little earlier when expounding on millenarian expectations, Michael spoke of the 'happier days' (XII 465) to come. But it now seems that we will not have to wait for the apocalypse. Adam can hope through faith to achieve an inner peace of mind that will amount to an internalised Paradise. Eden was a 'happy' state but this paradise within can be 'happier far'. Unexpectedly, the debate over the comparative merits of innocence versus experience remains open and the arguments of *Areopagitica* (see **pp. 18–20**) remain valid. Michael is not condoning the Fall itself but he does seem to be saying that mankind will value the choice of willing obedience more after the Fall. We might think that this is no more than a somewhat fallible argument meant for postlapsarian consumption but the Son says as much to the Father at XI 26–30. It would seem that, within Milton's epic, the choice of volitional obedience when made by a repentant individual is to be valued more by both God and man than is innocent behaviour.

This having learned, thou hast attained the sum
Of wisdom; hope no higher, though all the stars
Thou knew'st by name, and all the ethereal Powers,
All secrets of the deep, all Nature's works,

1 Cf. X 720, see **p. 145**

Or works of God in Heaven, Air, Earth, or Sea,
And all the riches of this World enjoyed'st,
And all the rule, one Empire; only add
Deeds to thy knowledge answerable, add Faith,
Add Virtue, Patience, Temperance, add Love,
By name to come called Charity, the soul
Of all the rest: then wilt thou not be loath
To leave this Paradise, but shalt possess
A paradise within thee, happier far.

Book XII 610–49: Eve's final speech and the Expulsion

Adam now descends the hill and returns to Eve. She has been asleep and says that she too has received guidance from God through her dreams. The woman gets the last word in *Paradise Lost*. It is obviously partial to say that she achieves in fourteen lines what Adam and Michael have been struggling with for a book and a half but her assimilation of the providential plan reveals an inner composure and a personalised faith that was not achieved through the formal pedagogy of Michael. The tone of Eve's speech is finely balanced as both elegy and love lyric (cf. IV 639–56): a farewell to Eden but an articulate expression of her trust in any new beginning undertaken alongside Adam. Eve identifies the continuation of her relationship with Adam as essential, making it possible for her to take 'paradise' with her. Through her words, marriage gains an even stronger metaphoric significance than it has previously held. It has been a definition of the human condition (God knows it is 'not good for man to be alone' VIII 445) and an inclusive metaphor for Edenic reciprocity. It was the first covenant to be renewed by the couple after the Fall, and now marital union offers a means of considering salvation theology.

Eve's ultimate consolation on losing Paradise is that 'by me/The promised seed shall all restore'. These concluding words in Paradise are rich in hope and assurance. Eve takes the Christian promise with her and her assurance begins to activate the intense potential in her words – the grain of faith will flourish and the movement towards the birth of Jesus as fruit of a woman's womb will begin. Michael's model of the 'one just man' therefore has its female equivalent embedded in the resonances of Eve's speech. Note that the very last human word spoken in the poem, and in Eden, is 'restore'. This is the essence of the Christian message and, as an expression of hope and faith, it is an active exemplar of how to live a Christian life. We have come full circle from the opening invocation, 'until one greater man / Restore us' (I 4–5). The poem, the narrator, and now Eve, are waiting and working for that great moment. In a bold move, the final line is also a conclusive political statement, rejecting the recent monarchical appropriation of the term 'Restoration' by the Stuarts, and reaffirming a final victory for those who are presently derided and denied toleration in religious worship. Such resonances in Eve's final speech, combined with its lyrical poise, embody a striking sense of compensatory calm at the moment of expulsion.

In contrast, the final events themselves are rushed. The air around Adam and Eve is changing and the appearance of the angels evokes terror not joy. Michael hurries the couple out of Paradise and disappears without further formalities. They are alone in the world. What could be more epic an undertaking? In the final nine lines the first human beings step into our world and begin our history. Their perspective is for the first time united with that of subsequent generations. We too can look back but the 'way' is forward. This is human heroism, based on hope and fear, grief and guilt, courage and reasoned commitment. The end of the poem is also a beginning. But the ways of God are now 'amplier known' (XII 544) than when, as readers, we began the epic. Most importantly, the assertion of eternal providence (I 25) can now be seen to unfold through the choice of providence made by the individual in every moment (XII 646–7). Our last image of the couple is of them 'hand in hand', setting out on that new heroic quest, a quest that is still continuing for every reader of this poem. The two last lines have been queried by commentators: Addison would have cut them, Bentley would have improved them (see **pp. 95–6**). Yet, the ambivalences contained here seem wholly justified. Only thus could a sufficient expression be achieved of the fallibility, individuality, resilience and loving commitment that define human experience.

Whence thou return'st, and whither went'st, I know;
For God is also in sleep, and Dreams advise,
Which he hath sent propitious,[1] some great good
Presaging,[2] since with sorrow and heart's distress
Wearied I fell asleep: but now lead on;
In me is no delay; with thee to go,
Is to stay here; without thee here to stay,
Is to go hence unwilling;[3] thou to me
Art all things under Heaven, all places thou,
Who for my wilful crime art banished hence.
This further consolation yet secure
I carry hence; though all by me is lost,
Such favour I unworthy am vouchsafed,
By me the Promised Seed shall all restore.
So spake our Mother *Eve*, and *Adam* heard
Well pleased, but answered not; for now too nigh
The Archangel stood, and from the other Hill
To their fixed Station, all in bright array
The Cherubim descended; on the ground

1 Favourably inclined.
2 To predict or make known.
3 Cf. *Ruth* 1.16 'And Ruth said, "Intreat me not to leave thee or to return from following after thee: for whither thou goest, I will go; and where thou lodgest, I will lodge: thy people shall be my people, and thy God my God".'

Gliding meteorous,[4] as Evening Mist
Risen from a River o'er the marish[5] glides,
And gathers ground fast at the Labourer's heel
Homeward returning. High in Front advanced,
The brandished Sword of God before them blazed
Fierce as a Comet; which with torrid heat,
And vapour as the *Lybian* air adust,
Began to parch that temperate Clime; whereat
In either hand the hastening Angel caught
Our lingering Parents, and to the Eastern Gate
Led them direct, and down the Cliff as fast
To the subjected Plain;[6] then disappeared.
They looking back, all the Eastern side beheld
Of Paradise, so late their happy seat,
Waved over by that flaming Brand, the Gate
With dreadful Faces thronged and fiery Arms:
Some natural tears they dropped, but wiped them soon;
The World was all before them, where to choose
Their place of rest, and Providence their guide:[7]:
They hand in hand[8] with wandering steps and slow,
Through *Eden* took their solitary way.

4 The angels are a dazzling phenomenon as they move along, gliding rather than walking on the ground.
5 Marsh.
6 The plain that lies beneath the cliff but more significantly a new location where postlapsarian man is reduced to a state of subjection (a) to mortality and (b) potentially to the dominion of kings, etc.
7 Providence means both divine direction and prudent self-government. The verb 'to choose' governs the entire phrase, emphasising once again man's free will in the decisions that lie ahead.
8 The couple were first seen, 'hand in hand' (IV 321), then, when Eve went off to garden alone, 'From her husband's hand her hand soft she withdrew' (IX 385). Her hand was later seized by Adam in a lustful moment (IX 1037) but this is an important indication that the marital bond is once again secure.

4

Further Reading

Further Reading

There is a vast body of critical material available on Milton. I make no attempt to provide comprehensive listings here but merely recommend a small selection of informative books and articles. I have not cited all the critical texts already reproduced in this book but I do of course recommend them highly. Students should also be aware of the dedicated journals, *Milton Studies* and *Milton Quarterly*.

Recommended Modern Editions of *Paradise Lost*

Paradise Lost, ed. Alastair Fowler (London and New York: Longman, 1998). Modern spelling and original punctuation. A truly admirable work of scholarship, with extensive footnotes. Fowler's edition of the epic was first published as part of *The Poems of John Milton*, ed. John Carey and Alastair Fowler (London and Harlow: Longman, Green and Co., 1968) and then as a single volume, *Paradise Lost*, in 1971. The revised second edition (1998) is more user-friendly but the first edition has supplementary information on Biblical and classical analogues.

Paradise Lost, ed. John Leonard (Harmondsworth: Penguin, 1998). Modern spelling, 'best practice' punctuation. A good, clean reading text with endnotes rather than footnotes.

The Riverside Milton, ed. Roy Flannagan (Boston and New York: Houghton Mifflin, 1998). A rich selection of Milton's prose is set alongside his poetry. The volume includes a full text of *Paradise Lost* in original spelling and punctuation and also presents the illustrations from the 1688 edition of the epic to advantage. The helpful introduction and editorial comments are intended to assist those new to the study of Milton.

John Milton: Complete English Poems, Of Education, Areopagitica, ed. Gordon Campbell (London: Dent, 1990). Modern spelling and punctuation. Pertinent annotation that wears its erudition lightly.

Biographies

Barbara K. Lewalski, *The Life of John Milton: a Critical Biography* (Oxford: Blackwell, 2000). Provides a clear narrative and considered critical analysis of Milton's texts, based upon a thorough awareness of the most recent critical, bibliographical and historical research.

Gordon Campbell, *A Milton Chronology* (Basingstoke: Macmillan, 1997). A timeline, documenting Milton's life and the publication history of his texts within the historical context. An excellent research tool and much more interesting to browse through than one might expect.

William Riley Parker, *Milton: a Biography* (Oxford: Oxford University Press, 1968). Revised and edited by Gordon Campbell. 2 vols (Oxford: Oxford University Press 1996). Immensely informative and erudite. Campbell has filled in many of the biographical and bibliographical gaps noted by Parker.

Helen Darbishire (ed.), *The Early Lives of Milton* (London: Constable, 1932). Reprinted by Scholarly Press, 1972. Contains six biographies, dating from c.1681–1734, by John Aubrey, Cyriack Skinner, Anthony à Wood, Edward Phillips, John Toland and Jonathan Richardson.

Collections of Critical Essays

There are numerous collections of essays on the market but I would single out the *Cambridge Companion to Milton* (Cambridge: Cambridge University Press, 1989; 2nd edition, 1999), edited by Dennis Danielson as an excellent primer in Milton studies and *A Companion to Milton*, edited by Thomas N. Corns (Oxford: Blackwell 2001) as the next step. While covering a wide range of Miltonic texts and themes, both contain a good number of essays on Milton's epic and both also offer impressive bibliographies.

Also useful in their own right and as a means of tracing shifting critical perspectives are:

William Zunder (ed.), *Paradise Lost: Contemporary Critical Essays* [New Casebooks Series] (Basingstoke and London: Macmillan, 1999).
Annabel Patterson (ed.), *John Milton* (Harlow: Longman, 1992).
Mary Nyquist and Margaret W. Ferguson (eds), *Re-membering Milton: Essays on the Texts and Traditions* (New York and London: Methuen, 1987, repr. 1988).
Frank Kermode (ed.), *The Living Milton: Essays by Various Hands* (London: Routledge & Kegan Paul, 1960).

Recommended Studies of *Paradise Lost*

Book-length studies precede any recommended essays under each heading.

As introductory guides:

Thomas N. Corns, *Regaining Paradise Lost* (Harlow: Longman, 1994).
Dennis H. Burden, *The Logical Epic: a Study of the Argument of Paradise Lost* (London: Routledge & Kegan Paul, 1967).

For discussion of Milton's style and language:

John K. Hale, *Milton's Languages: the Impact of Multilingualism on Style* (Cambridge: Cambridge University Press, 1997).
John Leonard, *Naming in Paradise: Milton and the Language of Adam and Eve* (Oxford: Clarendon Press, 1990).
Barbara K. Lewalski. *Paradise Lost and the Rhetoric of Literary Forms* (Princeton, NJ: Princeton University Press, 1985).
Christopher Ricks, *Milton's Grand Style* (Oxford: Clarendon Press, 1963).
John Creaser, 'Prosodic Style and Conceptions of Liberty in Milton and Marvell', *Milton Quarterly* 34 (2000), pp. 1–13.
In addition, William Ingram and Kathleen Swaim (eds), *A Concordance to Milton's English Poetry* (Oxford: Clarendon Press, 1972) will prove an extremely helpful aid to any student undertaking a close study of Milton's language.

On the classical tradition:

Charles Martindale, *John Milton and the Transformation of Ancient Epic* (London: Croom Helm, 1986).
Richard DuRocher, *Milton and Ovid* (Ithaca, NY: Cornell University Press, 1985).
John Steadman, *Milton's Biblical and Classical Imagery* (Pittsburgh, PA and Atlanta Highlands, NJ: Duquesne University Press, 1984).
Louis Martz, *Poet of Exile: A Study of Milton's Poetry* (New Haven, Conn., and London: Yale University Press, 1980). Reissued as *Milton: Poet of Exile*, 1986.

On *Genesis* and its exegesis:

James G. Turner, *One Flesh: Paradisal Marriage and Sexual Relations in the Age of Milton* (Oxford: Clarendon Press, 1987).
J. Martin Evans, *'Paradise Lost' and the Genesis Tradition* (Oxford: Clarendon Press, 1968).
Arnold Williams, *The Common Expositor: an Account of the Commentaries on Genesis 1527–1633* (Chapel Hill, NC: University of North Carolina Press, 1948).

On Christian theology in the epic:

Hugh MacCallum, *Milton and the Sons of God: the Divine Image in Milton's Epic Poetry* (Toronto: University of Toronto Press, 1986).
Dennis Danielson, *Milton's Good God: A Study in Literary Theodicy* (Cambridge: Cambridge University Press, 1982).

On Milton's heterodoxy:

Stephen B. Dobranski and John P. Rumrich (eds), *Milton and Heresy* (Cambridge: Cambridge University Press, 1998).
John Rogers, *The Matter of Revolution: Science, Poetry, and Politics in the Age of Milton* (Ithaca, NY: Cornell University Press, 1996).
John P. Rumrich, *Milton Unbound* (Cambridge: Cambridge University Press, 1996).
Stephen Fallon, *Milton amongst the Philosophers: Poetry and Materialism in Seventeenth-century England* (Ithaca, NY: Cornell University Press, 1991).

On seventeenth-century nonconformity and radicalism:

David Loewenstein, *Representing Revolution in Milton and His Contemporaries: Religion, Politics, and Polemics in Radical Puritanism* (Cambridge: Cambridge University Press, 2001).
Neil H. Keeble, *The Literary Culture of Non-conformity in Later Seventeenth-Century England* (Leicester: Leicester University Press, 1987).
Georgia Christopher, *Milton and the Science of the Saints* (Princeton, NJ: Princeton University Press, 1982).
Christopher Hill, *Milton and the English Revolution* (London: Faber, 1977).

On the politics of the period:

David Norbrook, *Writing the English Republic: Poetry, Rhetoric and Politics 1627–1660* (Cambridge: Cambridge University Press, 1999).
Andrew Milner, *John Milton and the English Revolution* (London & Basingstoke: Macmillan, 1981).

On gender and feminism:

John Guillory, 'From the Superfluous to the Supernumerary: Reading Gender into *Paradise Lost*' in Elizabeth Harvey and Katherine Maus (eds), *Soliciting Interpretation: Literary Theory and Seventeenth-Century English Poetry* (Chicago and London: University of Chicago Press, 1990), pp. 68–88.
Mary Nyquist, 'The *Genesis* of Gendered Subjectivity in the Divorce Tracts and in *Paradise Lost*' in Mary Nyquist and Margaret W. Ferguson (eds), *Re-membering Milton: Essays on the Texts and Traditions* (New York and London: Methuen, 1987, repr. 1988), pp. 99–127.

Christine Froula, 'When Eve reads Milton: Undoing the Canonical Economy', *Critical Inquiry* 10 (1983), pp. 321–47. Reprinted in Annabel Patterson (ed.), *John Milton* (London: Longman 1992), pp. 142–64.

Joan M. Webber, 'The Politics of Poetry: Feminism and *Paradise Lost*', *Milton Studies* 14 (1980), pp. 3–24.

Reception:

Steven N. Zwicker, *Lines of Authority: Politics and English Literary Culture, 1649–1689* (Ithaca, NY and London: Cornell University Press, 1993).

John T. Shawcross (ed.), *Milton 1732–1801. The Critical Heritage* (London and Boston: Routledge & Kegan Paul, 1972).

John T. Shawcross (ed.), *Milton: The Critical Heritage* (New York: Barnes & Noble, 1970).

Joseph A. Wittreich (ed.), *The Romantics on Milton: Formal Essays and Critical Asides* (Cleveland and London: Case Western Reserve University Press, 1970).

Nicholas Von Maltzahn, 'The First Reception of *Paradise Lost* (1667)', *Review of English Studies* 47 (1996), pp. 479–99.

Carolivia Herron, 'Milton and Afro-American Literature' in Mary Nyquist and Margaret W. Ferguson (eds), *Re-membering Milton: Essays on the Texts and Traditions* (New York and London: Methuen, 1987, repr. 1988), pp. 278–300.

Paradise Lost and the visual arts:

Roland Mushat Frye, *Milton's Imagery and the Visual Arts: Iconographic Tradition in the Epic Poems* (Princeton, NJ: Princeton University Press, 1978).

Marcia R. Pointon, *Milton and English Art* (Manchester: Manchester University Press, 1970).

On ecology:

Diane McColley, 'Milton and Nature: Greener Readings', *Huntington Library Quarterly* 62 (1999), pp. 423–44.

Glossary

Anagnorisis: recognition of present circumstance. Used particularly for the dénouement of a drama. Helpful when considering the shifting emotional states of man after the Fall.

Apocalypse: the revelation of the future granted to St John of Patmos. His vision relates to the last days and the Second Coming of Christ and comprises the last book of the New Testament (also known as the Book of Revelation).

Apostasy: the abandonment of one's faith or moral allegiance.

Apostate: one who has abandoned their faith or moral allegiance.

Bard: a poet who composes and sings his verses. Often used to refer to the narrator of an epic within the Homeric tradition.

Exegesis: explanation or interpretation. Used particularly of interpretation of Scripture.

Heterodox: an adjective used to describe an opinion which is not in accordance with the established view or doctrine.

Hexameron: a history of the six days of Creation as described in *Genesis*.

Invocation: the action of calling on a god in prayer or supplication. Often used to refer to the set piece in epic poetry where the bard calls on his muse as a source of inspiration.

Metaphysics: a theoretical consideration of the first principles of things, including concepts of space, substance, time and identity.

Monism: a denial of the duality of spirit and matter as two essentially distinct kinds of substance.

Monist materialism: a term used to describe Milton's belief in a holistic creation where matter and spirit are both manifestations of the same substance.

Monotheism: the doctrine that there is only one God.

Omnipotent: all-powerful. Used particularly of God as the Almighty.

Omniscience: knowing all things. Used particularly of God's infinite knowledge.

Peripeteia: a sudden change in circumstance or reversal of fortune. Used particularly for the depiction of such events in tragedy.

Postdiluvian: after the Flood.

Postlapsarian: after the Fall.

Prelapsarian: before the Fall.

Protevangelium: literally 'first gospel'. The term refers to *Genesis* 3.15 where the earliest scriptural indication of God's redemptive plan is to be found.

Regicide: (a) the act of killing a king or (b) a person involved in the killing of their king. The term 'regicides' can be used to refer specifically to those who signed the death warrant for King Charles I or who were notable supporters of his execution in 1649.

Restoration: the recovery of an original, unimpaired, condition. Used to refer to the re-establishment of monarchical rule in England in 1660.

Theodicy: the vindication of God's justice and goodness.

Theophany: a manifestation of God or a revelation of His power.

Index

Note: Bold numbers indicate extracts